19 Cowshed
20 Fodder store
21 Stables
22 Stables store
23 Scrap iron shed
24 Hospital buildings
25 Provisions store
26 Communal showers and
   laundry
27 Bakery and kitchen
28 Dining hall
29 Wheat storage (lower floor),
   clothes store, sewing room,
   and library (upper floor)

30 Plant nursery
31 Children's houses
32 Dwelling shacks
33 Depot and repair shop
34 Carpentry shop
35 Chicken coops
36 Tannery
37 Toilets
38 Remains of old Arab flour mill
39 Water pump
40 Dwelling shacks
41 Dwelling tents
42 Harnessmaker's and shoe-
   maker's shop

Gideon's Spring

Gideon's Spring

A Man and His Kibbutz

Zerubavel Gilead
and Dorothea Krook

TICKNOR & FIELDS · NEW YORK · 1985

Library of Congress Cataloging in Publication Data

Gilead, Zerubavel.
Gideon's spring: a man and his kibbutz.

1. Gilead, Zerubavel—Biography.   2. Authors,
Israeli—Biography.   3. 'En Ḥarod (Israel)—Biography.
I. Krook, Dorothea.   II. Title.
PJ5053.G473Z464   1985   892.4'16   [B]   85-6066
ISBN 0-89919-308-0

Printed in the United States of America

V 10 9 8 7 6 5 4 3 2 1

*This book is dedicated to
the founders of the House of Ein-Harod
and its succeeding generations*

Contents

viii CONTENTS

Acknowledgments

We wish to acknowledge the help we received from various people in writing this book. Our first debt of gratitude is to our good friends Professor Hillel Daleski of the Hebrew University of Jerusalem and his wife, Shirley Kaufman, the American poet, both of whom read the whole typescript, chapter by chapter, before we submitted it to the publisher. Their penetrating comments, criticisms, and suggestions were invaluable to us and helped to make the book a great deal better than it would have been if it had not had the benefit of their keen scrutiny.

We are also grateful to our two readers in England, Anita Jackson and Peter Sanders, who were most helpful at an early stage of the book's growth, making suggestions that became a valuable guide in our final planning and composition.

At Ticknor & Fields, we wish to thank Katrina Kenison for her brilliant editing of the typescript. Her taste and discrimination were constantly matched by her sympathy with the book and its authors, making it a delightful experience to work with her. We also thank her gifted manuscript editors, Laurence Cooper and Geraldine Morse, for numerous improvements. Chester Kerr, recently retired president of Ticknor & Fields, and his wife, Joan, generously read the whole typescript and offered many excellent suggestions. The whole idea for the book was Mr. Kerr's: a typical example of his bold enterprising spirit, which creates manuscripts rather than waiting for them to appear ready-made. We want to thank him warmly for his confidence in the book from the start, and for his constant encouragement at every stage.

Returning to home ground, we want to thank Yosske Rabinowitz of Kibbutz Na'an for carefully reading Chapters 11 and 12, "Mission to Poland," and suggesting important additions. We are also most grateful to Avraham Brum of Kibbutz Sh'fayim and Ze'ev Tsur of Yad Tabenkin for supplying, and then checking and rechecking, many of the figures in Chapter 19, "The Kibbutz: Changes and Continuities." Dr. Ze'ev Ivyansky of Ein-Harod kindly supplied us with valuable material on Orde Wingate and Chaim Sturman, and made other suggestions we found very helpful.

We are grateful to Kibbutz Ein-Harod Meuchad for permission to use material from its fiftieth anniversary volume, *Pirkei Yovel,* and from documentary material in its archives; to Kibbutz ha-Meuchad Publishing House, Tel Aviv, for permission to quote from Zerubavel's and others' books to which they hold the copyright; to Kibbutz ha-Meuchad Publishing House and the Institute for Translation of Hebrew Literature for permission to quote from *Pomegranate Tree in Jerusalem,* Dorothea Krook's translations of a selection of Zerubavel's poems; and to Yad Tabenkin and Beit Lochamei HaGeta'ot for permission to use their published documentary material and unpublished material in their archives. The photographs that are not Zerubavel's personal property are from the Ein-Harod (Meuchad) and Beit Sturman archives, and are reproduced with the kind permission of Ein-Harod and Beit Sturman.

We wish to thank Amnon ("Monni") Ophir, of Ein-Harod, and Israel Falk, of Moshav Merhavia, for their admirable reproductions of the old photographs, and Monni again, Michael Etz-Chaim, and Ilan Nitzan for the new photographs included in Chapter 20, "Ein-Harod, 1984." Ruth Kalusky, of Kibbutz Revivim, kindly provided reproductions of her father's photographs. Eyra Gal, Zerubavel's sister-in-law, made the guide for the unique photograph of Ein-Harod in 1924, and we want to thank her for the time and care she generously bestowed on the task.

Z.G.
D.K.

Preface

It was a vain ambition to try to tell the whole story of a life in Eretz Yisrael covering a span of sixty years in the space of a single, not very long book. I decided, therefore, to concentrate on my first thirty years here, 1924 to 1954, which included the formative period of my life, the life of my kibbutz, Ein-Harod, and the birth of the State of Israel in 1948. I have treated the years 1954 to 1984 briefly and selectively, though that story could easily fill a second volume.

Because this book is a personal record, I have deliberately chosen to write only of events, actions, people, and places of which I had firsthand knowledge, and that made a special impact on me, or influenced my development, or seemed symbolic of the spirit of the times, or were just vivid or amusing or sad or piquant enough to have lingered in my memory. I have sketched in as much historical and ideological background as seemed necessary to make the personal experiences intelligible, resisting the temptation to write a potted history of my times. Like every autobiography, the story I have told is *my* story, and it could not have been told by anyone else. But my object was also to make it a brief biography of the kibbutz community in which I have lived since early boyhood, and of the land in which both the kibbutz and I grew to maturity. I would like to believe that, in writing my personal history, I have also, in some measure, written the history of Kibbutz Ein-Harod and of Eretz Yisrael.

I have spent a good part of my life recording other people's life stories, so I found it an unusual, and somewhat strange, experience to have my own story recorded by someone else. I was lucky, thanks to Chester Kerr and Ticknor & Fields, to have had that task undertaken by my wife and co-author, Dorothea Krook. To my mind she has entered into my story and Ein-Harod's with an imaginative insight that is beyond praise. I find it difficult to believe that someone who did not live through the experience could understand so well and recreate so beautifully the general spirit and finest details of the story I was struggling to tell. There would have been no book but for her interest, her gifts, and her love. Ein-Harod and I both owe her an unrequitable debt of gratitude.

ZERUBAVEL GILEAD

Ein-Harod
September 1984

This book has been, in many ways, a perfect collaborative enterprise. Zerubavel supplied almost all the raw material, I did the shaping and writing: a clear, clean division of labor. The planning of each chapter and the book as a whole, and the selection of the material, were done jointly. The division of labor gave us, for a while, the pleasant illusion that we had undertaken a relatively easy project. In fact, it wasn't easy, but by the time we discovered this, it was too late to draw back; and we didn't really want to, because the difficulties, though formidable, were also intensely interesting and challenging.

The prime difficulty turned on the mass of material stored in Zerubavel's memory and records, which could easily have filled a book twice the length of this one. But we didn't want it to be a long book; consequently, selection and compression became our greatest challenge. Which of a dozen exemplary episodes, stories, personalities to include and which to leave out; how to present a complex character in a brief space without oversimplifying or distorting; what to do about essential historical, political, and ideological background material when one is not writing history, but a personal record of the life and times of one man. We tussled with these problems in chapter after chapter, and I think we sometimes solved them satisfactorily, though probably not always.

Then there was the problem of style, which was exclusively my problem. My aim was to be as faithful as possible to Zerubavel's personal style and spirit in his native Hebrew — in other words, to write the book he might have written if he had been able to write it in English. He is satisfied that I have succeeded; I hope other people who know him and his Hebrew writing will think the same.

All the translations from the Hebrew are mine: the documentary material; the quotations from Zerubavel's poems; and all the stories, dialogues, descriptions, and so on, he recounted from memory. But I could not have done it without his constant, ever patient help; so this, too, was a completely collaborative effort. To the best of our knowledge, none of the material from Zerubavel's Hebrew sources has ever appeared in English, which, we like to think, adds to the value of the book.

DOROTHEA KROOK

Ein-Harod
September 1984

Note on Transliteration

The technical problem of transliteration was one to which I could find no satisfactory solution: how to write Hebrew words, including proper names, in English so the English-speaking reader would have a fair chance of pronouncing them correctly. Feeling it would be pedantic to devise a special phonetic script for a book like this, I settled on a rough-and-ready system of transliteration, widely used in this country, which is based mainly on German. Thus I use *u* as in German *suchen* and *Mutter* for all English vowels pronounced *oo*, both long (tool) and short (took), *a* as in German *haben* for English *ah*, *i* as in German *richten* and *lieben* for English *ee*, both long (keen) and short (kin), and so on.

The most intractable Hebrew letters proved to be the consonants *khet* and *khaf*. The sound does not exist in modern English, and the *kh* I have used in *khet* and *khaf* is probably the nearest approximation to an accurate transliteration. But, though commonly used in the transliteration of roughly the same sound in Arabic, it is never used in the transliteration of the Hebrew sounds. What is used instead is either *ch* as in German *lachen*, or just *h*. The result is, if the name of the striking force of the Haganah, for example, is written *Palmach*, the English-speaking reader is likely to pronounce it "Pal-match" (as, Zerubavel tells me, many British Mandate officials actually did); if it is written *Palmah*, it comes out "Pal-ma"; and if written *Palmakh*, it may be pronounced "Pal-mack." The same is true of the initial *khet*, as in

Zerubavel's father's name: if written *Chaim,* it is likely to be pro-nounced "Chayme"; if *Haim,* it will be "Hayme"; if *Kha-yim,* it may come out as "Kay-yim." In any case, no Hebrew Chaim/Haim has ever spelled his name *Kha-yim* in English, and would doubtless regard it as outlandish to do so.

So, to avoid the outlandish, I simply used — I hope consis-tently — the transliterations the bearers of the names themselves habitually use when they were known to me: thus, Chaim Glass, Chaim Sturman, but Haim Hazaz, Haim Hefer. And when I didn't know, I used the German *ch,* for these and all other *khets* and *khafs,* hoping for the best, but knowing it is likely to become *tch* on English tongues. The reader who cares about the correct pronunciation of Hebrew words will, I'm afraid, have to consult a dictionary or guide to Hebrew pronunciation that transliterates in a systematic phonetic script.

D.K.

Gideon's Spring

Prologue:

Gideon's Men

I HAVE OFTEN FELT there was symbolic significance to the accident that brought me, as a boy, to live on the banks of the biblical spring where Gideon's men were chosen by the divinely prescribed test recorded in Judges.

> So he brought down the people unto the water: and the Lord said unto Gideon, Every one that lappeth of the water with his tongue, as a dog lappeth, him shalt thou set by himself; likewise every one that boweth down upon his knees to drink.
> And the number of them that lapped, putting their hand to their mouth, were three hundred men; but all the rest of the people bowed down upon their knees to drink water.
> And the Lord said unto Gideon, By the three hundred men that lapped will I save you, and deliver the Midianites into thine hand . . .
>
> Judges 7:5–7

The test itself remains mysterious and inexplicable: no one knows exactly why those who lapped the water were chosen and those who cupped it rejected, but the central idea is clear enough. It is that of being called to the fulfillment of a mission or vocation, and of having to pass a test of fitness for it. These are the threads that have guided and unified our lives: the twin ideas of vocation and test. Being distinctly secular-minded, we did not care to think of ourselves as "chosen" — God's Chosen People, or Gideon's chosen three hundred. Yet the sense of having been called to carry out a great historic task was strong in us, and with it the sense that our every act, indeed our every thought, feeling, and attitude, was a test of our fitness for it.

The task was to transform the dream of Zionist-socialism into reality. We had been called to reclaim and rebuild Eretz Yisrael, the land of Israel, the historic home of the Jews, not through the work of others, but by our own individual efforts. We had been called to the pioneering life as an exemplary way to achieve this goal, leading where we hoped others would follow. And above and beyond the reclamation and rebuilding of the land, we had been called to create a new society, a new way of life that would realize the historic ideals of social justice, equality, and humanity. The kibbutz was to be a nonacquisitive, noncompetitive, nonexploitative society: committed to absolute democracy in the government of its communal life; committed to absolute equality in the distribution of the community's material and spiritual goods — the great spiritual goods of education and culture, as well as housing, furniture, clothing, and all the material amenities of life; and committed also to the principle of mutual aid, mutual care, mutual responsibility, which is humanity in action in the daily life of a society.

The vision kindled the hearts and minds of the young pioneer Jews of my parents' generation to a blazing fire, and it was transmitted to us, the second generation, with almost undiminished brilliance and power. In the more than sixty years that have passed since the flame was lit, it has sometimes burned higher and sometimes lower, but it has never been extinguished. The sense of vocation has lived on, and the testing and retesting of the fit has continued almost without remission. They have been, for the most part, objective tests, originating in external conditions and events flung up by our wars, our ideological battles, our new immigrants, our expanding economy, our changing values. But more and more in recent years, the tests have also been internal and self-initiated, the severest of all.

The commitment to this vision has been the guiding thread of my life, shaping its joys, pleasures, and comedies, as well as its griefs and disappointments. But perhaps its deepest continuity is that they have all been experienced in the same place. Ein-Harod, which rose beside Gideon's spring, has remained my home all these sixty years. It has been the scene of the retesting and rededication, the main source of inspiration and strength for my creative endeavors; and it continues to nourish and sustain the roots of my being.

I have tried to express something of this experience in a poem called "Transparency," dedicated to the memory of Yitzhak Tabenkin, a founding father of Ein-Harod.

> The late rain cast
> a transparency over the tree.
> Its opened leaves
> were covered with fine lines
> pure as a blackbird's song.
> Then in one stroke, with a puff of wind,
> its veins thickened
> as if all anguish and bitterness
> were poured into them.
>
> Your forehead, rounded and smooth,
> arouses a tender pity.
> Old fool, who has faith still
> in the stubborn root.

This faith in the stubborn root, waiting for life in its ancient soil, brought Ein-Harod into being.

On a scorching day in September 1921, seventy-five men and women planted the sapling from which the root grew on the banks of Gideon's spring. They were inspired by their faith in the power of the Jewish pioneering spirit to create something out of nothing: a settlement fit for human habitation out of the deadly malarial swamps and stony wasteland of the valley at the foot of Mount Gilboa, a home on a historic biblical site for the young pioneers who were ready to redeem the land by their labor and love. Yehuda Almog, one of the leaders of the seventy-five, left a vivid record of the day they came to found Ein-Harod, called in Hebrew *yom ha-aliya al ha-karka,* "the day of the ascent to the land."

The pioneers set out from Merhavia, the first Jewish settlement in the Jezreel Valley, led by Zvi Nisanov, a famous member of the Hashomer, the first Jewish self-defense organization of Turkish Palestine. Nisanov, on horseback, was followed by a small motor car and a line of wagons loaded with tents, tools, and provisions. The settlers came on foot. In Ein-Harod's fiftieth anniversary volume, *Pirkei Yovel* ("Jubilee Chapters"), Almog recalled,

No road, no path, between the marshes. The heat was terrible. It was already past midday, and we advanced slowly, with great difficulty, along a narrow track leading to the foot of the Gilboa. That's the place where the spring of Harod emerges — the water source of the whole surrounding area. Our first task is to take possession of the spring and put up our tents there, even though the place is all marsh. This is the key to the conquest of the Emek; and we are about to get the key into our hands.

We marched between pools of water and patches of marsh until we reached the slope of the Gilboa and·the cave from which the spring leaps out: Ein-Harod, the Spring of Harod. The hour was half-past-four in the afternoon. Like our lapping fathers who followed Gideon for the salvation of the people of Israel, we knelt down beside the water and lapped it with joy . . . I gazed at the accursed earth around us, and knew that the Emek would exact sacrifices, inhuman effort, and limitless dedication of the spirit. Shall we find these powers in ourselves? Yes, we shall. I have not the shadow of a doubt that we shall!

They did. The Ein-Harod of 1984, sixty-three years hence, is a living monument to the sacrifices, effort, and limitless dedication of the spirit of its first generation of pioneer builders.

I

I Was Born on the Road to Eretz Yisrael

I WAS BORN in the town of Benderri in Bessarabia, a part of czarist Russia, on the fifth day of Hanukkah in the year 1912. In the Christian calendar I have the curious privilege of having two birthdays. My birth was first registered according to the old Julian calendar and then reregistered, six years later, according to the new Gregorian calendar, which was adopted in Russia in 1918 after the Bolshevik Revolution. My parents, however, following a traditional Jewish practice still widely observed in Israel, ignored both my Julian and Gregorian birthdates and simply celebrated my birthday at the lighting of the fifth candle of Hanukkah.

My parents expressed their Zionist aspirations by giving me the rather ponderous name Zerubavel, after the biblical hero who led the Jews out of the Babylonian exile and built the Second Temple in Jerusalem. According to my father, the words *zru Bavel!* meant, literally, "Throw off Bavel" or "Get out of Babylon!" — exactly what my parents wanted to do. From the time they first met in the Zionist movement in Benderri, their most passionate dream was to "throw off" the new Babylonian exile of Eastern Europe and sail to a new life of freedom and dignity in the ancient home of the Jews, Eretz Yisrael. Eretz Yisrael, "land of Israel," was the name Jews used to designate the biblical land of the Jewish people in the area that came to be known as Palestine, which for the first time in eighteen hundred years was being revived and rebuilt as a center of Jewish life.

This page: Zerubavel, age four

Opposite: With my mother, Chaya, when I was ten. She was practical, rich in common sense, and calm and matter-of-fact in handling the daily affairs of our life.

We did not sail until I was ten years old, and even then, for lack of money, we could not all go together. My mother and I went first; three years later my father was finally able to follow. But in all those years, in spite of the upheavals of the First World War, the Russian Revolution, and the Russian Civil War — when the battle for bare survival blotted out all other ambitions — my parents continued to prepare in spirit for the joyous hour of departure: sitting on their suitcases, as we used to say, ready to set out at an hour's notice. This was the air of expectancy I breathed from earliest childhood, and it has made me feel that I was indeed a child born on the road to Eretz Yisrael.

This yearning for Eretz Yisrael was the deepest bond between my parents. In other respects they were widely different. My father, Chaim Glass, was a professional Hebrew teacher. A lover of books and learning, a man of sensibility with a reflective cast of mind, he was also high strung and excitable.

In his native town in Poland he had been sent to a yeshiva to receive the traditional education of an intellectually gifted Jewish boy. He might have become a rabbi or a biblical or Talmudic scholar, but the spirit of the age decreed against this. At the age of eighteen, like many other young Jews of Eastern Europe at the time, he was converted to secular Zionism. Abandoning the yeshiva and the religious-scholarly life, he set about acquiring an education that included Russian, German, and other secular subjects. This kind of independent study was common among young Russian Jews avid for learning, and so was my father's way of supporting himself, by giving private lessons for little pay.

At the age of twenty-two he resolved to go to Eretz Yisrael to help rebuild the land. This was the period of the Second Aliyah, the second wave of Jewish immigration to Eretz Yisrael, primarily from Eastern Europe. The Hebrew word *aliya* means, literally, "ascent," and is used exclusively for immigration to Eretz Yisrael. You "immigrate" (*mehager*) to every other place in the world; you "ascend" (*oleh*) only to Eretz Yisrael. My father paid his own way to Jaffa in 1909 and immediately went off to join the Jewish workers of Petah Tikva, the first Jewish moshava, or agricultural village, in Turkish Palestine, which had been founded more than thirty years earlier. With many of his fellow pioneers, he worked chiefly in the citrus orchards — hard, back-breaking work for a former yeshiva student, made all the more difficult knowing that he was competing for his job with the cheaper and more expert labor of Arab workers.

At this time, my father became a devoted admirer of the Hebrew writer Yosef Chaim Brenner, a powerful influence on the young Jews of that generation, who has recently enjoyed a revival among literary-minded young Israelis. Brenner lived near Petah Tikva at Ein-Ganim, the first workers' village in the area. My father, who came to know him personally, revered him as a spiritual mentor to the end of his life. I still remember gazing at the picture of Brenner on my father's desk when I was a child. I think what appealed to my father and his generation was Brenner's realism about his people. He saw Jewish life and values as profoundly distorted and heading for disintegration, first in the Diaspora, but also in Eretz Yisrael, which was in too many ways merely a disappointing, depressing extension of Jewish life in exile. Fiercely unsentimental and unromantic, Brenner declared open war on all pious cant, particularly on the Zionist establishment of his time. He proffered no easy, universal salvation; indeed, if there was to be any salvation, Brenner intimated, it would be achieved only on a strictly individual basis and only by hard, unremitting, productive labor. This, if anything could, might one day bring about the normalization of the Jewish people — the only goal worth pursuing. It was a fundamentally pessimistic, Dostoevskian vision, but always there was that gleam of hope struggling to survive amid the surrounding despair; and this, it seems, is what spoke to the hearts and minds of my father's generation.

Brenner was killed in 1921 at the age of forty in an Arab pogrom on the outskirts of Jaffa. His death sent a shock of horror through Eretz Yisrael that reached Jewish communities abroad and that reverberates to this day.

My father's first attempt to settle in Eretz Yisrael ended abruptly about a year after his arrival. He was struck first by malaria and then yellow fever, and the doctors told him there was no cure except a change of climate. Accordingly, he was put aboard a cargo boat bound for Odessa, where he remained until his health improved. In 1910 he moved to Benderri, began to teach Hebrew, and became active in Zionist youth groups, where he met my mother. They married and immediately began to plan and save for their aliyah.

His first aborted attempt to settle in Eretz Yisrael deeply affected my father. In the thirteen years he had to wait before he could return, he threw himself with passion into his Hebrew teaching, regarding it not merely as a breadwinning profession but as a mission for the advancement of the Zionist cause. He also became a leading *madrich,* or instructor, of the young Zionists, preparing them for pioneer settlement in Eretz Yisrael. Recently I met in Tel Aviv a survivor of one of these groups of young Jews of Benderri, who remembered distinctly and with gratitude how my father had inspired him and others to take the momentous step of settling in a new land. My father's power to kindle his students' imaginations with his own ardor no doubt helped to sustain him through the many setbacks and disappointments of those long years of waiting. But they took their toll nevertheless. He was often restless and moody, sometimes angry and bitter, falling into fits of melancholy at the seemingly never ending delays and postponements.

My mother, Chaya, had a quite different personality. She was practical, rich in common sense, calm and matter-of-fact in handling the daily affairs of her life. The eldest of four children, she was born and brought up in the small town of Ananiev in the province of Cherson, not far from Odessa. It was hard to make a living in Ananiev, and in due course the family moved to Benderri, where my mother's father opened a small grocery store. My mother, then fourteen or fifteen, entered a vocational school to learn dressmaking. She also joined the Zionist youth group in Benderri and began to dream of going to live in Eretz Yisrael. Dressmaking, she felt, would be a useful skill to take to her new home. (Indeed, it proved so useful that she began and ended her working life at Ein-Harod at her sewing machine.) Meanwhile, she became a much sought after dressmaker in Benderri, helping substantially to support the family. My mother assumed responsibility at an early age, taking care of her two sisters, Adela and Bathsheva, and then of her mother after her father's death.

My grandmother Bracha was quite a character in her own right, but as a child I was particularly attached to my aunt Adela and to my grandfather. Young, pretty, and gay, Adela loved to play with and fuss over me, and in every way earned her status as my favorite aunt. My grandfather, of course, enjoyed the privileged place in my affections that every small boy reserves for his grandfather. I was very proud that he owned a shop and presided over such a wealth of good things to eat; I used to present myself regularly to receive my share of them: a fistful of sticky red sweets drawn out of a tall grocer's jar, which had the magical property of always being brim full no matter how much you took out of it. Besides keeping the shop, my grandfather also practiced his original craft of glazier to supplement the meager family income. He worked in a corner of the kitchen behind the shop, and I remember how fascinated I was by his tools and how I loved to watch him work with his minute diamond, drawing the fiery little sparks from the glass. He taught me to make dolls and all sorts of animals with glazier's putty, and this became one of my favorite entertainments in a life not overrich in children's games. In a poem called "My Grandfather Was a Glazier," I tried to evoke the vivid sensations associated in my memory with the diamond, along with an episode whose meaning I barely understood at the time:

> My grandfather was a glazier
> mending panes in the houses of simple people
> and windows broken in the market
> by evil men.
> He had a tiny diamond for cutting glass
> which he kept in his breast pocket
> next to his heart.
> When he used to take me in his arms
> I smelled the smell of the golden sparks
> which flew in the air
> when the tiny diamond split
> a sheet of glass.

One day Grandfather came back from the market
and his face was ashen.
He drew me between his knees
silently.
Suddenly he sighed and murmured,
"A Jew needs a brave heart,"
and began to tremble.

I was about four years old when my grandfather died. It was the first family death I experienced, and the memory of it is ineradicable. My parents thought I was too young to be told what had happened and sent me to stay with friends not far from our house until after the funeral. Long afterward, I learned that my mother was especially anxious that I be spared the sight of the body, laid out on a bed of straw on the living room floor, according to the Jewish custom of those days. But I sensed, as children do, that something portentous had happened, and I managed to slip out of the neighbor's house and run home. Our house was locked, with no sound coming from it, but peering through the uncurtained living room window, I saw an empty, flat bed of straw on the floor and my mother's long dressmaker's mirror covered with a white sheet. Although I still didn't understand what had happened, I began to cry, and kept on crying with a nameless desolation.

I remember my mother as very energetic, hard working, and scrupulously thorough about everything she undertook, whether she was cleaning a room, making a skirt, or teaching me to make my bed properly. Though she was quite well read in the Russian and Yiddish classics, she was not an intellectual like my father—not analytical, not passionately interested in ideas or ideologies, not given to the heated arguments about theoretical issues that were common in our circle. But she had a firmly rooted, more or less intuitive, sense of moral values; she was fiercely loyal to the people she loved and to the ideas and ideals she believed in; and she had a highly developed sense of responsibility, first to her family, but also to almost everyone who needed help or comfort. When the need arose, she was decisive, resourceful, and courageous. Shortly after her death in 1964, I heard for the first time the story of how she had helped a young member of a Zionist family in Benderri who had deserted the czar's army to be a pioneer in Eretz Yisrael. Despite the danger of aiding a deserter, my mother found him a safe refuge, provided him with civilian clothes, helped him to acquire the false papers he needed, and watched over him until he was able to leave undetected.

I received from my mother all the love and tenderness a child could wish for. But I was never pampered, even though for sixteen years, until the birth of my brother, Yuval, I was an only child. My mother firmly believed that a young child should be assigned regular tasks to promote independence and responsibility. Accordingly, from the time I was five I was required to make my own bed, help to keep my room clean, take proper care of my clothes, toys, and books, and as I grew older, to do my fair share of the rest of the housework. I was thankful to have had this early training when, at the age of eleven, I arrived at Ein-Harod and became a member of a children's community based on the principles of self-reliance and mutual aid.

To my father, I owe my fairly rapid intellectual development in early childhood. His love of books and taste for things of the spirit inspired me, and by the age of four I had started to leaf through the Hebrew books in his library, learning the letters of the Hebrew alphabet long before I was taught to read. I also started to pore over the drawings and photographs in his books about Eretz Yisrael, and I remember my excitement as I gazed at a picture of the Wailing Wall in Jerusalem, or the Gymnasia Herzliya in Tel Aviv, or the pioneers draining marshes in the first settlements, or the men of Hashomer, the Jewish self-defense group, in their Arab garb riding handsome horses. There was also an old book of color drawings of ten or fifteen wildflowers of Eretz Yisrael, which I studied with keen interest. Afterward, when I saw the wildflowers on Mount Gilboa above Ein-Harod, I recognized the cyclamen, anemone, and crocus, and felt I was encountering old friends.

Most of all, perhaps, I have my father to thank for my knowledge of Hebrew. Though I always spoke to my mother in Yiddish and we spoke Russian outside our home, my father always insisted on speaking to me only in Hebrew. Thus it became a mother tongue to me, and I became *yeled ivri*, a Hebrew child, like those of Eretz Yisrael — an unusual phenomenon even in our Zionist circle. This fluency has proved to be one of the great ad-

vantages of my life, enabling me to escape the "language crisis"
that most European immigrants to Eretz Yisrael, including children, experience in their first years there. When I arrived, all I
had to do was get rid of my Ashkenazic and adopt Eretz Yisrael's
Sephardic pronunciation. Because I was young, this didn't take
long; but I was made aware of the pain and embarrassment I had
been spared when occasionally I did pronounce a word in the
Ashkenazic way, drawing gales of derisive laughter from the other
children.

Most of our early-modern Hebrew poets, including Chaim
Nachman Bialik himself, learned Hebrew from traditional prayers and classical written sources — the Bible, Mishnah, the Talmud, the medieval poets and commentators — and never really
used Hebrew naturally as a spoken language. Others, like the
famous poet Rachel, came to the country with no Hebrew at all
and had to learn it from scratch at a relatively mature age — a
daunting task. I was spared all these problems, and I can scarcely
thank my father enough for having ensured for me a rootedness
in my language, which is surely one of the most precious assets of
a poet.

My Zionist upbringing in those early years was intensive indeed. Visiting Zionist leaders and lecturers gathered at our house,
where they would have animated discussions in Hebrew and sing
songs, in which I enthusiastically participated, thus learning some
of the favorite Zionist songs still sung by our song-loving Israelis.
On one occasion the guest of honor was David Vardi, one of the
first Hebrew actors in Eretz Yisrael, who came to Benderri to perform at our local Jewish hall. He stayed with us and told wonderful stories about Eretz Yisrael, mimicking the principal
dramatis personae, who included some of the leading Zionists of
the time. I watched him spellbound, and for weeks afterward
mimicked his mimicries.

My love of the actor's art was put to a more public test when I
was about four. I was chosen to perform a leading, though mainly
silent, part in a Hanukkah play about the Wandering Jew, who
symbolized the persecuted Jews of Eastern Europe fleeing from
the pogroms to the land of their fathers. The long line of refugees
was headed by an aged, white-bearded grandfather, the figure of
the Wandering Jew, holding his small grandson by the hand. I

was the grandson, dressed in a huge coat that reached down to my feet. I had no lines, only a Hebrew song about the Maccabees, the heroes and saviors of Israel, and as I sang I felt I *was* the child I represented. The identification was so complete that when everyone clapped enthusiastically at the end of my song, I burst into tears — of excitement, exaltation, pride, grief, and goodness knows what other confused emotions.

Shortly thereafter, my childhood became a story of perpetual flight. I was two years old in 1914 when the First World War broke out. By 1916 the German armies were approaching Bessarabia, and to escape them we were forced to flee from Benderri to Tiraspol on the other side of the Dniester River, and from there to Odessa. When famine struck Odessa, we fled to my mother's birthplace, Ananiev, and stayed there for a time. When the Russian Civil War started and Jews were being killed in the pogroms of the Whites and in clashes between Whites and Reds, we fled again toward the Dniester back to Tiraspol.

In spite of our refugee existence, my family tried to live a reasonably normal life in the intervals between flights. My formal education, though constantly interrupted, was at least begun, and my Zionist education continued unabated. While we were in Odessa, I went to a Hebrew kindergarten. Then, in Tiraspol, I entered the first grade in a regular Russian elementary school, where my first exercise book had a picture of Lenin on the cover. I knew enough about the history of the Bolshevik Revolution to ask my parents, "Why have they got Lenin on the cover? Why haven't they got Trotsky?"

The Civil War was well under way when a band of Whites intent on massacre entered Tiraspol. They fell upon people in the streets, calling them Bolsheviks or Jews or both. They killed some on the spot; they hanged others from the trees that lined the town's main road. My mother, unaware of what was happening in town, had come to fetch me from school as usual. As we entered the main road and she caught sight of the row of hanged victims, she put her hands over my eyes to prevent my seeing them. But she was not fast enough, and I did see. For weeks afterward, night after night, I would wake up, leap out of my cot, and run wildly back and forth, crying in Hebrew, "Save them! Save them!" A few years ago I wrote a poem, "The River," recalling this episode:

> The river that flowed on the outskirts of the town
> in which I was born beyond the seas
> did not come to me in a dream nor the forest
> that hung over its bank.
> But at night when I wake in the dark
> I hear the sound of the river: the room fills with
> the noise of bubbling and gushing and a rushing stream
> of water.
> A small boy, his hand in his mother's hand, stands on the bank
> among Jews whose faces are pale like the light of the moon
> and around them daylight.
> Suddenly a cow lows in the meadow.*
> My mother hurried to cover my eyes with the palm of her hand.
> She was too late: in the blink of an eye I saw
> a man hanging on a tree, swaying like a branch,
> and in my eyes beneath the palm of my mother's hand
> red, red.
> Be silent, silent, silent! I cry within
> in a hoarse voice to the river.
> But its voice rises, refusing to be silent.

All this time my parents were still "on the road to Eretz Yisrael," trying by all means to get to Palestine, which was under British rule. The Bolshevik regime was beginning to clamp down on Jewish immigration to Palestine, and the last emigrants allowed to leave sailed in 1919 from Odessa on a ship called the *Ruslan.* My parents had planned to be on this ship, and made frantic efforts to get our papers together in time. But they failed, the *Ruslan* sailed without us, and we lost our last chance to leave Russia legally. So our only hope was to try from the nearest place outside Russia, which happened to be my birthplace, Benderri, on the other side of the Dniester, then under Rumanian rule. My parents resolved to recross the Dniester illegally, from Tiraspol to Benderri, there to await a fresh opportunity to get away.

The crossing was an experience none of us ever forgot. The Russia-Rumania border had been sealed, but there were plenty of peasant "guides" willing, for a substantial payment, to smuggle

---

*According to Talmudic legend, the lowing of a cow signaled, simultaneously, the destruction of the Temple and the birth of the Messiah.

people across the Dniester into Rumanian Bessarabia. We did not have enough money to pay for the whole family to cross together, so it was decided that my father and I would cross first, leaving my mother and grandmother to follow later. This was the first time I was to be separated from my mother, and I cried a great deal at the thought of going without her. It was midwinter, the Dniester was frozen over, and there was thick snow on the ground in the forests on both sides of the river. Twelve of us were to be smuggled across in a sledge.

Like all refugees, each member of the group carried his meager possessions in a suitcase or pillowcase or awkward-shaped bundle. At seven, I was too small to carry a suitcase, so I wore most of the clothes I owned. There was the long overcoat I had worn in the Hanukkah play, and under this another overcoat, two pairs of trousers, several pairs of socks, and heavy galoshes over my shoes. Not surprisingly, it was all I could do to waddle in this strange outfit, and my movements were hampered further by the set of four books, tied up in a huge kerchief, that I clutched in my arms. These were the only books my father had allowed himself to take from his library in Tiraspol, and he had instructed me to hold them tight and never, never to be parted from them. The books were Bialik's poems, Shául Tchernichovsky's poems, Zalman Shneour's poems, and Henry Wadsworth Longfellow's "Hiawatha" in Tchernichovsky's translation. They were all de luxe editions with gilt lettering on the covers and spines.

We had been warned to remain absolutely silent because the border guards on both sides would shoot at the slightest sound. Although we heard shots as we approached the border, we reached the other side of the Dniester without mishap. There, our sledge-driving smuggler handed us over to his Rumanian partner, a Moldavian peasant who was to take us on foot through the snowbound forest to his cottage in the village on the other side of the forest.

Now my ordeal really began. We walked along a path single-file, in complete silence, hearing the shots of the border guards at intervals. I stumbled and fell repeatedly and, because of the weight of my clothes and the bundle I was clutching, I couldn't get up again — rather like a medieval knight in full armor who falls from his horse. My father had to help me up each time, causing the whole line to come to a halt. In the end our burly guide lost patience with the constant stops, seized me, tucked me under his arm beneath his huge fur cape, and carried me like a parcel for the rest of the journey. Several times he hissed at me angrily to throw away the silly bundle I was clinging to. But I obstinately refused and, hugging it to my chest, carried it into the peasant's cottage like a trophy.

Our stay in Benderri lasted three years, during which my father went back to teach at Dr. Zvi Schwartzman's Hebrew gymnasium. I was enrolled there, exempt from paying tuition fees because my father was a member of the staff. Dr. Schwartzman, the headmaster, was an imposing figure in the traditional European style of the time. Always formally dressed in a starched shirt and buttoned-up coat, he stalked about with a stiff, unbending gait and a severe expression on his face. There was nothing easy or informal about his relations with his pupils, and we were all in great awe of him. Nevertheless, despite his nonpioneering appearance and personal style, he was a dedicated Zionist, a pioneer of Hebrew education in czarist Russia, who fought successfully for the right to establish Hebrew schools in the main centers of Jewish life. He inspired many of his pupils with his fervor, came to live in Eretz Yisrael in his last years, and is still remembered in Israel by surviving contemporaries from Benderri as a decisive influence in their lives.

The Zionist atmosphere he created in the school had the effect, it seems, of inducing Dr. Schwartzman to relax from time to time into uncharacteristic informalities. One day, to our astonishment, he strode into my class of eight-year-olds, imperiously stopped the lesson, and announced that he was going to teach us two Hebrew songs. He then wrote the words on the board, commanded us to recite them in unison, and proceeded to sing them to us in a shaky, uncertain voice that was strikingly, and to us comically, at variance with his booming, confident speaking voice. The first song was a rousing ditty called "There in the Pleasant Land of Our Fathers," about the joys of the return to Zion, where all our dearest hopes would be fulfilled and we would create a life full of light and freedom. It was typical of the earliest Zionist songs and is still sung on festive occasions like Independence Day; only now we sing *"Here* in the pleasant land of our fathers." The unusual spectacle of the great Dr. Schwartzman bursting into song was itself unforgettable, but I had a special reason for remembering the episode. The second song was a marching tune, "Be Glad and Rejoice, Our People," and its refrain ran as follows:

> Come back to me, the days of *Zeruba-vel, Zeruba-vel!*
> Hurrah! Long live the people of *Isra-el!*

The rather feeble rhyme did not prevent me from swelling with happy pride, as we all sang the lines energetically and my classmates turned around to stare at me in admiration and envy. For once I was glad my parents had given me that burdensome name!

During our three years in Benderri, my parents were always struggling to save for our journey to Eretz Yisrael. At last there was enough money to enable three of us to go. It was decided that my mother, grandmother, and I should go first, leaving my father to follow as soon as he could pay his way. It was hard for me to be parted from my father again, as hard as it had been to leave my mother behind in Tiraspol for nearly six months. But there was no choice. This was clear even to me, and it has struck me since how early I was obliged to learn the meaning of that pregnant phrase, *ayn brera,* "no choice." Again and again in Eretz Yisrael we had no choice but to fight for an independent Jewish existence. And there was no choice but to go without my father, so, in the early summer of 1923, we sailed from the Rumanian port of Galatz on the Black Sea on the cargo boat *Constanza.*

It was night when we first sighted the coast of Eretz Yisrael. As we approached Haifa Bay and saw the flickering lights of the town, tremendous excitement swept our shipload of immigrants, composed for the most part of four hundred *chalutzim,* or pioneers. Spontaneously, as with one voice, they sang Hatikva, the song of yearning of Jews in exile, which has since become the national anthem of the State of Israel, and broke into the hora, the famous dance of the chalutzim. We reached the port of Jaffa in the morning. There were huge rocks in the approaches to the port, so our ship had to anchor some distance from the shore, and we were taken ashore in small boats manned by Arabs. Dressed in the

Turkish style, in billowing trousers caught at the ankle, the boat-men shouted and squabbled in shrill, raucous voices as they competed fiercely for the passengers. Once in the boats, we were thrown about like baggage; and this first encounter with the Arabs of Eretz Yisrael was bewildering and frightening to my child's soul.

Our boats were met by a few seedy British officials, who treated us with cold indifference; although not positively hostile, they definitely were not friendly. So our first encounter with the British authorities of Eretz Yisrael was not very encouraging either. It was offset, however, by the single Jewish official who had come to meet us, a representative of the Immigration Department of the Zionist Executive in Palestine, who ran back and forth among the impassive British in a frenzy of excitement, waving his arms in welcoming gestures and crying out the traditional Hebrew greeting, *Bruchim haba'im* (Blessed are they who arrive). He may have been ridiculous but he was human, and by this time we were greatly in need of a sign of humanity in the alien surroundings.

Jaffa port was dirty and dilapidated, and beyond the port bleak sand dunes were visible all along the coast. We were given various injections and told we would be kept in quarantine for a week. Thus we spent our first days in Eretz Yisrael herded together in barrackslike dormitories in a compound surrounded by a barbed wire fence. The friends and relations who came to welcome the new immigrants that week were not allowed beyond the fence, and we felt distinctly like prisoners. It was a depressing start to our new life. Nevertheless there was one beautiful moment in those first cheerless days. As we were taking a walk in the quarantine compound, my mother suddenly seized me and started to twirl around in a sort of dance, crying joyously, with tears in her eyes, "We're in Eretz Yisrael, Eretz Yisrael!"

We began life in Eretz Yisrael with an unsettled, unsatisfactory year in Tel Aviv. The first week or two we stayed in a small flat with old friends of my mother who had emigrated from Benderri before the First World War. Then we moved into a single room of our own, with a small outdoor stove and an outdoor washbasin and toilet. There in that one room we all slept and ate, there I did my lessons, and there my mother did her dressmaking. The one large piece of equipment we had brought with us was her Singer sewing machine, and it proved its worth from the start. My mother received dressmaking commissions almost immediately, starting with *bnei-ir* (literally "town mates"), old friends from Benderri, who in turn recommended her to other women. This custom of helping newcomers continues to the present day. So my mother's modest clientele grew fairly rapidly; it was proof of her foresight and practical wisdom in choosing her profession that she was able to earn a living by it immediately on our arrival in the country.

Then my mother heard from friends in Tel Aviv that three fellow Zionists of her youth in Benderri had gone to live in a new kibbutz, Ein-Harod, in the Emek, the Jezreel Valley. The settlers in this kibbutz were experimenting with the new study-and-work system of education of which I had already had a taste in my school years in postrevolutionary Russia. My mother decided that this was what she wanted for me: study and work combined, a child taught to be a scholar and a worker simultaneously. She knew almost nothing more about the organization of a kibbutz, but this, along with the knowledge that old friends from Benderri were there, was enough for her. So in the spring of 1924 we set off for the unknown Kibbutz Ein-Harod in the Emek. We left my grandmother in a home for the aged in Tel Aviv as a temporary arrangement. If she liked it there, she would stay; if she didn't, she would join us once we were settled in our new home.

I

Ein-Harod

2

First Encounters

THERE WERE NO tarred roads, no buses, no other forms of public transport to Ein-Harod. We took the train from Tel Aviv to Haifa, and there boarded the narrow gauge popularly known as the Emek Train, which stopped at Ein-Harod, went on to Tzemach in the Jordan Valley, then crossed the Jordan River into Transjordan, and proceeded to Damascus. This Emek Train, I learned later, was a homely, familylike train in the Turkish tradition. The engineer and conductor were Arabs, and for a small consideration they would let you off at any unscheduled stop you requested. If the conductor saw you running and waving in the distance, he would obligingly keep the train waiting until you were safely on board. When you bought your ticket from him, he would give it to you at a reduced price. You would pay, say, seven grush instead of the full fare of ten and get no ticket; the conductor pocketed the seven and you saved three grush. As children we loved to travel on this friendly Emek Train, and we all sadly missed it after it was discontinued in 1948 during the War of Independence.

The shabby little station at which we got off was graced rather incongruously by an imposing sign bearing the name AYN-HAROD in big black letters on a white ground. It had been put up by the British Mandate authorities and was an exact replica (as I learned on my first visit to England forty years later) of the British Railways signs on all English stations. Ein-Harod was about a kilome-

ter away, and we set out on foot, carrying our possessions in a
modest suitcase. It was an April day in the week of Passover, and
we approached the settlement in the evening light. Mount Gilboa
towered over us, with empty fields all around, no people in sight,
and only the howling of jackals and hooting of owls to break the
oppressive silence. Sensing my fright, my mother held my hand
tightly in hers until we reached the outskirts of Ein-Harod. It was
a settlement in the wilderness — this is what I felt, though I could
not have expressed it then. My mother said nothing and her face
was impassive, but I sensed obscurely that she shared my feelings
of trepidation, and I found comfort in this.

Trepidation was soon supplanted by the interest and excitement of taking in my new surroundings. And indeed Ein-Harod
in 1924, three years after its founding, offered a great deal to absorb the mind and imagination of a newcomer of eleven. For a
start there was the natural scene, bare and arid, especially to the
eye of a boy from a European country rich in forests, orchards,
and cultivated fields. I think I must have been struck first by the
absence of trees. There was just one ancient fig tree at the entrance of the cave from which Gideon's spring emerged, one cas-
tor-oil plant behind the cowshed near the remains of a cactus
fence, and a eucalyptus grove on the banks of the stream near the
spring. The bare mountain slopes yielded only thorns, thistles,
and keel, which burst briefly into green in the short wet winter
months, then turned to gray and yellowish brown all through the
long hot summer. There were birds of prey but no others except
sparrows, larks, and finches, which I came to love in this nearly
birdless world. One heard almost no birdsong by day, and at
night only the eerie cries of night birds mingled with those of the
jackals and hyenas — strange, disagreeable music to the ears of a
town-bred child.

It was a land of stones, thorns, and dust. There were rocks
everywhere: on the paths, between the tents and huts, even in the
fields, despite the fact that they had been cultivated for three
years. The stones absorbed the heat, remaining hot even after
sundown and adding greatly to the tormenting discomfort of the
long summer. They also provided hiding places for scorpions and
sometimes poisonous snakes as well, and we were constantly
warned to beware of lifting stones without the utmost caution.

The dust was everywhere, too. Great clouds of it rose from the unpaved road leading to the fields every time a wagon or cart or horse passed through; it settled on the huts, the tents, the children's house, the hospital — on everything. The one dust-free place was along the banks of the stream, and this is where we used to take our refuge, especially when the eucalyptus grove grew larger and offered shade as well. In winter the dusty earth turned to deep, thick mud, as impassable as a quagmire. The only way to get from one part of the settlement to another was by means of little paths we carved out with a homemade mud plow, fashioned of wooden planks in the shape of a triangle and drawn by mules. We became quite expert at cleaning the mud off our shoes several times a day, but drying them out was a problem. Boots were still an unimaginable luxury, as were heaters. So we dried our shoes by stuffing them with newspapers or rags at night and putting them close to the oven in the bakery, which was alight all night to produce the next day's supply of bread. My mother was the inspiration behind this method, which was soon adopted by others as well, and during the wet months the bakery nightly became a crowded repository for steaming shoes.

The settlement lay at the foot of Mount Gilboa, which formed its southern boundary. It was bounded on the east by a chalk quarry in a natural valley, and on the west by the Spring of Harod, widening into the Stream of Harod, which curved around to form its northern boundary and flowed on eastward to the Jordan River.

Mount Gilboa was a magnificent backdrop, inspiring for its rich biblical associations. But in daily life it could become oppressive, especially in the summer. It loomed over and encroached upon us, the gray rocks and tangled masses of dry thorns reaching right down to our tents and huts giving us a sense that the mountain was bearing down on us, cutting us off from air, enclosing us. It was different in the winter and early spring, when the Gilboa was all green and covered with masses of wildflowers. Then it beckoned with an exhilarating freshness, spaciousness, openness, and climbing its slopes to breathe the bracing winter air or to pick the spring flowers was a favorite recreation. From the top of the Gilboa on a clear day — and most of our winter days, then as now, were beautifully clear — we could see Mount Carmel to the

Ein-Harod in 1923 was still little more than a settlement in the wilderness.

west, the Gilead Mountains to the east, Mount Hermon to the north, the hills of Samaria to the south. For valley dwellers like us this was a fine, liberating experience.

The physical components of Ein-Harod in 1924 are as clear in my memory as those of the Ein-Harod I live in today. The settlement, including the fields, covered an area of 9600 dunams, about 2400 acres. Its farm buildings — the cowshed, sheep pen, stables, forge, repair shop, and so on — were on the southern perimeter, immediately below the Gilboa. In the center stood the long wooden hut that was the communal dining hall; it also served as assembly hall, clubhouse, theater, and dance hall. Adjoining it were the kitchen, bakery, and administrative office; to the west of it, the storehouses and the laundry; and to the north, near the stream, the residential quarters, composed of three rows of wooden huts interspersed with tents. The chicken runs, the nursery and greenhouse, the children's quarters, and the small hospital and maternity ward (the first in the area) were on the eastern perimeter. Also to the east of the dining hall, near the chicken runs, stood a large, rather odd-shaped two-story building, which housed the kibbutz granary on the first floor and the library, sewing room, and communal closet on the second. There were no pri-

The Stream of Harod, 1924

vate storage spaces in the huts and tents, and no personal ownership of clothes or bed linens; all clothing was communal, and we
just wore what the *machsana'it,* "clothing keeper," put into our
cubbyholes, and were satisfied if the size was approximately right.
Beyond the eastern perimeter lay the vineyards, orchards, and
fields, the chief crops at the time being wheat, barley, maize, and
sunflower. Just three roads led out of the kibbutz: two dirt
tracks — one running east through the fields, the other north
through the vegetable garden — and one pebbled road going
north to the railway station in the valley.

The population of the settlement was as unique as the land. In
1924 Ein-Harod was a community of 276 people; by 1926 it had
grown to 382: 287 adult members, 75 children, and 20 "aged parents," many of whom were hardly past fifty but were considered
aged because the members, whose parents they were, were so
young. At that time, no other kibbutz was as large as Ein-Harod;
the maximum number in the others was about fifty, and even
most modern kibbutzim in their third or fourth year number
fewer than a hundred people.

The adult members of the kibbutz fell into two categories, the
chalutzim (pioneers) and the *vatikim* (veterans). The eighty or so

The children's vegetable garden, with the schoolhouse at left and the children's house in the background, 1926. I am hoeing at right.

veterans were mostly immigrants of the Second Aliyah (circa 1904–1914), who had settled in Eretz Yisrael before the First World War and had come to Ein-Harod from older settlements, mainly from Kinneret on the shore of the Sea of Galilee. By 1926 there were about two hundred pioneers, who had recently arrived in Eretz Yisrael in the Third Aliyah (circa 1919–1923). Primarily from Russia and Eastern Europe, but including a small group from Germany for the first time, the young pioneers were a very mixed lot: many of them were former students, secular and religious; some were former shop assistants; there were a few artisans and a few farmers. The majority knew little or nothing about farming and had to learn the hard way, on the job, instructed by the veterans, most of whom had been farmers in the country for a decade or longer.

The so-called aged parents had a separate dining room and kitchen in an old stone hut that also doubled as a synagogue. This special arrangement had been made because many, if not all, of the parents had been brought up as observant Jews, and they wanted to worship in a synagogue and observe *kashrut*, the traditional dietary laws. The rest of the kibbutz, on the other hand, did not observe kashrut or other Jewish religious practices. The parents, who were assigned the lighter communal tasks, had shorter work hours and other exemptions. The men, for example, were postmen, accountants, glaziers, or keepers of the tools store; the women usually worked in the kitchen, peeling potatoes, preparing the traditional *lokshen* (homemade noodles) and *pashtida* (noodle pie) for the Sabbath, and baking challah for their own dining room. This is how, in 1925, one of the mothers recorded her experience of lokshen making:

> My goodness, what masses of lokshen one has to prepare here! In the old days before the Russian Revolution, I used to make lokshen with eggs for the whole family, and it used to last us the whole winter right up to Pesach. But here — bless their hearts — it's a whole sack of flour each time! They do know how to eat here — may they be healthy and strong! [*Pirkei Yovel*]

There were tension and comedy in the relations between the pioneers and the veterans that might by themselves form a chapter in the history of Ein-Harod's first years. They arose partly from the difference in age, what we now call the generation gap. Most of the young pioneers were between eighteen and thirty-five; most of the veterans of the Second Aliyah were thirty-five to forty-five. The difference, then, was one of only about ten years, but it seemed to count for a great deal, for it marked a fundamental difference in spirit and attitude between the two groups.

The older immigrants had shown heroic powers of resistance and endurance in those early years, and a total dedication to the idea of building the land by their own labor — in preparation, they hoped, for a mass immigration of young Jews after the war. But by the early 1920s they were suffering from weariness and depression induced by the hardships they had endured under Turkish rule during World War I. The regime had expelled the Jews in Palestine who were not Turkish subjects, either to Egypt or back to their mother countries in Eastern Europe. Those who remained had been reduced to poverty, in some cases to the point of starvation. They had felt isolated, cut off from the outside world during all those hard years of the war. So by the time they arrived at Ein-Harod in 1921 and the years immediately following, many were somewhat depleted. Nevertheless, they retained brave hope for the future and faith in the power of the young pioneers of the Third Aliyah to carry on the building of the country that they had begun.

In contrast to the veterans, the young chalutzim were fresh and full of energy. They were also more radical in their political views, more open and uninhibited in their attitudes and behavior, and more receptive to new ideas. Those who came from Russia were bursting with idealistic enthusiasm, inspired by the Russian Revolution, to build in Eretz Yisrael a model communist society. Those who came from central and eastern Europe saw Europe as corrupt and decaying (this was the Kafka generation), and were fired by the ideal of creating a new and better society free of the ugly injustices of the countries they had left behind. Of this second group, many belonged to the intelligentsia. Indeed, there were so many young intellectuals in the Third Aliyah that a few months after the founding of Ein-Harod, two other kibbutzim, Hephtziba and Beit-Alpha, composed almost entirely of pioneers from the educated stratum of European society, were founded in the eastern Jezreel Valley.

So there were both psychological and ideological differences to account for the undercurrent of tension at Ein-Harod between the young pioneers of the Third Aliyah and the veterans of the Second Aliyah. It sometimes percolated down to the children who, though they could scarcely have understood what the conflicts were about, were certainly adept at aping their elders with a great show of smugness. Soon after his arrival at the kibbutz as a new chalutz, Chaim Shifroni, one of our first three permanent teachers, was doing his dining room duty in the children's house for the first time. A boy named Yossik and I had been assigned to work with him, and while I was washing the breakfast dishes in the kitchen, Shifroni and Yossik were washing the dining room floor. Yossik had ostensibly shown Shifroni what to do, namely, to pour pails of water on the floor and then mop up the water with a cloth. Having gotten Shifroni started, Yossik abandoned his senior partner and ran off to play in the nearby threshing field. Shifroni, who had never washed a floor in his life, simply went on emptying pails of water, but had no idea how to get rid of it. He stood there helplessly in the rising flood around him and finally, in despair, called me from the kitchen to help him.

Yossik's conduct was considered a serious dereliction of duty, and he was called before the children's disciplinary committee. Would he please explain why he had abandoned Shifroni when he was supposed to guide and help him?

Yossik, unrepentant and defiant, vigorously defended himself: "Why, what's wrong with it? I'm a *vatik* — I've been in this country eleven years. He's a new *chalutz*, so why shouldn't he do some work? Why shouldn't he learn things the hard way, the way we did?"

Whether the committee was amused or scandalized by this defense from eleven-year-old Yossik was not recorded, but it does illuminate the kind of talk the little pitchers with big ears must have heard often enough among their elders.

Despite the tensions and the talk, however, the vatikim and the chalutzim seemed to work together well enough in the overriding task of building and developing the kibbutz, and there was a great deal of mutual warmth, kindliness, and good humor in their day-to-day relations. The older men and women were often won over by the very freshness of their young fellow members — by their unconventionality, their frankness and forthrightness, and the spontaneous way in which they were apt to break the established norms of behavior.

Second Aliyah veteran Batya Brenner recalled her own adjustment to the ways of the kibbutz. The sister of Yosef Chaim Brenner, the writer who so profoundly influenced my father as a young man, she was a founding member of Ein-Harod who had come there from Kinneret. She arrived with only two valuable possessions, a watch and a rain cape, which had been given to her as gifts. But, alas, she was not to retain possession of them for long: She wrote in *Pirkei Yovel*:

> On the very day after the day of my arrival at Ein-Harod, a young *chavera* [female member] approached me, saying, "Ah-ha, I see you've got a watch! You're unmarried, aren't you — so why do you need a watch? I'm a nursing mother, and I do need a watch. Let me have your watch!" I wanted to say to her, "But this watch is a gift!" Instantly, however, I was converted to the logic of the communal life. She really needed the watch more than I did, so I gave it to her.

Then, not long afterward:

> It was raining, so I drew out my rain cape and walked to the dining hall. Our kibbutz guard was standing at the entrance. He caught sight of me and cried, "Hurrah! A rain cape!" — and took off my cape. I stood there and he looked at me, opened the wings of the

cape, smiled, and said, "If it rains hard, I will come to your tent and take you under my cape." *His* cape? "What, *yours?*" I said. He answered, "Yes, it's mine, because I'm on guard duty this week. And next week it will be someone else's." I smiled, too, and said, "Don't worry about me, I'll go without a rain cape. My position, after all, will then be the same as that of many others." And that is how the two gifts I had received from a friend who had returned from the Jewish Battalion [of the British army in World War I] became the property of the commune.

She also gives good insight into the work ethos of the time.

There was a great readiness for work. It was a willingness to do work that, according to the prevailing notions of the girls of the small Jewish towns of Eastern Europe, was never done by Jews. One Sabbath a *chaver* [male member] holding a heavy stick, his hands covered with gloves made of rags, approached me. He said, "Come! Today it's our turn to do the toilets." We went. We emptied the pails into the sewer pit and washed and scrubbed them. Afterward, I washed myself thoroughly, and changed all my clothes — but I couldn't go into my tent. For nearly an hour I stood outside, fighting my nausea.

We rotated in every kind of job. For example, my permanent work was in the vegetable garden, but I was also required to take my turn at cooking. We didn't sleep all night before our day of cook duty. Tomorrow — I'm going to do the cooking. And nobody told me how much water or how much salt to put in. The spirit of readiness to take on any task supplied all the answers. But we felt good. On days when things were easy, we said, "What a tremendous job we did today, and it wasn't all that hard. How marvelous!" And on a bad day we said, "What a hard day it was! But see how we survived — how marvelous!" [*Pirkei Yovel*]

This was the community my mother entered in 1924. My place was in the community of children. Of the sixty-nine children who were there when I arrived, sixty-two were babies, tots, and kindergarten children, and only seven were of school age. I made the eighth, and my mother liked to tell me afterward that she was accepted as a member of the kibbutz because of me. At that time Ein-Harod was reluctant to take in new members because it had not yet been recognized by the Settlement Department of the Zionist Executive in Jerusalem for financial aid and had received no budget for development. Consequently there was a shortage of

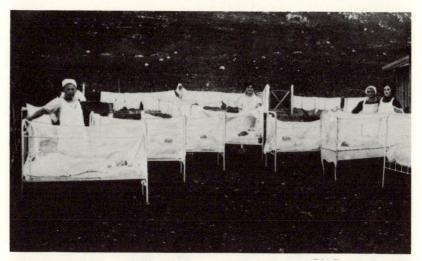

Babies' cots covered with mosquito netting, 1926. From the beginning, the children were a focal point of kibbutz life, embodying the future of the kibbutzim and of Eretz Yisrael.

work, food, living quarters, and everything else the settlement needed to expand its membership. Nevertheless, it was very eager to increase its number of school-age children, which is what finally persuaded the community to accept us.

The community of children I joined was designed to be a separate, self-contained social unit of the kibbutz. Its physical center was the children's house, a single, long wooden structure that housed all the children from ages three to fourteen. The babies and the tots had separate quarters. The children's house was composed of a kitchen, dining room, bedrooms, and a playroom for the kindergarten children who also had indoor showers and toilets. Next to it was the schoolhouse and a smaller three-room wooden hut called the Green Hut, which included a nature room. Along one side of the schoolhouse was a vegetable garden worked by the children and a carpentry and general workshop. When our numbers increased, we had a second, experimental vegetable garden and half a dunam of wheat, worked under the supervision of an agricultural expert from the Experimental Station of the Zionist Executive. Later a small flower garden was added.

Behind the schoolhouse was the children's yard, which featured a stable containing three sheep, two donkeys, and a small donkey cart. The provisions for the children's house arrived each day

Sabbath elegance in a tent

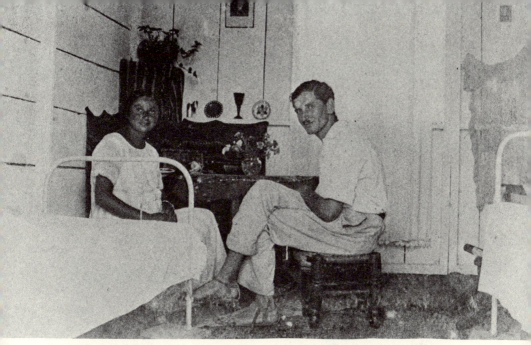

In 1926, interiors weren't considered worth photographing. Thanks to photographer Ya'kov Weissenberg (*right*), we have this picture of a typical dwelling shack.

from the kibbutz store in this cart, and the donkeys played a central part in our lives. The tall brown one was called Shloimele (Little Shlomo) after the first treasurer and leading ideologue of the kibbutz, Shlomo Lavie, who was tall and thin; the small black curly haired one was named Moishele (Little Moshe) after the first librarian, Moshe Schweiger, because the donkey had the distinction of having been born in the kibbutz library.

Next to the stable was a chicken run that housed about fifty hens and roosters, forty chicks, and a few ducks. Behind the chicken run were the primitive bucket toilets used by the schoolchildren and their teachers, and nearby we had a small zoo of birds, snakes, lizards, white mice, hedgehogs, a jackal, a wildcat, and other creatures. The whole children's compound was situated at the eastern perimeter of the kibbutz next to the threshing field. This was our playground: a big open space covered with green grass in the winter, full of haystacks and bundles of wheat in the summer, in which we could tumble about to our hearts' content, play hide-and-seek, cops and robbers, cowboys and Indians, and other games.

We were playing cops and robbers one summer day when I had an encounter I have never forgotten. I was in the field doing my bit as a robber, when I suddenly saw a rather stately man, dressed in a suit and tie, surrounded by a group of our field workers. His clothes marked him as a visiting townsman, but I had no idea who he was and only afterward learned that he was Shlomo Tzemach, a professional agronomist and respected author, who had come to assess our wheat output for the purpose of determining our wheat tax — a kind of tithe that was regularly levied in those days. He was explaining how he made his assessment to the workers, and I stopped to listen, curious to hear what he was saying. Noticing me, he called me over and announced flatly, "Tomorrow I'm bringing Bialik on a visit here."

"Oh, yes," I said indifferently, and headed back toward my game.

At this he shouted angrily, "Stand still, boy, when a grown-up is talking to you! Do you know who Bialik is?"

"Yes, yes. I know," I replied, not quite liking this stranger and his questions, and trying again to get away.

But he stopped me again, fixed his eyes on me, and said, slowly and solemnly, "Do you know, boy, that but for Bialik there would have been no Ein-Harod?"

I made my escape at last, but his strange remark left me puzzled and worried. What *could* he have meant? That evening, still mystified, I sought out one of my favorite grown-ups, Eliyahu Satt, our harness maker and a veteran of the Second Aliyah, who always had plenty of time and patience for talk with the young. "What did that man mean by saying that but for Bialik there would have been no Ein-Harod?" I asked.

Satt gazed at me thoughtfully for a few moments, then answered, "He's right, you know. Oh, yes, he's right. Shall I tell you why I came to Ein-Harod? Because I read Bialik's poem about the Kishinev pogrom. You know which one I mean — 'The City of Slaughter,' that one — I read it, and *that's* what made me decide to immigrate to Eretz Yisrael. And I'm not the only one, I assure you. I know that others, plenty of others, came for the same reason — directly inspired by 'The City of Slaughter.' Oh, yes, that fellow was right."

I have often thought since about this unusual proof of the

power of literature to move men to action. And I have thought, too, how typical it was of the spirit of that period in our history that a poem — just a poem — should have had that power.

Bialik's poem eloquently describes the horror of the Kishinev pogrom of 1903, in which forty-seven Jewish men, women, and children were killed and ninety-two injured by Jew-hating inhabitants of the Bessarabian town. But it also speaks of the shameful timidity and submissiveness of the victims, who never stood up to their tormentors, never fought back, but instead fled or hid like terrified mice. This fierce critique of the victims acted as a clarion call to young Zionists like Eliyahu Satt, inducing many of them to immigrate to Eretz Yisrael, to build a national home in which Jews would never again know the shame and humiliation of Kishinev.

Our community of schoolchildren, growing in size from year to year, was run on the same principles as the kibbutz as a whole. A microcosm of the kibbutz, it was based on self-government, self-help, and mutual aid, and its governing body was the General Assembly, of which all the children and their teachers were voting members. We met once a month to discuss problems and make decisions bearing on every aspect of the life of our community. Any proposal put before the assembly was democratically debated, then accepted or rejected by a simple majority vote. One of us acted as secretary and kept the minutes, and each work group was required to submit monthly reports, including comments and criticisms of the work record of the group's individual members, to the General Assembly. Like the kibbutz, we had an elected "work organizer" who scheduled the weekly work assignments of the children and teachers: who was to do the potato peeling, vegetable cutting, floor washing, dish washing, toilet cleaning, and so forth. There were also elected officers for other rotating jobs — the librarian and clothes keeper, for example — who held their positions for six or twelve months and were then replaced. And, like the kibbutz, we had a host of committees. There was a committee for the farm, for clothing, for parties, for editorial affairs (of which I was always a member), and for discipline, which was tactfully called the committee for "clarifications."

All the work of the children's house and schoolhouse — including the cleaning, maintenance, repairs, farm chores, and so on —

was done jointly by the children and their teachers. The only outside help we were allowed was our cook, but we were expected to
help in the preparation of the food and were taught to cook from
an early age. The boys and girls shared equally in all the work;
the boys did mending along with the girls, and the girls worked
beside the boys on the farm. We were expected to keep accounts
of income and expenditure, of the weight of our produce from the
vegetable gardens, of the number of eggs produced by our
chickens, and other bookkeeping records. In addition to our normal tasks in the children's house and on the farm, we and our
teachers also did our share of the seasonal work of the kibbutz in
the fields and later in the vineyards. This work was a full-time job
for about six weeks of each year, requiring the virtual suspension
of lessons and most of our other jobs.

Our lessons were a rather haphazard affair in the first two years
or so after my arrival. As there were just eight students, all of different ages and at different stages of development, we were taught
almost individually by just one teacher, all in one room, receiving
different assignments according to age and ability — almost exactly as if we were in a *cheder,* the traditional Jewish religious elementary school of Eastern Europe. Our teachers changed often in
these first years. They were generally new arrivals who weren't
members of the kibbutz, and they spoke Hebrew with their funny
Ashkenazic accent, were raw to the ways of the country, and had
little teaching experience. I am afraid we gave them a bad time,
teasing and tormenting them mercilessly, reducing them to despair about ever teaching us anything, and practically forcing
their departures.

Later, when there were more school-age children, the situation
changed. We got our first three permanent teachers; all members
of the kibbutz, they viewed teaching as a pioneering vocation,
and they were persons of striking character and personality. Unlike their unfortunate predecessors, they were treated with great
respect, indeed with reverence, by children and parents alike, and
they exercised a great formative influence on our lives.

The children were a focal point of kibbutz life from its beginning. For the founding fathers and mothers, they embodied the
future, of the kibbutzim and of Eretz Yisrael as a whole. They
were to be the new Jews, living a healthy, free, dignified life in the

"The Three Graces," the first kindergarten teachers at Ein-Harod.
Left to right, Rivka, Frumka, and Natalka.

restored homeland of the Jewish people, liberated forever from the oppression and humiliation of Jewish life in exile. This is what the visionaries of the return to Zion yearned to witness, and the settlers of Ein-Harod, with those of the other kibbutzim, set out to create this reality with purposeful vigor. The children were given privileged treatment from the start. They got the best food — plenty of milk, eggs, and chicken — even when the adult members never saw meat, except on festivals, and had a ration of two eggs a week. Whatever amenities the community could afford were first given to the children. Toys, pictures, and other decorations, cheap but gay, somehow appeared in the children's house long before there was anything to please the eye in the tents and huts of their parents. In the summer, the high-risk season for malaria, we schoolchildren were sent to Nazareth in the hills, where we had our first direct contact with Arabs, whom we found as interesting and exciting as the change of scene.

Our Nazareth interlude lasted six to eight weeks each summer, during which time we lived in a rented house under the care of two women and one man from the kibbutz. Each week our provisions were brought from Ein-Harod in a wagon drawn by mules, and the steep ascent and descent to and from Nazareth were considered such a nerve-racking business that only our most expert wagoners were given the job. Our parents came to visit us on the Sabbath, and we enjoyed seeing them, rather like children at a boarding school on parents' visiting day. Nazareth seemed very picturesque and delightfully exotic to us. The Arab houses were surrounded by gardens with pomegranate, almond, and fig trees, trellises of vines, and boxes of geraniums in many colors. There were fine views of ancient cypresses from almost any high vantage point, and I spent one summer industriously painting the trees and other views from the long verandah of our house. My father, when at last he joined us at Ein-Harod, had brought me a gift of a box of water colors, and this set me off on my brief painter's career, which peaked that summer in Nazareth.

The highlights of our Nazareth summers were usually provided by our Christian Arab friend, Hananiya, and his extended family. Hananiya was a master quarrier who had come to Ein-Harod from Nazareth to teach our men the art of quarrying — how to blast a rock the right way and other esoteric skills. He became a great friend, often helping the kibbutz to find a suitable house to rent for the children and acting as our host throughout our stay. He would invite us to his home, where his womenfolk — wife, daughters, mother, and grandmother — made a fuss over us, giving us rose wine to drink, delicious Arab sweetmeats to eat, and rose perfume with which to anoint ourselves. He often took us on excursions to the churches, monasteries, and other holy places in and around Nazareth. I particularly remember a visit to the French monastery on the hill, where I first heard organ music and the singing of a church choir, both of which made a great impression on me.

Hananiya's kindness to us was evidence of the friendly coexistence of Jew and Arab that was possible in those far-off days. But such friendliness as his was by no means universal. There were hostile Arabs as well, as we learned when we once went on our own to an Arab village on the site of an ancient Jewish town called Tzipori, where there were antiquities we wanted to see. As we entered the village, Arab children started to throw stones at us while their elders looked on, doing nothing to stop them.

Another proof of the importance of the children of Ein-Harod was the central place assigned to them in the new and vigorously developing cultural life of the kibbutz. The most striking example was the children's role in new variants of the traditional Jewish festivals that the kibbutzim were creating as a vital expression of their Jewish-Zionist communal life. From the start children were given leading roles in the beautiful new songs and dances introduced into the celebration of festivals: Hanukkah, the Festival of Lights; Tu B'shvat, the New Year of the Trees; Purim, the carnival based on the story of the Book of Esther; Pesach, the Passover Festival; Shavuot, also called Chag ha-Bikurim, the Festival of the First Fruits; Rosh Hashanah, the New Year; and Succot, the Feast of the Tabernacles. To these were added the birthday of the kibbutz, called Yud Chet Elul (its date in the Hebrew calendar), which soon acquired the status of a traditional festival and developed its own original character; and the celebration of the First of May, with the red flags flying alongside the Star of David on the blue and white ground, to mark the union of historic socialism and Zionism in the life of the kibbutz. The participation of the children, in ever fresh forms, in all the festivals (including, since 1948, Independence Day) continues and remains one of the most moving and delightful features of the communal cultural life.

3

A New Childhood

EIN-HAROD GAVE ME back the childhood I had lost as a refugee child. During these first kibbutz years, my deepest desire was to put my past in exile behind me and to become, as quickly and completely as possible, like a child born in Eretz Yisrael — a sabra.* This was scarcely a conscious goal, of course, but it was powerful enough to make me change some of my favorite activities and habits and adopt new ones with a child's eager alacrity. I practically stopped reading for a time, at least with the avidity with which I used to read my Hebrew and Russian books. I joined the other children in adoring the romance of horses and hero-worshiping their riders, going wild with excitement when the two former members of Hashomer, who acted as the mounted security guards for our area, came riding into the kibbutz on their magnificently accoutered Arab horses. For the first time in my life I enjoyed children's games, some of them childish indeed. My mother was once horrified to catch me blowing soap bubbles with obvious enjoyment and scolded me for being such a baby — a big boy of eleven playing silly infants' games! I don't think she can be blamed for not understanding what I myself came to understand only long afterward — that I was trying to make up for the lost childhood of my first ten years.

My new childhood was also part of my effort to adapt to my

*Sabra means "a prickly pear" in Arabic. As the colloquial name for a native Israeli, it signifies a prickly exterior combined with a tender heart.

new community of children. This process was neither easy nor quick, but I did learn, in time, to make the most of such advantages as I possessed. I soon became the recognized storyteller of my group, and in the absence of any of the forms of entertainment available to kibbutz children today — theater, cinema, radio, and television — my homely gift for holding an audience proved a valuable social asset. At about that time I also made my modest mark in the adult community of the kibbutz by my prowess in public declamation, giving my most memorable performance at the celebration of Ein-Harod's fifth anniversary, in September 1926.

The festive program of speeches, songs, dances, and recitations was performed at night in our quarry in the valley of the Gilboa, which formed a natural amphitheater. The quarry was lit for the occasion with homemade paraffin flares and bonfires, the main bonfire burning in one corner of the huge flat rock that formed the stage. With its leaping, dancing flames the stage was reminiscent of the sacrificial altars of the Bible, and emotion ran high in the large audience that sat and stood around it.

There were hundreds of guests from all the surrounding settlements and from other parts of the country, up to and including Jerusalem. The crowd was a sign of the fame Ein-Harod enjoyed as the leading kibbutz of the country, and of its good relations with the Arab population of the area. Distinguished guests included Edwin Samuel, son of Herbert Samuel (later Lord Samuel), the high commissioner; Araf el-Araf, the Arab governor of the Beit She'an district, representing the Arab notables of the area; and several senior British officials, who had come from Nazareth to represent the Mandatory government.

The Ein-Harod choir opened the program by singing the first verse of Psalm 42: "As the hart panteth after the water brooks, so panteth my soul after thee, O God." Then I stood up on the stone stage of the quarry and recited the famous passage from Ezekiel about the dry bones in the valley that the Lord God caused to live again, covering them with sinews, flesh, and skin, and putting breath into them, and proclaiming that "these bones are the whole house of Israel."

> And ye shall know that I am the Lord, when I have opened your graves, O my people, and brought you up out of your graves,

And I shall put my spirit in you, and ye shall live, and I shall
place you in your own land: then shall ye know that I the Lord
have spoken it, and performed it . . .

These two verses particularly stirred the Zionist emotions of
the audience. They felt the valley they were sitting in was Ezekiel's valley, the resurrection of the dry bones their resurrection,
the fulfillment of the divine promise to be placed in their own
land already begun here at Ein-Harod at the foot of Mount
Gilboa.

This, however, was one of my last great successes in public declamation. Two years later, when I had to perform at our First of
May celebration, I forgot my lines about halfway through, struggled to remember, failed, and fled from the stage. I was so morti-
fied by this catastrophe that I refused to take the risk of another
ever again. Thus the actor's boldness and savoir-faire I appeared
to command at the age of thirteen passed from my life, like other
transitory talents of the very young.

Our community of children also had its deficiencies and limitations. The sheer small size of our society, with its children of different ages, was in itself painfully restrictive. Added to this was
our rural isolation, which cut us off from virtually all contact with
other groups of children our age. The result was a certain narrowness of mind, which I would now call provincialism, and a
conspicuous absence of cultural development. At this time my
group had very little interest in books and very little intellectual
curiosity. They were not inclined to exercise their imaginations;
they much preferred purely physical and practical activities. I
was so intent on adapting to the group that I was only dimly conscious of this. But I think I must have missed what they lacked,
especially intellectual curiosity and imagination, and so I often
sought the company of adults of the kibbutz, drinking in their superior knowledge and wisdom.

Perhaps the worst side of our group was its proneness to the
cruelty peculiar to village children, over and above the kind of
bullying of the weaker by the stronger common to all societies of
children. I was haunted for years afterward by a *Lord of the Flies*
episode of this period. An alarm had reached the children's house
about the danger of rabies from infected dogs that had strayed

into the kibbutz, endangering our precious cows as well as the human population. We children had a small pet dog whom we all loved and cherished. Though he was in perfect health, showing no sign or symptom of the dread disease, it was decided to put him to death by stoning, to save the kibbutz *in case* he should get rabies. Each child in turn was required to throw a stone, and to go on throwing, in strict rotation, until the little dog was dead. They all did, watching the slow dying of the animal to the last piteous twitch. But I couldn't. I watched with the rest, but I couldn't throw my stones. Years later I recorded the episode in a story, and only then was I liberated from the horror that shook me each time I remembered it.

Yes, there were some ugly, painful episodes to live with and through in our community of children. But for the most part it was decent and jolly enough, and in spite of the physical hardships and deprivations we had plenty of the normal fun enjoyed by early-teenage children the world over. When our good friend Uri Brenner heard that we were writing this book, he volunteered to tell how he had first met me when he was about twelve. Uri, the son of Yosef Chaim Brenner, is a founding member of Kibbutz Maoz Chaim in the Beit-She'an Valley on the Jordanian border. He was deputy commander of the Palmach when Yigal Allon was its commander, and has published several books on the history of the Haganah and the Palmach.

"I must have been about twelve when my mother took me from our home in Tel Aviv to visit my Aunt Batya at Ein-Harod," Uri recalled. "Guest accommodations were extremely limited in the hut in which Batya had her little room, so it was decided to put me in the children's house for the night while my mother stayed in Batya's quarters. Exhausted by the midsummer heat and unaccustomed to fresh country air, I was fast asleep in my dormitory bed when suddenly, some time after midnight, I woke up to find five ghostly figures looming over me from both sides of my bed. Zerubavel was one of them. They were dressed in long white nightshirts, and around his waist each had slung a leather scout belt, from which was suspended a heavy, dangerous looking penknife — they looked as if they meant business. 'Come on, get out of bed!' commanded the ghostly ringleader. 'You're coming with us!' Still dazed with sleep, not knowing what on earth they could want of me, I nevertheless obediently got out of my bed and followed them as they trooped out of the dormitory. Once outside, they ran across the children's compound and out toward the stream, sending out wild whooping and whooing cries such as I had never heard in all my town-boy life. When they reached the stream, with me just behind them, they stopped. Then, to my blank amazement, each threw off his scout belt, stripped off his nightshirt, and plunged into the stream stark naked. 'Come on in!' the ringleader commanded from the water. 'You've got to come in, too, d'ye hear?' So I stripped off whatever improvised nightwear I had on and joined them in their midnight bath, trying to enjoy it as best I could. Having splashed and ducked joyously for a while, they finally got out of the water, flung on their nightshirts and scout belts again — dripping wet — and ran back to the children's house with more whooping and whooing, followed by their poor, bewildered town guest, now more than ever dying to get back to bed."

Though I didn't remember this particular episode, I do recall many other such midnight excursions, especially one when we frightened a nervous elderly chavera into hysterics as we went flying past her tent wailing our Indian war cries. The cemetery was nearby; she thought our white nightshirts were shrouds and screamed from her tent opening, "Dead men! Dead men risen from the grave! Help! Help!" The war cries, I remember, were taken directly from *The Last of the Mohicans,* which had been translated into Hebrew and was one of our favorite books.

The stream in which we took our midnight swim was then a focal point in my life. Its plant and animal life held a perpetual fascination, and I spent countless hours gazing at the reeds growing thickly along the water's edge, the small fish playing in its shallows, the dragonflies skimming its surface, the butterflies and bees hovering over the bushes that grew on its banks, and the patches of yellow water lilies floating in its more sheltered parts. You could hear birds twittering in the bushes and sometimes singing in the early morning or at twilight. The play of sunlight and shadow dappled the waters, and if you sat very still you might see a badger peeping out from the reeds or a marten darting out of the bushes and quickly vanishing again. Some of my most intense memories are of experiences that happened by this stream. And the one my grandchildren and their little friends like to hear re-

counted again and again is my dramatic adventure with Yugedeni the mule. It was a tragicomic trauma typical of the kind
every child has known: the tragedy lies in the child's capacity to
be plunged into an abyss of helpless misery by a trivial failure,
and the comedy lies in the triviality of the failure and the power
of imagination to magnify it into tragedy. Yugedeni was the
doyen of the twenty or so kibbutz mules housed in the stables next
to the cowshed. He was very old, bone lazy, and having long since
been retired from active service, generally conducted himself like
a privileged pensioner, doing little but eat, sleep, and occasionally
perform some old-timer job, like drawing the cart that carried a
water barrel from the stream. He had been bought from the British army along with other castoffs, and it was rumored that he
had been in the mule corps at Gallipoli which, if true, would have
made him of a venerable age indeed.

Yugedeni's great charm for us children was that from time to
time we were allowed to take him out for a ride. We were rarely
permitted to take the horses or the younger serviceable mules, but
decrepit old Yugedeni was considered expendable enough to be
entrusted to any child's care for an hour or two. So we used to
hang around the stableman, ready to help him, do errands for
him, or do anything he asked in the hope that we might earn a
ride. One Sabbath afternoon my turn came. The stableman on
duty was a rather surly fellow named Yosske, whom none of us
particularly liked. What I didn't know — I was still a new boy —
was that he also liked to play nasty practical jokes.

"I suppose you'd like to take Yugedeni for a ride," said Yosske,
in his offhand way.

"Oh, yes!" I answered rapturously.

"Well, okay, you can take him now, for an hour. But mind you
bring him back safely — safely, you hear?" said Yosske.

"Oh, sure, I'll bring him back safely — in not more than an
hour." And quickly, before Yosske could change his mind, I seized
Yugedeni's bridle, tossed a sack over his bare back, vaulted on,
and digging my heels into his aged sides, trotted off briskly in the
direction of the fields, where I knew I could have a good ride.

I held my head high as I rode, feeling like a king on his royal
charger, and I was humming a song as we approached the stream.
When we reached the bank, Yugedeni pulled up sharply and,

jerking his head down as if to drink, shot me clean off his back. I
had scarcely gotten back on my feet, shaken but not hurt by my
fall, when he took a long leap across the stream and galloped off
at great speed. I quickly waded across and set off in hot pursuit.
Panting with anxiety, I stumbled through the clods of the plowed
field, ran into clumps of thorns that tore at my bare legs, shouted
and hallooed at the ever receding mad mule. But all in vain. He
soon disappeared from sight and I had to give up, knowing it
would be useless to go on pursuing him.

The field was empty because it was the Sabbath. I crept toward
the dirt track that ran alongside the field and sat down on the
ground nearby. My heart was a huge heavy stone in my chest,
and I started to cry. "I've lost Yugedeni, *lost* Yugedeni" was the
sentence hammering in my brain. I couldn't go back to Yosske
and tell him what had happened. I couldn't tell *anybody* what had
happened; it was too terrible and shameful to tell. No, I would
never tell anybody. I would never go back. I would stay here forever, until I died. Yes, I will die here, I said to myself, sobbing at
the thought of being dead but also relieved, almost glad, to have
hit on this alternative to the impossible disgrace of going back
and telling.

So there I sat in the field near the dirt track awaiting death, the
stone in my chest growing heavier and heavier as the day waned
and it began to get dark. I must have fallen asleep in my misery,
for the next thing I knew, a dog was leaping about in front of me,
barking wildly. Dazed and confused, I looked past the dog and
saw Shlomo Buchbinder, our cowherd, approaching on the dirt
track behind a herd of cows he was bringing back from the pasture. I knew Shlomo well. A warm-hearted, cheerful fellow, he
was a veteran of the Second Aliyah from Benderri and an old
friend of my mother.

"Zerubavel, child, what are you doing here?" said Shlomo, his
face full of surprise. At the sound of his voice, I broke into tears
again, crying as if I would never stop. "What's the matter, Zerubavel, my boy? Why are you crying?" Shlomo's face was all kindness and concern. I could scarcely speak for sobbing, but somehow
I brought out my dreadful story. To my astonishment, Shlomo
burst into a great roar of laughter. "That stupid Yugedeni!" he
cried. "He's done it again! D'you think it's the first time he's done

it? Not on your life! He's *always* doing it. Going off, for two or three days at a time, the devil knows where, then just coming back, without apology or explanation, as if nothing had happened! So you've no need to worry about that stupid mule. He'll find his way back all right — he always does, and he will this time."

Then, as if a fresh thought had suddenly struck him he asked, "Which stableman gave you Yugedeni to ride?" When I said it was Yosske, he broke into an angry shout. "So it was Yosske, the practical joker! He knows perfectly well what Yugedeni's likely to do when someone gets on his back. And he didn't tell you! I'll give him what for, I promise you, the moment I see him. Oh, yes, I'll tell him exactly what I think of a grown man playing dirty little tricks on children." Shlomo's face brightened again. "And now, my child, you're coming right back with me. Come on, we'll go back together, and you won't worry anymore — will you? — about that ridiculous Yugedeni!"

As I walked by his side in the falling light with the cows ambling before us, I felt the relief and happiness of a doomed man who has been saved from execution at the eleventh hour. I didn't have to worry about Yugedeni. I didn't have to stay in that field until I died. I could go back to my mother, to my classmates, even to Yosske, holding up my head without fear or shame. Nowadays when I catch one of my smaller grandchildren sobbing with an unspeakable woe, I remember Yugedeni and know exactly what the child is feeling, and I try to deliver him from his suffering as Shlomo the cowherd delivered me.

The limitations of our small community of schoolchildren contrasted sharply with the adult community of Ein-Harod, which was highly developed, richly varied, and full of vitality. Many first-generation members had brought their European backgrounds with them. They had strong cultural habits and needs, they had education, intelligence and imagination, good will and faith, and a great fund of creative energy. It is not surprising that they gave Ein-Harod its golden age of cultural development.

From the start they set up numerous study circles — for Bible study; for Hebrew language and literature; for contemporary problems in politics, society, and education; and for *yediyat ha-*

aretz, literally "knowledge of the land," encompassing the history, geography, archaeology, geology, and flora and fauna of Eretz Yisrael. Every week there were lectures, by members of the kibbutz or guests, which were followed by lively discussions. Political leaders, writers, artists, and academics came from Tel Aviv, Jerusalem, and Haifa to speak. Everyone wanted to come and considered it an honor to be invited.

Music was everyone's passion; the members could never have enough. When people were living in wooden huts without indoor toilets or running water, and subsisted on watery soup, bread, and two eggs a week, Yehuda Sharett's Emek Quartet gave regular concerts at Ein-Harod; and in 1926 Jascha Heifetz came to give an unforgettable concert in the same hillside quarry in which I had declaimed from Ezekiel the previous year. Indeed, most of the celebrities who came to perform in Tel Aviv gave a concert at Ein-Harod, and neither audience nor musicians ever forgot these events. Then there were our own performers, such as the Ein-Harod choir, started in 1921 by Shmuel Shapira, another Second Aliyah veteran who had come to Ein-Harod from Kinneret. It was a big choir for a community the size of Ein-Harod — forty to fifty men and women, joined by the children with the best voices — and they sang at every festival, memorial service, and communal event.

But the most popular forms of local entertainment were singing and dancing the hora. After the evening meal in the communal dining hut, the tables and benches would be pushed back against the walls, and a circle of dancers would start the hora in the center. They would be joined within minutes by another circle around it, and the second by a third, and the third by a fourth, until the whole company swayed and whirled in concentric circles to the accompaniment of their own rhythmic singing and hand clapping. The children often formed their own innermost circle, whirling, stamping, and clapping along with the grown-ups. This would go on for two or three hours at a stretch and they danced with a joyous abandon that drove out the tensions of body and mind accumulated in the day's usually grueling work. These few hours were pure pleasure, enjoyed without thought for the morrow. And when the morrow came, everyone would be up for work punctually, often before dawn, no matter what time they had gone to bed. There was the same spontaneity about communal singing. On a Friday night before the Sabbath Eve meal — or after the meal or at any gathering, big or small — someone would start to sing a familiar song in Yiddish or Russian or Hebrew; others would join in, and within minutes the whole kibbutz would be singing as in one ever swelling voice. They sang song after song of the old country, expressing their lingering homesickness, their yearning, in spite of themselves, for the remembered scenes of their childhood and early youth. Of course, they also sang the songs of their new country, Eretz Yisrael, and again the singing would go on for an hour or longer, giving cathartic relief to the weariness of the body and the oppressions of the spirit that were the price constantly paid for a pioneering life.

Of all Ein-Harod's cultural achievements in that period, the most original and lasting was its creation of new forms of traditional Jewish festivals, which were soon adopted by most of the secular kibbutzim, each with its own variations. While retaining many elements of traditional religious celebrations, the new forms were designed with a twofold object: to bring into greater prominence the aspects bearing on the national history of the Jews and to restore the element of the agricultural festival, which had been an integral part of the biblical celebrations of Pesach, Shavuot, and Succot in particular, but which had been lost in the centuries of dispersion. The innovations of Ein-Harod's first years have constantly been developed and modified. Almost every year something new is added, something old revised or completely dropped. But the basic features remain, and I rejoice when I recognize them in their updated forms, nearly sixty years since I first experienced them.

The two festivals that have come to diverge most radically from religious tradition but are still a blend of the old with the new are Pesach and Shavuot, which is six weeks after Passover, in late May or early June. The new Shavuot celebration started in the 1920s as a regional festival for the whole Emek, in which all the kibbutzim and moshavim* of the area participated. Each year a different kibbutz or moshav would act as host to the rest, who all

*The *moshav* (plural, *moshavim*) is another form of pioneering cooperative settlement, which retains some private ownership but, like the kibbutz, practices a high degree of mutual aid based on collectivist principles. The first moshav, Nahalal, was founded in 1921.

brought their first fruits in a caravan of wagons. Later, the rabbinate put a stop to this regional fiesta. Getting the wagons to the
host settlement meant traveling on a Jewish holy day, which is
strictly forbidden by religious law. Determined to stop such hea-
then practices, the rabbinate threatened to boycott the settlements' newly formed cooperative marketing board. *Cherem,* the
Hebrew word for "boycott," also means "excommunication."
Since the settlers themselves could not be excommunicated, the
next best punishment, the rabbinate reckoned, would be to im-
pose sanctions on their produce. The threat proved completely
effective: the settlements could not afford to lose the business
of the large religious sector of the Jewish community, so the regional festival was replaced by separate celebrations in each
settlement.

In 1928, however, it was still a regional festival, and Ein-Harod
was the host kibbutz. Although many of the details had become
vague in my memory, they were revived by a vivid account of the
festival written by Yitzhak Michaeli in a letter home to his parents in a small Russian town. The letter was published after his
death by his son, in a volume called *From My Satchel: Letters and
Sketches, 1925–1943.*

After explaining how the Festival of the First Fruits was celebrated in the days of the Second Temple, Michaeli proceeded to
its modern revived version at Ein-Harod in 1928:

> The preparations start in the early hours of the morning. In the
> kibbutz yard you see people busy decorating wagons with green-
> ery, fruits, flowers, and work tools. Each work group endeavors to
> do something original and surprising and to outdo the others in the
> splendor of its decorations. The children have their own wagons
> according to age group: the toddlers, the kindergarten children,
> the schoolchildren. All the settlements of Emek Harod are to come
> to us, each with its own procession of wagons. The Ein-Harod
> wagons will join up with those of Geva and Ein-Tivon [now Kfar
> Yehezkiel] at the railway station in the north, and with those of
> Beit Alpha and Tel Yosef at the quarry in the east. Ein-Harod will
> lead the grand parade of wagons, which will start at one o'clock in
> the afternoon.
>
> At the appointed hour, the long caravan of wagons turns into
> the threshing field of Ein-Harod through a gaily decorated gate.
> They line up facing the stage set up for the festival to await the

start of the parade. What a blaze of color, what excitement — and
what noise! The whinnying of the horses and the cries of the wagoners mingle with the laughter of girls to fill the air with humming, bustling sound. And how good it is to meet comrades you
have not seen for a long time!

For Michaeli the scene recalls the market days of his little Russian
town, which he had left behind just three years before. But here,
of course, the scores of wagons loaded with fruit and wheat, and
the tractors and threshing machines are all driven by young Jewish men and women speaking Hebrew. "That," he notes, "is the
real revolution!"

The young men wear white shirts, riding breeches, and high
boots, "as becomes guardsmen on horses." To this outfit the more
fashion conscious have added a fringed sash around the waist.
The girls wear black pinafores or blue "pioneer" skirts with white
blouses. The children, in cream-colored raw silk blouses with em-
broidered stand-up collars, are sitting packed together on their
wagon "like little lambs in a pen." Some of them are crying with
excitement; the women in charge try to calm them by giving them
sweets and drinks.

And now the crier announces, "The parade is about to start!"
Yitzhak Henkin, son of a famous founder of Hashomer, is the first
to pass through the gate, riding a mighty chestnut horse. He is
followed by a procession of girls in brilliant dresses with flower
wreaths on their heads, carrying jars on their shoulders in the
graceful oriental style. After the girls come young men carrying a
huge bunch of grapes suspended from a long horizontal pole and
then the long line of wagons, led by Ein-Harod's: "A group carrying a selection of the first fruits leads the procession. It is followed
by the field workers and their exhibits, in the following order:
tractor and plow first, then a pair of animals pulling a 'discus'
plow and another pair drawing a drill. Then two pairs of animals
drawing the sheaf binder, another pair drawing a wagon loaded
with sacks of wheat, followed by a wagon loaded with loaves of
bread, and finally the big threshing machine drawn by a tractor."
After the field crops come the other agricultural groups, each with
its own wagon: saplings of fruit trees on one, produce from the
vegetable garden on another, tobacco on a third. These are followed by the products of the chicken coop and the beehives. Then

come the workshops, with the fruits of their labor: the foundry, the wheelwright's, rein maker's, and carpenters' shops, the repair shops and others. Finally, winding up the Ein-Harod procession is the schoolchildren's wagon, displaying the first fruits of the children's farm, drawn by their own donkey Moishele.

All told there are twenty Ein-Harod wagons — thirteen from the work branches, the remaining seven divided among the children and various other enterprises — and even if each of the four guest kibbutzim had only half that many, it would have made a spectacular procession of some sixty wagons.

The parade is followed by the concluding ceremony, the bringing in of the first fruits. The audience, kibbutz by kibbutz, take their places in rows facing the stage. A trumpet sounds and the ceremony begins. The children's choir sings the song of the first fruits, accompanied by violins. Then representatives of each kibbutz come on stage and the master of ceremonies enumerates the bountiful gifts received from each kibbutz: two sacks of wheat grain, six sheep, three pitchers of milk, seven combs of honey, and so on. The cash value of these gifts will be donated to the land buying fund and, in the name of the treasurer of Ein-Harod, the announcer calls out the total: three hundred lirot (Egyptian pounds), a substantial sum in those days. "Thus," Michaeli observes, "we have succeeded in donating the first fruits of our lands for the purchase of more land for our people."

Michaeli takes particular joy in this renewal of the ancient biblical form of the Festival of the First Fruits as a symbol of the renewal of the Jewish people in their historic homeland. "This," he tells his parents, "is how we have renewed the festival in accordance with ancient forms, and not as our ancestors celebrated it in Exile. For them, because of the harsh and unsettled condition of their life, it became a festival of the synagogue and the home: full of spiritual content indeed as the festival of the giving of the Torah, and the splendor of the ancient agricultural festival symbolized by the greenery with which they decorated their homes. But now we are celebrating it anew as our forefathers did in ancient times." Michaeli earnestly advocates that we continue to return to our biblical origins: "As pure water is drawn from the depths, so our ancient Jewish culture has to be drawn from the depths of Jewish tradition and allowed to stream once more through the channels blocked in the years of the Exile. By this means we shall attain to a new fullness and richness of life."

Today this enthusiastic consciousness of Zionist renewal in our Festival of the First Fruits has doubtless dimmed, along with other ideological enthusiasms of that early period. But no one today can fail to perceive how the element of the agricultural festival still predominates and how the spirit of our biblical ancestors lives again in the whole great show.

The crier of 1928 is gone now, replaced by microphones and loudspeakers, which are strung across the huge playing field of the kibbutz sports stadium, where the celebration is now held. The field is the stage, and the audience of more than a thousand sits facing it in a semicircle of tiered seats rising high above it. But the gifts of the first fruits are still "sold" for hard cash sent to the Keren Kayemet for land purchase, and the procession of today is as gorgeous and as noisy as it was in 1928. Instead of the plow, sheaf binder, and threshing machine, the combine harvester lumbers forward, with head held high as if proud to replace them all. It is followed by a splendid assortment of the newest, most sophisticated farm machines, which are put through their paces before the spellbound audience. Then come the trucks, still twenty or more of them, representing the work branches: the chicken coop, the cowhouse, the grapefruit orchards, the beehives, supplemented now by the stainless steel and furniture factories. Brilliantly decorated with flower garlands, branches of greenery, colored streamers, and balloons, they flaunt large banners and placards inscribed with witty, humorous legends advertising the year's work and achievements. They pass slowly, one at a time, across the stage, to give the audience time to read the placards and to point out children and grandchildren as they swarm all over the trucks, singing and shouting, or sometimes crying with excitement, just like the children of 1928.

The carnival atmosphere is perhaps even more prevalent than it was sixty years ago. There are new group dances and more choral singing than there used to be, and the performances are a shade more polished. But to a veteran spectator like myself, the spirit is the same and the link with our biblical past as exhilarating and moving as it was for Yitzhak Michaeli.

4

Lessons for Life

PEOPLE INTERESTED in the history of the kibbutzim often ask me what, in the early days, the prevailing attitude of the settled Jewish population of Eretz Yisrael was toward Ein-Harod, the leading kibbutz of the country. The answer is that it was a fairly even mixture of hostility and admiration.

The hostility, like a hard, cold wind, blew from several directions. First it came from the Zionist establishment, which was ideologically divided on the question of the Big Kibbutz, of which Ein-Harod was the sole example. The difference of opinion turned on the relative merits of what was called the *kvutza ktana*, the "small commune," and the *kibbutz gadol ve gadel,* literally "the big-and-growing kibbutz." The small commune was the intimate, familylike kibbutz exemplified by the "mother" of the kibbutzim, Degania, founded in 1910. It deliberately restricted itself to a maximum of about fifty members, claiming that a truly organic, cohesive communal life was impossible with a larger membership. The big-and-growing kibbutz like Ein-Harod refused to restrict its numbers, wanting to be an ever open, ever growing community. Its advocates believed that the loss of the intimacy and cohesiveness of the Degania-type kvutza ktana was more than compensated for by the diversity of personalities and talents Ein-Harod could accommodate, the richly varied development it would allow, and — a very important consideration — the special opportunities its size would offer for the absorption of new immigrants from the Diaspora in fulfillment of one of the prime goals of Zionism, "the ingathering of the exiles."

The dispute in the Zionist Executive between the supporters and opponents of the big kibbutz was protracted and characteristically fierce. Those who opposed it argued that it had no chance of survival, that its agricultural enterprises were doomed to failure, and that the whole idea was a megalomaniacal absurdity. They bitterly begrudged the development funds they were expected to disburse, saying these would just be wasted. So it was a hard fight for Ein-Harod to gain official recognition and the desperately needed funds; its opponents, even after they were democratically defeated, continued to view Ein-Harod with cold, unfriendly eyes.

The attitude of the rest of the *yishuv*, the "already settled," was similarly divided, though on different grounds. The propertied and moneyed bourgeoisie of the country — principally the wealthy citrus growers of the coastal plain, the businessmen and financiers of Tel Aviv, and many professionals — were openly hostile to the very idea of the kibbutz. They disliked its socialist ideology, its cooperative methods, its egalitarian principles, regarding them as a bag of utopian nonsense, which they expected — and, we often felt, wished — to be an unmitigated failure. In this hostility they were vigorously supported by their counterparts in Jewish communities abroad, represented by the bourgeois political parties of the World Zionist Organization (WZO) headquartered in the United States, which at the time exercised a decisive influence on the direction and form of Zionist enterprise in Eretz Yisrael.

Since the creation of the State of Israel, the influence of the WZO has waned somewhat, but the hostility of the country's bourgeoisie tends to persist, intensified by the success of the kibbutzim in the very areas of life in which they were expected to fail. It cannot be pleasant, I have often thought, to have one's expectations so cruelly disappointed; consequently, I view the unfriendliness of our present-day bourgeoisie with rather more equanimity than I did that of their predecessors in the late twenties and early thirties.

In contrast to the citrus growers, the big businessmen, and many of the leaders of the WZO in the United States, a substantial part of the Jewish community, in Eretz Yisrael and abroad, admired and honored the kibbutzim. These people saw in the kibbutzim a fulfillment of the Zionist ideals in which they most ardently believed. For them Ein-Harod represented a new Jewish reality that had the power to excite and inspire like almost no other creation of modern Zionism. They saw it as a unique fusion of some of their most cherished values. Of these, the first was the pioneering life: they had always believed that Eretz Yisrael could be redeemed only by pioneer effort, and Ein-Harod was doing it, visibly proving the truth of their belief. In the same way, the kibbutz realized other fundamental elements of the Zionist-socialist vision: the return to the land and manual labor as the key means to the "normalization" of the Jewish people; the socialist dream of absolute social equality, democracy, equality of opportunity in education and employment; and the ideal especially dear to the hearts of European Jewish socialists, who rejoiced to see a community of Jews combining high standards of education, culture, and intellectual creativity with the utmost simplicity, not to say primitiveness, in the material conditions of life.

The Zionist-socialist, labor-orientated section of the yishuv included not only the workers of the country, who were already an organized force within the Histadrut (Labor Federation), but also a high proportion of writers, artists, and musicians — the intelligentsia, in the Russian and European sense. After the opening of the Hebrew University in 1925, many academics also counted themselves members of this group. Many of these kibbutz loyalists had spent some years in a kibbutz and, though they had left, felt a lasting attachment to it — often reinforced by a lingering feeling of guilt about not having stayed. They still tended to call it "their kibbutz," which they visited regularly to see relatives or old friends from the Zionist movement. They returned for the Passover Seder and for birthday celebrations, weddings, funerals, memorial services, and other communal or family events; they encouraged their children to become kibbutz members or at least to work in one for a time; academics or performing artists gladly came to give lectures or performances and, in general, maintained close, warm relations with the kibbutzim throughout their lives.

* * *

My new childhood at Ein-Harod did not last long — at most two years, when I was eleven to thirteen. By September 1926, when I was nearly fourteen, our school community had grown to seventeen boys and eleven girls, between the ages of eight and sixteen, and we had at last gotten our first three permanent teachers. The days of the old-world cheder were over; we had a curriculum of studies for each age group and grade level, and serious homework for the first time. Although our school now had the framework of a regular school, the number of pupils in each grade was still so small that classes were often combined: for example, grades two and three had some of their lessons together, and grades three and four joined up for other classes.

We had a regular timetable and attended class five to six hours a day, though the actual times of the older children's lessons varied according to their kibbutz work schedule, for everyone from the age of fourteen up did a daily stint of four to five hours' work. We studied the Bible, Hebrew language, arithmetic, elementary geometry, elementary chemistry, zoology and botany ("nature study"), geography, Jewish and general history, and the comprehensive study then called *moledet* (native land) and later *yediyat ha-aretz* (knowledge of the land). Elementary English and Arabic were added a few years later. Generally this was the curriculum in schools throughout the country at the time, but the social framework and discipline in our school were unique. Relations between teachers and pupils were extremely informal. We always called the teachers by their first names, did not rise from our seats when a teacher entered the room, and classroom discipline was maintained only by the teacher's power to hold our interest. This thoroughly unconventional atmosphere made great demands on the teachers, but they, it seems, were unconventional enough to meet them and enjoy this special challenge. In the Ein-Harod annals, *Pirkei Yovel*, Chaim Shifroni, one of our three teachers, described his view of the relations between teachers and pupils at Ein-Harod in 1927.

> The teacher is in every respect a member of the children's community; he is superior only in knowledge and experience, which he endeavors to transmit to the children. Our children's house reminds you of the warmth and intimacy of a family home, or of the direct, simple closeness and mutual trust that used to exist in the good *cheder* of the past.

The children sometimes show great discrimination about the teacher's opinions, which have to stand up to their criticism; and often the teacher is obliged to relinquish his opinion in deference to the children's. He does it with a secret pleasure, knowing that it leaves unimpaired the special spirit of mutual good will and trust that prevails here. This spirit is the outcome of our special conditions: teachers and children meet here not only for lessons, but live together, sharing a full and rich life, in a living society, in close contact with nature . . .

Chaim Shifroni, who had taught in Russia before coming to Ein-Harod, became in effect the first principal of our school, though the office as such did not yet exist. Having attended a yeshiva, he had a thorough grounding in Jewish studies, and he acquired his secular education at the well-known Yellin Teachers' Seminary in Jerusalem, where he spent two years after his arrival in Eretz Yisrael. He soon decided that teaching in a kibbutz was the best pioneering service he could give to the country, and that brought him to Ein-Harod in 1924.

Shifroni was a thin man, of average height, and physically not especially prepossessing. But he had a pleasant deep voice, and though gentle by nature, an air of authority that commanded respect. He was only about twenty-seven, yet there was something fatherly in his attitude which, combined with his warm, relaxed manner and quiet humor, drew the affection of the children. Completely dedicated to our education and care, he always stood up for, and if necessary fought for, our rights when they seemed to be threatened by an overzealous work organizer. He made sure that teaching hours were not too drastically reduced during seasonal work periods, kept a vigilant eye on the children's house budget, and personally supervised and inspected all the work of the children's farm. He was always accessible to the children and their parents for any problem or difficulty that might arise, hearing them out patiently and proposing wise and humane solutions.

He taught only the twelve- to sixteen-year-olds, and his favorite subjects were in the humanities — the Bible, literature, and history. But he also taught mathematics, and later chemistry, which he went to study at the Technion in Haifa for the sole purpose of being able to teach it. He subsequently published a textbook on chemistry in collaboration with Ephraim Katzir, who was to become a distinguished professor at the Weizmann Institute and

president of the State of Israel in the late 1970s. Shifroni constantly pressed for the development and expansion of the school,
and his labors finally bore fruit in the late 1930s, when a regional
high school was established to serve most of the kibbutzim in the
eastern Emek. It combined the scholastic standards of a gymnasium for the academically gifted with a vocational program for
the nonacademic.

The second of our trio of teachers was always called Shoshanna
ha-morah (Shoshanna the teacher). Her surname was Czenste-
chovski, but few people knew it. Short in stature, dark-skinned
and dark-haired, with conspicuously bright black eyes, she, too,
had had a thorough Jewish education and knew her Bible and
Talmud almost as well as if she had studied in a yeshiva, though
she had actually been taught at home by her father, a traditional
man of learning. She had also had a good Polish secular education, received her training in a Hebrew teachers' college in Warsaw, and had written and published poetry, mainly in Yiddish.

Shoshanna came to Ein-Harod at the invitation of two close
friends from Poland, Natalia Tabenkin and Fruma Asherovsky,
always called Natalka and Frumka. Both were trained kindergarten teachers and founding members of Ein-Harod who had
played a leading part in creating the framework of the children's
community. Natalka, Frumka, and Shoshanna became a forceful
triumvirate in the teaching and care of the youngest children,
leaving their mark on all their charges and on Ein-Harod as a
whole. Shoshanna never married; she devoted her life to the
school and the children, performing the duties of housemother
along with her teaching. Later in life, after the establishment of
the State, she became a chief inspector of schools, primarily in the
new kibbutzim, moshavim, and development towns founded after
1948, and was very successful in her new role.

In our school she taught the junior classes and as housemother
supervised all the domestic work of the children's house. She was
a bit of a martinet about cleanliness, tidiness, and punctuality,
which often led to lively conflicts with her less disciplined charges,
with fur flying on both sides in our egalitarian atmosphere. Then
Shifroni would act as a court of appeals, listening to both sides
with his customary patience and somehow contriving to restore
peace and amity. But when she was not bemoaning our domestic

failings, Shoshanna was the ideal teacher that parents dream of. She held a monthly meeting with the parents to give them detailed reports of their children; many at Ein-Harod today remember the special loving discrimination that informed her reports, and how often she helped them to understand and appreciate their children.

Shoshanna made her most permanent contribution to the cultural life of the kibbutz by starting the tradition, continued to this day, of celebrating the Sabbath and the festivals in the children's house, infusing them with a spirit that may well have sprung from poetic talents she possessed in her Polish youth, although she hadn't written poetry since. At any rate, her innovations were highly original and imaginative and earned general admiration. With Shifroni and Shmulik Shapira, the choirmaster, she trained and rehearsed the children for their performances at the big kibbutz festivals, year after year, with ever increasing success. Later she wrote the first guide to these children's performances, which included a small anthology of songs and readings she had collected. It was widely used in schools throughout the country and in almost all the kibbutzim.

Of our first three teachers, the most original, most variously gifted, and most powerful personality was Moshe Carmi. More than anyone he, with Chaim Sturman, our other idol, put his stamp on my whole generation at Ein-Harod. Born in Petah Tikva, he was the only sabra among our teachers, and he had the further distinction of having been educated at the Gymnasia Herzliya in Tel Aviv, the first Hebrew high school in Eretz Yisrael. Moshe was a member of its first graduating class, which produced many of our earliest national leaders in politics, defense, and diplomacy, as well as education.

His gifts and accomplishments were wide ranging indeed. He was a talented linguist and, having been brought up in close contact with Arabs, had a fluent command of Arabic. He loved music, played the violin, and was a fine amateur musicologist. His other dominating passions were nature, the Bible, and the land of Israel, but he also loved classical and modern literature, and I remember his reading to us, on a typically bold impulse, the whole of Bialik's translation of *Don Quixote* — a reading spread over many weeks, even though the text was abridged. Another time he read us Tchernichovsky's translation of "Hiawatha," the same one I had carried across the frozen Dniester.

Moshe Carmi was constitutionally averse to routine. He cared nothing, for instance, about our formal curriculum, and simply taught us whatever happened to interest him most at the moment in any way it happened to spring from his teeming brain. His enthusiasm, always at boiling point, his uninhibited spontaneity, and his zest in pursuing an idea, an impression, an association wherever it might lead, utterly captivated us and more than compensated for the absence of the systematic and orderly in his teaching technique.

His greatest achievements as guide and mentor, however, lay outside the classroom. No one of my school generation at Ein-Harod will ever forget the great excursions on which he took us, on foot or by wagon, to all parts of the country, including the most remote and out-of-the-way places. They usually lasted from four to fourteen days, and they inspired us with a love of Eretz Yisrael based on an intimate knowledge of every inch of its length and breadth and every particle of meaning hidden in its ancient earth. Moshe seemed to know everything about every place we came to: its history, its archaeology, its biblical associations, its geology, its flora and fauna, its contemporary human interest. He was one of the first to initiate the practice of learning to know the land "on foot," which has since become widespread, indeed a favorite national recreation of Israelis of all ages. It was carried a big step forward by the Palmach, which required of all its fighters an intimate knowledge of the land they had undertaken to defend. It is a standard part of the training program of the Israel Defense Forces as well. In civilian life, the Society for the Protection of Nature, and hundreds of schools, youth clubs, workers' associations, and senior citizens' homes actively perpetuate *yediyat ha-aretz*, "knowledge of the land," which we were privileged to experience directly through one of its founders, Moshe Carmi.

Our excursions frequently took us to Arab villages, where we stopped for rest and refreshment and, as often as not, to spend the night. It was a lesson for all of us to see how Moshe conducted himself in these encounters with Arabs. He was always warmly received, partly because he spoke Arabic fluently, but chiefly because he treated the Arab villagers, from the sheik or *mukhtar* down to the simplest villager, with respect and an easy, open friendliness. At the same time, he made no bones about deploring what he saw as their shortcomings: their laziness, unsanitary living conditions, and most of all their ferocious cruelty, not only to Jews but to each other. My adult attitudes toward the Arabs of Eretz Yisrael were greatly influenced by the example of Moshe Carmi's conduct in their villages.

Moshe's physical appearance was somehow of a piece with his character and spirit. He had a very open, mobile face and his early baldness had given him a high forehead, which was always conspicuously suntanned. His body was broad and strong, his walk firm and confident, and he had striking blue eyes, which could become unexpectedly dreamy in repose. He had a short temper, and when he was angry he could shout in a way that his more timid pupils found terrifying and the spirited ones resented, often returning his anger with their own. My younger brother, Yuval, disliked him intensely during all his school years because Moshe used to tease and torment him about his mop of curly hair, which no comb or brush could subdue to decent tidiness. Moshe was demanding in small matters as well as large, and very insistent, often too peremptorily, on having his demands executed exactly as he wished. But in another mood, he would be tenderly considerate and helpful to a child lagging behind on a job; and beneath his impulsive temper he was sensitive to any injustice he may have caused. When he was proved wrong in a dispute he would apologize, recognizing his error with a generosity of spirit and a sincerity that left no doubt about his concern for fairness and his freedom from false pride.

I remember an episode, amusing in retrospect though serious enough at the time, that exemplifies the way the impulsive harshness of which he was often capable was balanced by his sense of justice and largeness of spirit. A boy in class had said something Moshe thought particularly stupid, and he had turned on him, shouting contemptuously, "What an *eglon* you are!" (An *eglon* is a wagoner.) The boy, Nachum Nitzan — one of my next-door neighbors and still a fighter for his own and other people's rights — would not let that pass. He promptly demanded that Moshe be brought before the children's disciplinary court on the ground that to use the word *eglon* as a term of abuse was an insult to an honorable profession, to the dignity of labor, and to the working class as a whole.

A full-scale trial was held, with Moshe the accused standing in the dock facing Nachum the plaintiff, with a court-appointed prosecutor, counsel for the defense, and all the other judicial appurtenances. The prosecution produced, in support of its charge, a piece of vital documentary evidence: a long narrative poem by David Shimonovitch, "Jubilee of the Wagoners," in which the poet, more than half seriously, lauds the invaluable service that wagoners have rendered to their people and country. Perhaps this evidence was decisive; at any rate Moshe was found guilty of the offense described in the charge sheet and was required by the judge to make a public apology for his gross lapse from the standard of correct conduct and expression. He did so handsomely, pleading in his extenuation that he had been brought up in Petah Tikva where, alas, an eglon tended to be a coarse and ignorant person. But this was no excuse, he fully acknowledged, for using the word as a term of contempt, and he apologized abjectly for having done so. An eglon, he concluded, was a noble human being, every bit as good as — in fact better than — a teacher. He would never again speak of wagoners in any terms other than those of the highest respect and appreciation.

Besides our unforgettable excursions, a dozen episodes with Moshe live on in my memory, but I shall recount just two. The first was his arrival at Ein-Harod in 1925, after having spent three years pursuing a course of advanced study in Germany. A few days after his arrival, a huge packing case, as large as a small wooden shack, was brought from the station on a flat-bed wagon drawn by a pair of mules and set down in the children's yard between the Green Hut and the chicken run. When it was opened, it seemed to us like an Aladdin's cave; we had never dreamed such a treasure-trove could exist except in fairy tales. Open-mouthed, we clustered around Moshe as he pulled out one fairy gift after another. Golden trumpets, carpentry tools with blades glittering like mercury, violins and flutes, folders stuffed with reproductions of famous pictures, and books, books, books. Books with gilt edges, bound in leather or gray cloth. Alfred Edmund Brehm's classic works on zoology and Otto Warburg's on botany, and great fat books full of pictures of animals, birds, reptiles, trees, bushes, and plants from all corners of the earth. There were pamphlets, pictures, and models of animal skeletons; collections of multicolored butterflies; a microscope with wonderful lenses in an ebony box with shiny brass latches; and all kinds and sizes of glass cylinders, test tubes, and mysterious dissecting instruments. And finally, to crown all, out came a small organ worked by foot pedals — what the Germans call a *Fussharmonium* — an instrument of ravishing beauty, made of dark red mahogany and carved and engraved with flowers, birds, leaves, petioles, and tendrils of vine.

As we gazed enraptured at the piled-up treasures, we felt that our world had suddenly, in this one moment, grown rich and varied. Before this we had never seen a real painting, or even a color reproduction; the nearest thing we had known was a very old catalogue of faded black-and-white photographs of world masterpieces, which had reached the children's house by chance and was passed from hand to hand until the pages fell apart. Yes, Moshe's treasure-trove, his magic box we called it, certainly enriched our lives. At the same time it put a restlessness in our spirit, a yearning for things we had never known existed to be yearned for; this perhaps was the best proof of its power to expand our intellect.

I said that music was a central passion of Moshe's life, and I cannot forget a small episode that was typical of his feelings and his power of transmitting them to us. Talma Yellin Bentwich, a cellist, had come from Jerusalem to give a performance at Ein-Harod of one of Beethoven's sonatas for cello and piano, the well-known Sonata no. 3 in A Major. Moshe had missed the concert because that evening he was lying sick in one of the hospital huts at the farthest boundary of the kibbutz, opposite the children's house. When I went to visit him the next day, I found him reading Paul Becker's book on Beethoven.

"How was the concert?" were his first words. I told him it had been wonderful. "The doctor wouldn't let me get out of bed, so I had to strain my ears to catch the sounds of the music floating in from the dining hall. But this helped me," he said, pointing to the book he was holding. "I made sure I had it with me when they pushed me into this hospital. As the music was being played last night, I read what Becker had written about it, and I felt as if I were hearing the concert. Yes, I felt I *heard* it!"

He softly started whistling the rich, delicate, melodic theme of

the sonata. His fellow patients looked at him reproachfully, surprised and annoyed at such strange behavior in a hospital ward.
Moshe smiled at them apologetically and fell silent. Then, in a
low voice, as if talking to himself, he said, "Everybody hears the
music in the measure of the answering echo from his soul. The
deeper the echo, the greater our power of understanding and as-
similating the music." I speak from memory and perhaps have
not quoted Moshe exactly, but I remember being strangely
moved by his words. To this day, whenever I hear that Beethoven
sonata, I hear it accompanied by Moshe's low voice, talking about
music and its echo.

In the later years of my school career I was always the youngest
among the older children and the oldest among the younger, by
about three years in each instance — in other words, I awkwardly
fell between two stools. Thus, when the older children reached the
age of sixteen and were obliged to stop their schooling and go to
work full time in the kibbutz, I was left without a regular school
class. I joined some of the classes of the younger age group, and I
was permitted to participate in the one "study day" a week allowed to the working sixteen-year-olds. But my chief means of
making up for the irregularities of my formal schooling was by
reading everything I could lay my hands on in the kibbutz library.
      The business of getting all the books I wanted was by no means
straightforward. The librarian was a surly, suspicious fellow who
took the view that books were meant to be kept on library shelves
rather than read, and flatly refused to give me the books I asked
for because, he cruelly informed me, he didn't believe I understood what I was reading. I protested and argued to no avail; then
I found my own illegal way of getting what I wanted. The library,
on the upper floor of the odd-shaped granary, was separated from
the wardrobe room and sewing room by a partition that did not
reach the ceiling, leaving a conveniently wide gap. So, during
siesta hours, when I knew nobody would be about, I used to creep
in quietly, use a ladder to climb over the partition into the library, take any two books I wanted off the shelves, read them
within twenty-four hours, and return them the following day by
the same method. The killjoy librarian never found out, and I had
no compunction about outwitting him.

He was right, of course, up to a point, about my not understanding what I read. The books I filched and secretly feasted on
were certainly somewhat above my head: Tolstoy's *Anna Karenina*
and *War and Peace* (the first volume only — the second had not
been translated into Hebrew); *Crime and Punishment* and almost
everything else by Feodor Dostoevski; the famous Scandinavians
of the time, like Knut Hamsun; the best-selling Romain Rolland;
Jacob Wasserman and other German novelists, like Bernard Kel-
lerman and Artur Schnitzler. I fancy I understood scarcely half of
what I read, but when I reread some of these books in later years,
I was surprised and pleased to discover how deeply they had entered my soul. So I had reason to be grateful for our kibbutz library in spite of the librarian.

Indeed it was remarkable how good a library it was, considering our pitifully limited resources. A budget for books had been
set aside from the very first year, even though the kibbutz lacked
money for food, clothes, building, machinery, and almost all
other necessities, and the library grew apace in the years I
climbed over the partition every day. It was the accepted practice
for members to give most of their own books to the library, partly
because there was no space for them in the huts and tents, chiefly
from the public-spirited motive of making a precious commodity
available to the whole community. There were also periodic gifts
of books from the central library of the Histadrut in Tel Aviv, and
kibbutz emissaries, as a matter of course, brought back books
from abroad, sometimes stacks of them. Accordingly, it became as
well-stocked a library as a boy with literary inclinations could expect to find in any rural area, let alone in a mouse-poor kibbutz in
the first ten years of its existence, and it made my self-education
possible where no other means were available.

5

In the Plant Nursery

I ENTERED A NEW PHASE of my life at Ein-Harod when I reached the age of fourteen and was required to do four to five hours of work each day in the kibbutz. My first assignment was in the kibbutz nursery, where I joined a group of twenty workers, mostly women, planting seedlings of pine, cypress, and other forest trees in pots and tins. When they had grown into saplings, they were wrapped in newspaper, carefully packed in boxes, and sent off to the Keren Kayemet, the Jewish National Fund (JNF), which since its founding in 1901 has been responsible for the afforestation of the country. Ein-Harod was one of the first kibbutzim to supply saplings to the JNF and continued for some time to be an important source of saplings for the forests of the Jerusalem hills, the Balfour Forest in the Nazareth hills, and the Galilee forests around Safed. We also grew saplings of fruit trees, mainly apples, pears, plums, olives, and citrus; flowers, which were sent to Haifa every day to be sold; and we had a greenhouse for special plants like ferns, indoor pot plants, and others.

My work among the adults brought me, for the first time, into close contact with some of the outstanding members of the kibbutz. It also gave me the opportunity to pick up a detailed inside knowledge of their lives. The women workers, especially, were well informed in these matters. There was nothing they did not know, it seemed, about the intimate lives of their fellow members, and they had no inhibitions about sharing these tidbits with one another and with anyone who happened to be listening. So I learned a great deal about the goings-on of my elders: about their "romances," as their flirtations and love affairs were delicately called; about the ups and downs of their marriages (usually the downs); about their social relations — whom they did or didn't get on with; and about the work morale of the members — who was a good or outstanding worker, who was a lazy good-for-nothing, and so on. The gossip flowed in an incessant stream as we planted or watered or packed, and I listened with fascinated interest. Though I didn't know it at the time, I was laying by rich stores of human material for my future stories and poems.

Some remarkable women among us played a central role in the life of the kibbutz, though in widely different ways. One of the most outstanding was Eva Tabenkin, the wife of Yitzhak Tabenkin. A founding father of the kibbutzim and of the whole labor movement of Eretz Yisrael, Yitzhak was regarded, with David Ben-Gurion, Berl Katznelson, and Golda Meir, as one of the giants of the first generation of national leaders. Their two eldest sons, Moshe and Yosef, were in their turn destined to become leading figures of the next generation — Moshe as a poet, educator, ideologue, and political writer; Yosef as a brilliant commander of the Palmach. I became closely associated with the whole Tabenkin family, so these first encounters with Eva, the matriarch, have a special place in my memory.

The sphere of Eva's activities was narrower, of course, than her husband's, but of supreme importance for the development of the kibbutz. She came from a well-to-do and cultivated Polish-Jewish family, had been a student at the University of Cracow, and joined the Zionist worker's movement to express, in the spirit of the times, her identification with "the people." She certainly achieved all the identification a young woman with her upbringing could wish for when she came to Eretz Yisrael as a pioneer of the Second Aliyah, doing every kind of hard, often menial, physical work at Kinneret and other places. By the time I came to know her in the Ein-Harod nursery, she was in her late thirties, a handsome woman with striking dark eyes, and a very erect carriage, a commanding figure in our group of workers. A great talker, with a tendency to dominate conversation with her energy and eloquence, she had clear and firm opinions on most topics, and in particular the two closest to her heart: the communal system of education and the role of the woman in the kibbutz.

The two issues were more closely connected than they seem. In those early years at Kinneret, before she and Yitzhak came to Ein-Harod, Eva had experienced firsthand the difficulties of bringing up young children in a tent or hut, in the grueling conditions of pioneer life, after a full day's work. Motherhood simply enslaved the woman, making a mockery of the equality-of-the-sexes principle of the kibbutz; for what time or energy was left for a woman to take an active part in community life and help direct its development if she was doomed to spend sixteen hours a day at her job and child rearing? From this experience — shared, of course, by almost all the mothers of her generation — was born the idea of communal education and upbringing of the children. Eva Tabenkin became one of its most vigorous exponents at Ein-Harod, and one of the architects of the entire system that was to become a unique feature of the kibbutz way of life.

At the same time — and it was typical of Eva that she should maintain apparently contradictory positions — she insisted on the central importance of family life in the kibbutz and on the physical closeness of parents and children as a sacred principle of child rearing. Accordingly, she became an active member of the group of mothers who succeeded in introducing at Ein-Harod the practice of having the children sleep in their parents' quarters from the ages of six to fifteen. They did everything else in the children's community: went to school, did their chores, washed, ate, and played. But they came home to sleep, and the first permanent houses that were built had a second "room" for the children. Although this was actually only a small enclosed porch off the one-room parental house, it was still a luxury in the poverty-stricken days of the early 1930s and represented a great concession to the demands of Eva Tabenkin and the other mothers. This practice remained peculiar to Ein-Harod for many years, continuing unchanged until about ten years ago. Then the children started to sleep at home at an earlier age, and now they do so from the day they are born. It is a development in the spirit of Eva Tabenkin, and I like to think that she would have approved.

Eva was also a passionate proponent of the absolute equality and independence of women, a principle that already held an honored place in the ideology of the kibbutz, but like principles everywhere, was all too often breached in practice. At the same time she insisted on the supreme value and virtue of motherhood and child rearing in the life of the kibbutz woman. It was typical of her energetic character that having herself succeeded in reconciling these seeming inconsistencies, she could see no reason why every other kibbutz woman should not do the same. Afterward, she fought vigorously for the equality of women in the Haganah, the underground self-defense organization of the Jewish community in Mandatory Palestine. Especially after the Arab riots of 1929 and the massacre of the Jewish community in Hebron, the Haganah intensified all the defense arrangements in the country, and the kibbutzim were required to set up defensive positions around their perimeters. Eva was one of those who insisted that women were to participate fully in the manning of these posts, carrying guns and knowing how to use them. She fought for this right in fiery speeches at Ein-Harod and at conferences of the Women Workers' organization, and it may well have been the success of Eva and her fellow fighters in persuading the Haganah to treat women as equals that led its striking force, the Palmach, to admit young women into its fighting units.

What a range of human types we must have had in the nursery that it could encompass both an Eva Tabenkin and a Rachel Kravtzov. Rachel, about twenty-two at the time, was the reverse of a commanding personality. Modest, shy, and unassuming, she loved literature and poetry, but most of all she loved her work, first in the nursery and later in the apiary. Our friendship began when we were both assigned to hoe two new flower beds. To my astonishment and mortification, she finished her bed long before I did mine; I would never have thought so slightly built and frail looking a young woman could work with such speed and efficiency. Her physical strength, I discovered later, was indeed remarkable, and so was her mental stamina. She loved to *study* the subject of her work and spent her evenings reading, with passionate absorption, every book and article bearing on her work that she could lay hands on. These, for the most part, were written in her native Russian — there was very little professional literature available in Hebrew at the time — and she learned to read English so she could follow the newest developments in her field. What particularly won my heart was that along with her detailed scientific knowledge, she also had remarkable powers of direct, firsthand observation and an intuitive grasp of everything in nature. It was a gift for entering imaginatively into the life of the flowers, plants, and trees she worked with; and even of the butterflies, insects, and bees, which were to become her life's work. This rare talent was matched by a power to express her imaginative insights precisely and vividly. Though I never actually worked in the apiary of Ein-Harod, I was always fascinated by the life and habits of bees and spent scores of hours with Rachel, asking her questions and delighting in her answers. Later I made extensive use of the bee lore I amassed from these talks in a book for children, *Story of a Beehive and the Queen Bee.*

Beekeeping in those early days was a tough, physically exacting job, so Rachel needed her exceptional stamina to cope with its demands. The heavy hives had to be moved by truck from one place to another, according to the seasonal flowerings: for the citrus flowering season, to the area in the plains around Petah Tikva and Rehovot; and for the wildflower season, to the Beit-She'an Valley and the Galilee. The apiary workers stayed with the hives for the flowering period, usually two to three months, quartered in a tent or hut in the nearest kibbutz, and they came home to Ein-Harod only for the Sabbath once or twice a month.

Rachel trained a succession of boys to become full-time workers in the apiary. One of Rachel's star pupils, Gil Lavie, described some of his best remembered experiences with Rachel in *Pirkei Yovel.* Gil himself became an expert apiarist, with a love for the work as ardent as Rachel's, and his account is a moving tribute to the special qualities of Rachel's character and spirit. At the same time, it gives a good impression of the hardships of beekeeping life in his apprentice years, 1946 to 1948.

> The first battles of the War of Independence were being fought when we set out to visit our swarms in the fields at the foot of the Gilboa. The work force in the fields had been sharply reduced because there was often Arab sniping from the Gilboa, and all work beyond the perimeter of the kibbutz had become very dangerous. But Rachel remained adamant about the beehives. "What! Who says we won't go down to look at our beehives? Who says we are going to abandon them?"
>
> So we went out to the fields. When we reached the slope of the Gilboa, Moshe Sturman [the son of Chaim Sturman, Moshe was

commander of the defense system of Ein-Harod] appeared and called out angrily, "What are you *doing?* Is this the time to visit beehives? Don't you know there is a battle going on on the mountain? We're at war. Come back with me immediately!"

But Rachel would not yield. "Wait a moment, Moshe — just a moment — until we've finished our inspection of the hives!" Her voice was soft but firm, and Moshe gave in. Only when we had completed our inspection of the hives was he allowed to take us home in his truck.

In later years I spent a good deal of time reading Russian poetry with Rachel. My Russian was not good enough to read it on my own, but with her help and guidance I acquired a lasting love of her favorite Russian poets, such as Sergei Yesenin, Alexander Block, and Anna Achmatova. These readings strengthened and deepened a friendship that remained one of my closest at Ein-Harod until Rachel's death in 1977.

My first encounter with Shlomo Lavie, the leading Ein-Harod ideologue after whom we had irreverently named our donkey Shloimele, also took place during my hours of work in the nursery. I knew him by sight, of course, and had heard the grown-ups speak of him in tones indicating he was a Very Important Person, but had never exchanged a word with him until the day I was sent to water the saplings in the citrus nursery, next to the grapefruit grove. The ground level of the nursery was slightly below that of the grove, and as both nursery and grove were served by a single water pipe, the water naturally flowed down to the nursery, leaving the grove without sufficient water unless the flow was properly regulated. When I arrived at the nursery, I saw Lavie in the grove; he had evidently been irrigating it that day. I asked him to please tell me how to open the tap so that the grove would get the water it needed. I was frankly excited, for this was the first time I had spoken to the great Lavie on an equal basis, as one worker to another.

He showed me how to open the tap and asked what citrus saplings we were growing. I told him we had grapefruit, orange, and lemon, and that we had grafted them all onto a *chush-chash* — a particularly hardy citrus tree we had recently started to use as understock. Then, wishing to impress him with my knowledge of the newest developments in our common field, I told him that I had read a long article in the monthly agricultural review published by the Histadrut, explaining that it was bad to graft citrus saplings onto an understock of lemon because this weakened the trees and exposed them to disease. This new knowledge, I told Lavie, was based on scientific experiments conducted in California, then regarded as the source of all the most advanced agricultural wisdom.

But my effort to impress misfired badly. "What!" cried Lavie scornfully. "You call *that* new? I've known it for nearly twenty years! Ever since I worked in the citrus groves of Judea. That's not new!" And he turned his back and stomped off without another word.

The response was typical of his weaker side: self-assurance bordering on arrogance, a sharp contemptuous tone that could be very wounding. I was not surprised to learn afterward that he was heartily disliked by many people, and respected rather than loved by the rest. He was a tall, bony man with a long, thin, unsmiling face, which habitually wore a severe and somehow remote expression, as if his mind were fixed on far-off things and barely saw either objects or people in front of him. He had no sense of humor, very little charm, and was so intently absorbed in his ideas and plans that he seemed to have no time or patience for human relationships. With the zealot's unshakable confidence in his own doctrines and opinions, he tended to dismiss with contempt any that differed from his own and to scorn and despise the advocates of the divergent positions. After stormy kibbutz General Assembly meetings at which Shlomo Lavie let fly at his ideological opponents, people would come away shaking their heads, saying, "A difficult man — yes, a very difficult man!" or more tactfully, "a very controversial personality."

Yet few did not respect and honor him for the qualities that helped raise him to his position of undisputed leadership: his originality and imagination, his integrity, his courage and fighting spirit, and his single-minded pursuit of his vision of what a kibbutz ought to be. The radically new concept of the big kibbutz was his brainchild, and won the support of the national kibbutz organization of the time, the Gdud ha-Avoda (Battalion of Labor), which started to build Ein-Harod in accordance with the broad pattern proposed by Lavie. But when the Zionist Executive was divided on the issue of the big kibbutz, it was Lavie who fought the battles with the establishment, tirelessly arguing for the idea itself and for Ein-Harod's claim to the financial means to develop as a kibbutz on that scale. If, as Shlomo Tzemach said to me in the threshing field, there might have been no Ein-Harod at all but for Bialik, it is fair to say that but for Shlomo Lavie, Ein-Harod would not have been the model of a big kibbutz it became within its first five years.

Lavie was also the first to insist that citrus, and in particular grapefruit and lemon, could be grown in the heavy soil of the Emek, at a time when it was believed that it could be grown only in the sandy soil of the coastal plain. When the experts from the Settlement Department of the Zionist Executive came to Ein-Harod to check out the situation, they pronounced the idea to be absurd. "If grapefruit can grow in this place," said one inspector, holding his hand out in front of him, "hair can grow on the palm of this hand." But the experts were wrong. Grapefruit did grow very successfully at Ein-Harod and remains one of our principal crops.

Shlomo Lavie's personal life was full of tragedy. His wife died at a young age and he never remarried. Both his two sons were killed in the War of Independence, leaving his one daughter. In his later years he was a lonely man, his loneliness aggravated by the disappointment of seeing many of the ideals he had lived and fought for in his prime go unrealized. Nevertheless, he managed to produce three volumes of memoirs in which he recorded, with all his characteristic force, his most original ideas, his varied activities, and his signal disappointments.

As I linger over my recollections of Lavie's character and personality, my thoughts return to the day I first met him. The water was flowing smoothly between my rows of saplings when suddenly a great flood shot out of my tap and began to spread rapidly. The cause must have been a tap turned off somewhere along the pipeline, but I had no idea how to stop the flood and desperately began trying to mend the collapsing walls of the furrows between my saplings. Lavie, still working in his grove, saw what had happened and immediately ran to close the main tap, saving my saplings from ruin. Then he came up to me, and perhaps observing my mortification, let his usually severe face break into a smile that caused soft wrinkles to form in the corners of his eyes. With unexpected gentleness he said, "This is the sort of thing that can happen to anyone. The important thing is not to panic — to know the cause — just to go and shut the main tap."

The most magnetic personality of Ein-Harod during my boyhood and early youth was Chaim Sturman, a father figure for his contemporaries, a hero and idol for the young. A natural leader with tremendous personal authority and charisma, he made his most distinguished contribution in defense, in land purchases for Jewish settlement, and in working ceaselessly for friendship and good neighborly relations between Jews and Arabs. Having come to Eretz Yisrael in the Second Aliyah in 1906 at the age of fifteen, he gained his first experience of Jewish defense in the famous Hashomer, which he joined three years later. From the start he was entrusted with the most responsible tasks, taking on, for example, the guarding of the whole Hadera area. By the time the Haganah was founded in 1920, he was regarded as one of the country's authorities on defense matters, constantly consulted by the Haganah's national command. When he joined Ein-Harod in 1921 as a founding member — coming from Kinneret, like most of the other Second Aliyah veterans of Ein-Harod — he immediately became its mukhtar, the Arabic title designating the person in charge of all the defense arrangements of a settlement and its environs. He continued to hold this office to the end of his all too short life.

Because he had become fluent in Arabic while his family was living and farming in the lower Galilee, he became Ein-Harod's spokesman in all its dealings with the Arabs of the area, and then the leading negotiator of the Emek and surrounding areas in land purchases from the Arabs. Once the land had been bought, he determined exactly where a new settlement was to be put up. As soon as the settlement was founded, he guided the new settlers in solving problems of defense and helped them to establish good relations with their Arab neighbors. Later, during the Arab riots of 1936, he was the leading spirit behind the new stockade-and-watchtower settlements, which could be built in a single night. Again, Chaim Sturman's main tasks were to negotiate the purchase of land, to ensure the defense of the new settlement, and —

the job he regarded as the most important—to build friendly relations between the new settlers and the local Arabs.

Though his expertise was mainly in land buying, Chaim also excelled at other kinds of purchase, which sometimes took him far from Ein-Harod, across the then open borders of the Middle East. He bought cows and horses in Damascus, mules in Cyprus, sheep in Turkey, and he always knew exactly which were the best specimens. He was what one might call the universal farmer. He had learned every side of the science and art of farming before he came to Ein-Harod, and there was nothing he couldn't do on the farm — from working with the cows and horses to immersing himself in the planning and organizational work of the kibbutz. I remember my first encounter with him, soon after my arrival at Ein-Harod. There was a tall fellow — broad-shouldered, solidly built, with gingery hair and complexion to match, and a distinctive short mustache — painting our newly built school hut a bright green. He gave me the warm friendly smile I came to love ever afterward and said, "Hullo, boy! That's our children's house, you know. I'm trying to give it a more cheerful face!"

He tended to speak little at meetings of the kibbutz General Assembly, listening carefully while others let themselves go in floods of excited talk. For this reason, perhaps, when he did speak he was accorded respectful attention, and his proposals were generally accepted unanimously. In private conversation he was easy, good-humored, and witty; and he loved children and loved to talk to them most of all.

"There was a special charm and flavor in his encounters with children," a woman member wrote after his death. "On returning from a journey in his car, he would always pick up children he happened to meet on the way, just to give them a ride . . . And there was something special about his way of telling a story to a child — in a whisper, and only when he was sure no grown-up was listening — only the child."

Chaim Sturman's life ended abruptly in 1938 at the age of forty-seven. He was killed by a mine laid by Arabs while on his way, with two companions, to fix the site of a new settlement in the Beit-She'an Valley on the Jordanian border. The tragic irony of his death was evident to all: that Chaim Sturman, who had loved and respected the Arabs, who had been admired and loved in return by his Arab friends — that he of all people should have

been killed by an Arab mine. The new settlement whose site he
never reached was named Ma'oz Chaim in his memory, and the
area where he and his two companions were killed was turned
into a national park. By a further stroke of irony, Chaim was
killed on Ein-Harod's seventeenth birthday, and the Yud Chet
Elul festival that year, to which he never returned, became a day
of bitter mourning.

Among the mourners at Chaim Sturman's funeral was his great
friend and admirer Orde Wingate, the brilliant, unconventional
British army captain who became an ardent Zionist and advocate
of Jewish self-defense and who helped develop the Haganah into
a formidable military force. Sent to Palestine to protect the Brit-
ish-owned Iraqi Petroleum Company's vital oil pipeline to the
Haifa refineries from attacks by Arab saboteurs, Wingate was
soon cooperating with the illegal Haganah units in the actions of
his Special Night Squads (SNS). He was deeply impressed by the
caliber of the Jewish fighters, and induced the Haganah, under
the military leadership of kindred spirit Yitzhak Sadeh, to abandon its mainly defensive posture and adopt instead the strategy
and tactics of an "active defense" against the Arabs. From his
SNS headquarters at Ein-Harod, Wingate provided the training,
guidance, and inspiration that transformed the character of the
Haganah and, according to its leaders, "shaped a generation of
commanders and fighters which in the days to come formed the
nucleus of the Palmach and the Israel Defense Army."

I was in Poland during the whole period Wingate was at Ein-
Harod so I missed him completely, but of course I heard all about
him — his great work for the Haganah, his devout Christianity,
and his warm friendship with our defense chief, Chaim Sturman.
At first Sturman, intent on maintaining Ein-Harod's good relations with its Arab neighbors, was opposed to Wingate's making it
a base for offensive military actions and treated him somewhat
coldly. But later he came to recognize the importance to the Haganah of Wingate's training, and they became close friends and
collaborators. "From the first, he perceived the qualities of maturity and humanity in Sturman's nature," wrote Wingate's friend
Emmanuel Yallan, the head of Haganah intelligence in Haifa at
the time. Wingate saw in Chaim Sturman a man who "was not
prepared to sacrifice his convictions even on the altar of the highest purpose, however sublime it might be." In due course, Yallan

said, "ties of deep friendship bound the two men. Although they had no language in common, they understood each other. Wingate once remarked how entertaining it was even to be silent with Sturman."

And, like others, Wingate came to have a profound admiration for Sturman's attitude and behavior toward the Arabs. "On one occasion," Yallan recalled, "a number of Arabs were taken prisoner. The nights were cold, and when Wingate went to inspect his prisoners before dawn he found Sturman in their compound distributing blankets. At that time Ein-Harod had no spare blankets and Sturman had collected them from his own men. Wingate was greatly impressed by this incident. He was happy to have met a brother in destiny." It may have been this incident, among others like it, that led Wingate to inscribe on the ribbon of the wreath he laid on Chaim Sturman's grave: "A great Jew, a friend of the Arabs, cut down by Arabs."

Orde Wingate was not alone in being impressed by Chaim Sturman's humanity. Some of the most moving memoirs that appeared after Chaim's death were those testifying to the mutual affection and respect that characterized his relations with his Arab friends. He had believed all his life in the possibility of peaceful coexistence between Jews and Arabs in Eretz Yisrael, and it seems his Arab friends appreciated what he had achieved, and loved and cherished him for it. The following episode, recounted by Yosef Fein, an old friend of Chaim, occurred in the midst of the Arab riots of 1936–1939, two days before Chaim was killed.

Fein had run into Chaim in town. They were standing in a side street, absorbed in talk, when suddenly an Arab crept up behind them and pressed his hands over Chaim's eyes.

"For a moment," Fein recalled, "we were taken aback. Then we recognized one of our good friends with whom we had worked for many years. He said, 'Ah, these are bad times, *Ya Ha'wadja* Chaim.* But when I see you, I think to myself, All hope that Arabs and Jews will live together is not yet lost. We can still, to-

---

*Ha'wadja, "sir" or "mister," was the title Arabs used to address Jews and Englishmen in Mandatory Palestine. The prefix *ya* was an exclamation, like "Oh" ("Oh, Mr. Chaim").

gether, build not only Palestine, but lots of other countries as well!' He paused, then said, 'We don't have many people like you, Chaim. Take care of yourself. There is great unrest all around you. Try to go as little as possible to Beit-She'an.'

"Chaim answered with a smile on his lips, 'Ya, chabibi, our good friend — I trust in Allah, and in the Arabs, and we will yet meet and talk about the hard days we are living through now.'

"Our Arab friend was afraid to remain in our company for long, and as he was leaving, he said, 'How precious you are to us, Ya Chaim! You know that I don't like to flatter people to their faces. But when I see you in these times, I feel bound to tell you what I have just said.' And he went."

Batya Brenner recalled that Chaim's murder reminded her of the murder of her brother, Yosef Chaim Brenner, in the orchard near Jaffa seventeen years before. Then she commented, in her bare, curt style:

Did Chaim have friends among the Arabs? Who knows? But he, on his side, certainly treated them as friends. I will tell of one incident. When we started to build our settlement on Kumi Hill and there were still only few of us here, an Arab from Kumi village threw a stone at me, wounding me. The Arab was immediately caught by our young men, and it was decided to hand him over to the police.

The sheik of the village came to Chaim to sue for peace. What Chaim said to the sheik I don't know. What he said to me was, "We will certainly have the Arab brought to trial. We can't let them think they can get away with this sort of thing. But we must not be too severe, because we are neighbors."

The Arab stone thrower was sentenced to twelve days in prison and a fine of twenty-two lirot, for court costs and as compensation for my injury. Again the notables of the village came to Chaim to ask for a reduction of the sentence. He received them in a friendly spirit. I didn't hear their conversation, but I remember what Chaim said to me: "I want you to sign a peace pact with them. We have reached a compromise. The twelve days' imprisonment will stand — he will lose nothing by it, and he will get his pita all the same. But in order to pay the fine, he would have to sell his pair of oxen. That would be a great pity."

I looked at Chaim, astonished. "Do you mean to tell me you're *sorry* for him?"

He answered, "What can we do? The money won't mend your injury, and we have to live together with them."

That's how Chaim always behaved with them, rationally and humanely. And we must say the same; we have to live together with them. But alas, we do it in mourning.

The death of Chaim Sturman was as shattering a blow for me as it was for everyone who knew him. I was on a mission to Poland when it happened and received the news in Warsaw. Stricken with grief, I sent home a letter expressing my thoughts in those hours of desolation. They seemed to turn mainly on the magnetism Chaim had for us, the confidence and courage he inspired, the standard of excellence he set for us in all our activities — our farming work, our defense duties, our human relationships.

As I think of Chaim, I remember the Ma'ayan Harod and the ancient spreading fig tree next to the cave from which Gideon's spring emerges. At midday in summer, when the bare Emek was flooded with burning light, your eyes turned to the dark green of the fig tree, and you said to yourself: here is one shady corner, one shelter, one refuge in which to hide yourself.

Such a shelter and refuge Chaim Sturman was for you, always. And it inspired you with confidence. We felt it from the days of our childhood, when he first taught us the meaning of work in the threshing field. Tall, quiet, confident, a smile playing beneath his short golden mustache, he taught us how to tame the foals, how to hold them firmly, how to hurry them on in their runs with the threshing sledge. Afterward he taught us how to use the pitchfork to turn the crops; and, at dawn, how to scatter the chaff before the wind. The touch of his large, warm hand transmitted courage and self-confidence. Chaim is pleased, you said; that means you've done your job well.

It was the same in later years, in your encounters with him during the Arab riots, when you were on guard duty at night in the citrus orchard on the slope of the Gilboa. When the Arabs started shooting down at us from the mountain, Chaim would silently appear out of the darkness, quiet, smiling, confident, pat you on the shoulder with his large, warm hand, and you knew: Good, you did the right thing. Chaim is pleased; that means you've done your job well. And your heart filled with happiness to know that you had stood the test. For with Chaim you became strong, brave, and tranquil.

With Chaim it was also good to be silent. It was not only that his silence was pleasant, but you also learned from him how to listen to silence. I remember meeting him once on our night train to Ein-Harod when he was returning from a journey to Damascus. He had been away for about two weeks and eagerly asked for news of home. It was good to meet him on the train; but even better to walk with him on a summer's night from the station up the hill full of lights. We walked in silence. Suddenly he stopped and said, "I can smell our fields." His voice sounded a little hoarse with emotion. I was startled. "Is *that* what Chaim's like?" As if he sensed my surprise, he turned his head and asked in his normal voice, "Have they finished cutting the crops?"

At our last meeting before I left for Poland, when we were returning from a trip to some of the new settlements in the Emek, he patted me on the shoulder with his large, warm hand. My heart swelled with confidence; I felt I could face my long journey.

Chaim Sturman's death was the beginning of what almost the whole country now knows as the Sturman Story. The destiny of the Jew in Eretz Yisrael to fight again and again, and if necessary to die, for his right to live in peace in his homeland pursued Chaim's family in the years that followed like an ancient Greek fate. His only son, Moshe Sturman, was killed in the War of Independence at the foot of the Gilboa in the Beit-She'an Valley not far from the place where his father had died. He was twenty-six. Moshe's only son, named Chaim after his grandfather, was killed at the age of twenty-three in the Green Island action of July 1969 in Nasser's War of Attrition following the Six Day War. Ten months later, Amir Brin, nineteen, the only son of Chaim the elder's daughter, was killed at the Suez Canal when his tank struck a mine.

I had known Moshe Sturman from childhood, and remember how strongly he resembled his father in his vivid, charismatic personality. Like his father, he dedicated himself from his youth to the defense of the Emek and the country; so it was not by chance that Moshe had appeared at the foot of the Gilboa when Rachel and young Gil Lavie came to inspect their beehives. In many ways less intellectual, more physical and intuitive than his father, Moshe loved farm work and did every job he undertook with an almost sensual enjoyment. Indeed, he was a man of nature to his sensitive fingertips, knowing every inch of the Emek intimately and loving all of nature — the trees, flowers, animals, rocks, and caves he had lived with from his earliest childhood.

His son Chaim belonged to my daughters' generation; I knew him as a handsome, brave, high-spirited young man with the natural gift of leadership of his father and grandfather, a great talent for friendship, an ardent love of life. His mother, Re'uma, who was awaiting his release from the army after a four-year period of service, heard instead how he had died. He had been in the special volunteer commando unit of frogmen in the action that captured Green Island and was killed by a grenade when the battle was virtually over. Amir, his cousin, was so young when he was killed that there was scarcely time to know him. But I knew his mother, Tama, and his father, Shlomo Brin, very well and knew what it was for Tama Sturman to have lost a father, a brother, a nephew, and an only son in our wars.

And of course I knew — we all knew — Atara Sturman, widow of Chaim, mother of Moshe, grandmother of Chaim the younger and Amir. She lived through it all, bearing her losses of three generations with incredible courage and fortitude. Like her husband, Chaim, she had been a member of Hashomer, and once said to someone who had marveled at her fortitude: "Hashomer people don't cry." At another time she said simply that she had believed all her life that the survival of the Jewish people and the continuity of Jewish life in Eretz Yisrael came before everything else, and she would go on believing it, whatever happened. The story of the Sturmans, though no longer unique, remains a symbol to the nation of the faith that every Jew here is obliged to take hold of and never let go, in spite of the price that has to be paid, and perpetually repaid.

6

Working Youth

WE DID NOT have long to wait for my grandmother Bracha to make it clear that she did not like the home in Tel Aviv at all. My grandmother was illiterate, but she was a woman of independent character with firm ideas of her own and self-confidence rooted in her experience of life and her wisdom about the vagaries of human nature. What she most disliked about the home was its old-fashioned discipline. The director, evidently a disciplinarian of the old school, treated his senior citizens as if they were wayward children in a boarding school, treatment my grandmother found intolerable. When my mother urged her to join us at Ein-Harod, she readily agreed, and she came to Ein-Harod in 1925, a year after our own arrival.

We were pleasantly surprised at how quickly she adapted to the life of the kibbutz. Recalling, perhaps, the atmosphere of the first years of the Russian Revolution, she seemed to like the idea of being part of a community of workers, particularly its social equality. She in turn impressed the kibbutz people with her energy and dedication to her work and her vivid, expressive Yiddish, full of homely aphorisms and sappy, colorful figures of speech and locutions that defy translation into any other language. She had a passion for order and tidiness; there are still those at Ein-Harod who remember how she pulled up the straggling thorn bushes that grew beside the hut in which she shared my mother's room, and how with her own hands she made a gravel path between the hut and the outside water tap, carrying the gravel all the way from the perimeter of the kibbutz in the lap of her skirt as if it were an apron. On summer evenings we used to light a bonfire to drive away mosquitoes, and as we sat beside it she would tell me Chassidic stories of the Thirty-six Just Men, who went about the world doing good deeds without ever revealing their real identity. Later I would retell the stories to an entranced audience in the children's house.

But my grandmother lived with an uneasy conscience, for she had left behind in Odessa her youngest daughter, Batsheva. Sheva had always been a sickly girl, and my grandmother felt that she ought to go back to take care of her. In the end, after about twelve months with us, she decided she must go, and she went. As my grandmother could not write, my favorite aunt, Adela, wrote to my mother periodically to give her news of Grandmother Bracha until, toward the end of the thirties, the letters ceased. This was the period of the Moscow Trials, Stalin's terrible purges of the old guard of the Bolshevik Revolution, and it had become dangerous for Jews to maintain contacts abroad. So we never knew what happened to my grandmother.

The one chance we had of finding out, much later, in the spring of 1956, was strangely and horribly frustrated. My brother, Yuval, by then a sailor in the Israeli merchant navy, happened to be on a cargo boat carrying Jaffa oranges to Odessa. He had tracked down Adela's address, and on his arrival in Odessa Yuval promptly went off to visit her, very excited at the prospect of meeting his aunt, bringing her our family greetings, and hearing all her family news to bring back to us. A young woman, evidently Adela's daughter, opened the door and showed him into the modest living room, announcing the identity of the guest. The moment Adela heard his name and that he had come from Israel, she waved him off frantically, crying, "Go away! Get out of here! I don't want to see you! I don't want anything to do with you!" Afterward we learned from my mother's brother, who had long since settled in Paris, that Adela's husband had been taken away by the GPU one night and had never returned; ever since, our aunt had lived in terror of any contact with the outside world — the kind of terror that only a Stalinist police state can inspire. Yuval, of course, had no choice but to go, without speaking a word to her. To this day we don't know what happened to the remnants of my mother's family in Soviet Russia.

My father, whom we had left in Benderri in the spring of 1923, soon thereafter went to Canada for a time. He had been invited there to teach Hebrew, the Bible, and other Jewish subjects. The school paid for his passage and he stayed for nearly two years. As the salary was much better than anything he could have earned in Benderri, he managed to save money for his journey to Eretz Yisrael and arrived at Ein-Harod at the end of 1925.

Before he left Canada, my father wrote to ask what gift I wanted him to bring me. I piously wrote back that I wanted no gift, only him. But I couldn't help being curious to know, I said, whether such a thing as a bicycle could be bought in Canada, and if so, whether it was very expensive, and if not too expensive, that was something I would someday, when we could afford it, very much like to have. My father found he could afford it then and arrived with it in December 1925, just in time to make it a bar mitzvah gift. This bicycle was the first ever seen in Ein-Harod, and indeed in the whole Emek; people came to gaze at it as if it were a rare animal from a distant land. Though it was formally my personal property, the communal ethos prescribed that the joy of riding it should be shared. Accordingly, there was an almost permanent line of children, who were each allowed a half-hour ride. The fame of my bicycle reached a peak when it became a recognized medical aid. Our kibbutz doctor prescribed regular bike rides for a delicate girl. The doctor came to the children's house to explain to us why it was important to the girl's health to have these rides, and to request official permission to use the bicycle for this therapeutic purpose.

After two years of glory, my bicycle met its end in a sad, dramatic, typically Jewish way. One holiday I set out on my bicycle for Haifa to visit a former Ein-Harod friend, Aharon Laskov, elder brother of Chaim Laskov, who later became one of the chiefs of staff of the Israel Defense Forces. Although I wonder now at my temerity in undertaking this two-day journey on my own, in view of the danger of attack from Arabs, I reached Haifa safely and spent some pleasant hours with my friend. As I was about to start on my return journey Aharon, on an impulse, asked a favor of me. He was working outside Haifa, a good distance from the wooden shack he lived in, and transportation was a constant problem. If I would let him keep my bicycle until he could afford his own, I would be doing a great mitzvah. I agreed — whether reluctantly or not I cannot remember — and went back to Ein-Harod by train. Within a few months the 1929 Arab riots broke out and Aharon's shack was burned by Haifa Arabs, my bicycle along with it. We said, when we heard about it, there goes another victim in the battle for our existence in Eretz Yisrael. The loss, of course, seemed a negligible one at a time when human beings were being killed in many parts of the country.

My father was thirty-eight when he came to Ein-Harod. He was not very strong and found the physical work difficult. For a short time he worked in the vineyard, and then in the stables, but in the end he had to settle for desk work in the kibbutz accounting office. Though he made some good friends, he felt like an outsider in the Second Aliyah group to which, historically speaking, he belonged. He had missed the common experiences of the pioneer life before and during the First World War that bound them together, and it made a gap in communication, which could not easily be filled. I suspect he also missed the public life he had been accustomed to since early manhood, and though he took part in all kibbutz activities, he did so in a passive way, unable, it seemed, to summon the energy and spirit for more active leadership roles. He did make his mark, however, as a guide to English-speaking visitors to the kibbutz, of whom there was a constant stream. He had learned English in Canada, and as only three other members of Ein-Harod knew English at that time, my father had this department of kibbutz activity almost entirely to himself.

My father was doomed not to realize his lifelong dream of a pioneering life in Eretz Yisrael. He was soon robbed of his second chance to make it, which was to prove his last. Within three years of his arrival at Ein-Harod, he came down with an illness the doctors here could not diagnose. He had severe stomach pains, suspected to be a kidney problem, but the doctors were not certain and urged him to seek medical aid abroad. Toward the end of 1928 he left for Paris, where my uncle Salamon and his family could be counted on to help. They were helpful in finding him work as a Hebrew teacher, so he could maintain himself while he was consulting doctors, but the Paris doctors were no more successful in diagnosing his illness than our local ones had been and were unable to suggest any treatment that might lead to a cure. My father struggled on for three years, his pains growing worse all the time. Then in the spring of 1931 he went into the hospital, where he died on May 5, at the age of forty-four.

In his letters home he had said very little about his illness, telling us instead how he missed us and how he longed to see his baby son, Yuval, who had been born after his departure. So we knew practically nothing about the course of his illness nor what had been the exact cause of his death. The only information we ever had came from our doctor at Ein-Harod, who by sheer chance had gone abroad for advanced study at the very hospital in Paris in which my father died. He saw my father shortly before his death, and all he could elicit from the hospital doctors about the cause of death was that he had suffered some form of blood poisoning — as mysterious, it seems, as his whole illness had been. More than forty years later, in 1973, my brother Yuval died at the age of forty-four of a rare kidney disease, which the doctors here said was almost certainly hereditary.

As I recall the three brief years I had with my father at Ein-Harod when I was a young teenager, the main impression that lingers is that of a man who was not altogether happy. He found joy, of course, in being with his family after his long separation from us and in his participation in some of the creative activities of the kibbutz. But his hovering illness (which must have sapped his strength long before he was conscious of it), his failure to find a natural place in the community, and the physical hardships of kibbutz life combined to have an oppressive effect. He was often withdrawn, sunk in his own thoughts, not wholly in touch with the world he inhabited. If I had been older, I might have found a way to help him, but I was too young to understand such complicated inner states and, without understanding, I could not enter into them; for the most part I found his moods puzzling and vaguely disturbing. But there were good times as well — we had some excellent talks, mainly about books, and he could still be wonderfully animated when carried away by a favorite topic, like his old love Chaim Yosef Brenner, whom he was rereading and whose work I had just discovered. Our talks about Brenner were highlights of our communication in those years.

By the time my father died, Ein-Harod had completed its move to a new and permanent site on Kumi Hill, four kilometers from Ma'ayan Harod. When we received my uncle Salamon's cable telling us of my father's death, my mother and I walked from our new quarters at Kumi to the kibbutz cemetery, which was still at the old site at the foot of the Gilboa. It was nearly an hour's walk, and we cried all the way. It was terrible for us not to be able to bury him in our cemetery, and we sat there in silence for more than an hour, as if we had come for his funeral and were sitting by his grave. The fiction must have helped us, for we walked back to Kumi calmer than we had come.

Many years later, on my first visit to England, I had an experience that led me, on my return to Israel, to write a poem called "Vine."

> He used to appear in my dreams
> in a worn khaki shirt
> as in the old photograph:
> bent over his spade
> planting a vine
> in the first vineyard.
> But when he suddenly appeared to me
> in the foreign village, he was
> dressed in black,
> the violet light of the lake
> gleaming in his glasses.
> Stooping on the path, with a pale hand he blessed
> a crowd of children hurrying
> out of Sunday school.
>
> I stood there, older than my father now
> by ten years or more,
> yearning for the sad look
> of his eyes.
> For a brief moment I saw a child
> laboring at a vine
> on a harvest day
> and whispered with parched lips,
> "My father
> my father planted
> this vine." *

*From *Pomegranate Tree in Jerusalem*, Kibbutz ha-Meuchad Publishing House, Tel Aviv, page 46.

In 1926 I entered a fresh phase of my life at Ein-Harod. That year all of us between the ages of thirteen and sixteen joined *Ha-No'ar ha-Oved*, the Working Youth movement, the nationwide young workers' organization affiliated with the Histadrut. This marked my entrance into the world of ideas of the labor and Zionist-socialist movements from which the kibbutz sprang and by which it was nourished and sustained. At about the same time I started to attend the weekly "study day" of our sixteen-year-olds, who had stopped their formal schooling to work full time in the kibbutz, and this was a further formative experience in my early education in the history and philosophical foundations of the kibbutz.

It may be difficult for the outsider to understand either the importance of this "education in ideas," as we call it, or its interest and excitement for us. Its importance rests on the plain historical fact that the kibbutz was the creation of people with passionate ideological convictions and would never have come into existence but for those strong convictions. Many of the founding members arrived with little or no passion for these ideas. Often they came for purely practical reasons: because they could not find employment in the towns; because they thought it would be easier to bring up their children communally; because they wanted to farm and felt the kibbutz offered the easiest way to do it. But once they had become members, they came to understand, to a greater or lesser degree, the raison d'être of the kibbutz. And they came to understand because they were *taught* to understand, on the assumption that a social organization like the kibbutz, which was both demanding and voluntary, could not sustain or perpetuate itself without a belief in the shared goals of communal life.

They were taught, from the first, through their participation in the life of the kibbutz, and by listening to and joining into the vigorous discussions and arguments about fundamental questions that went on all the time. What is a kibbutz? What are its essential features — those that make it a kibbutz and not something else? What are the rights and wrongs of this or that aspect of communal life, this or that economic plan, this or that decision about the education of the children, the living conditions of the members, the procedures of the general assembly, or whatever? The "philosophy" of the kibbutz always made itself felt somehow in these discussions and arguments, and this was doubtless the most immediate, concrete way of absorbing it. But the kibbutz also provided a more deliberate, systematic education in ideas for those who had the taste and the gift for it, and the value of this education for the survival and self-perpetuation of the kibbutz has been amply confirmed in the more than half century that has passed since my youth. The preoccupation with ideas and ideology was the heart's blood of our communal life in those days, and I could not tell my story or that of Ein-Harod without recording here the prominence it had in our lives.

As for our interest and excitement in coming to understand the historical and philosophical foundations of the kibbutz, these sprang from the intrinsic satisfaction that all knowledge gives, but also from our more or less intuitive recognition of the crucial importance of this knowledge for the survival of the kibbutz. By knowing and understanding we would somehow help Ein-Harod to live on — this was the thought that moved us, though in forms admittedly dim and vague, and it proved to be a most powerful motive in my own studies.

The Working Youth movement, as I said, launched our education in ideas. It also wrought radical changes in our lives. The movement came into being as a direct consequence of the appalling conditions in which the youth of Tel Aviv, Jerusalem, and the smaller towns worked and lived in the early 1920s. They were obliged to put in ten to twelve hours a day in their workshops, primitive factories, and other workplaces; they were very badly paid; and they were often unemployed because of the widespread shortage of work. The Histadrut, founded in 1920, protected the rights of workers over the age of eighteen, but had no provision for the under-eighteens. So in 1924 the young workers started to organize themselves, with the support of the Histadrut, against the exploitation of employers. From the beginning, the No'ar ha-Oved organization undertook to provide elementary education for those young workers who as children had been obliged to help support their families, and further education for those who had had some. Having started in Tel Aviv and Jerusalem, the movement spread first to Haifa, Tiberias, and the *moshavot* (agricultural villages), and in 1925 to the kibbutzim and moshavim — whose members were all, by definition, workers. Ein-Harod willingly agreed to join as a "branch" of the No'ar ha-Oved national organization, and before long I was elected its secretary.

We soon felt the beneficial effects of our new link with the No'ar ha-Oved, both intellectually and socially. On the intellectual side there was the new experience of receiving monthly visits from members of the national secretariat, who came to report on the activities of the No'ar ha-Oved and to give lectures explaining its economic and social problems. Under their inspiration we formed a study circle at Ein-Harod for the purpose of examining the foundations of Zionist socialism. We read such classic socialist works as Friedrich Engels's *Development of Socialism from Utopia to Science,* and Zionist books like Leon Pinsker's *Auto-Emancipation,* Moses Hess's *Rome and Jerusalem,* and of course Theodor Herzl's *The Jewish State.* But the expansion of our social and communal life through these studies and lectures was scarcely less important for us than the new knowledge itself, and for this we had to thank chiefly our two dedicated instructors, David Cohen and Yisrael Galili.

David Cohen, thirty-four, had become the principal guide and mentor of the No'ar ha-Oved movement. He had a warm, vivid personality and was no ordinary lecturer. At the end of his talks he used to tell us Chassidic stories in which the hero was almost always a poor, simple fellow who in times of crisis disclosed shining virtues of goodheartedness, helpfulness to others, and loyalty to his people. We lapped them up, perhaps because we were also poor and simple fellows, and we sang with gusto the Chassidic songs he taught us. David came from a Chassidic family in Lithuania, and we could feel his love for them in his storytelling and singing, even though he had long since abandoned the religious side of his upbringing. In the summer David often gave his talks outdoors under an arbor in the vineyard, in the eucalyptus grove by the stream, or on a haystack in the threshing field, and these pastoral settings greatly added to our enjoyment of his discourses.

Yisrael Galili was to become a national leader of the first rank and one of my closest friends and mentors over a period of fifty years, so it is particularly pleasant for me to recall these earliest beginnings of his public career and of our friendship at Ein-Harod in 1926, when I was fourteen and he seventeen. He was to become one of the leading members of the Haganah and was its last commander in chief before it was transformed into the Israel Defense Forces. Afterward he was Ben-Gurion's deputy minister of defense in the first government of the State of Israel, a cabinet minister in several Labor governments of the 1960s and 1970s, and the closest adviser of Golda Meir, who was said never to have made an important decision without consulting Galili first. Throughout his long career he was a political leader and representative of the kibbutzim. A founding member of Kibbutz Na'an, the first kibbutz established by the No'ar ha-Oved, he lives there still.

Galili's connection with the Working Youth movement was direct and intimate: himself a working youth, he had grown up in Tel Aviv, started to work as a plumber at an early age, and had little formal education. So he knew firsthand the deprivations and most urgent needs of young workers. All his knowledge and wisdom, and the beautiful literary Hebrew for which he became famous, were the fruits of self-education and self-discipline. Though I have known Galili since we were teenagers, I never cease to wonder at his natural gifts and force of character, and at how his ascent to positions of eminence and power has left inviolate his modesty, simplicity, and integrity, which even his political adversaries have granted are almost without peer among our national leaders.

Some of these endowments were already evident in the handsome, golden-haired, blue-eyed youth who came to talk at Ein-Harod. They really were talks rather than lectures; the immediacy and intimacy of his style of address made each member of our group feel that he or she was being engaged in a personal, private conversation, in which any question could be asked, any doubt or uncertainty or criticism aired openly and frankly. What made the greatest impression on us was his intellectual power, expressed in his remarkable lucidity, analytical acuteness, and talent for exact definition. Naturally eloquent, he had a gift for vivid, pictorial description in a rich and subtle Hebrew. The people of Israel were destined to enjoy the benefits of Yisrael Galili's talents for many years to come. It was said in the sixties and seventies that there was probably not a single official statement of policy issued by the Labor governments of that period that had not been formulated by Galili. When people sometimes expressed astonishment at his remembering verbatim not only every statement, declaration, and proposal of these Labor governments, but also every amendment proposed, accepted, or rejected, he would answer, "Well, if you've spent many hours, and sometimes days and weeks, formulating them, you can scarcely help remembering them, can you?"

Having been elected secretary of the Ein-Harod branch of the No'ar ha-Oved, I was sent as our representative to a meeting of the central committee of the organization in Haifa. This was to be my first independent encounter with the world outside the children's community, and I went alone and unescorted on our Emek Train. I was practically the youngest representative there, but I was treated as an equal by everyone, and felt very proud and pleased. Full of fresh impressions from the discussions and arguments at the meeting, I returned to Ein-Harod that evening. The Emek Train was full of Arabs, but I was too happy and excited to be nervous.

I was feeling very grown up and confident, but someone else had not forgotten that I was, after all, only a young boy. As I stepped out onto the platform of our little station, into darkness illuminated only by a single paraffin lantern suspended from a pole, I saw to my surprise the thin, slightly bowed figure of Chaim Shifroni standing under the light. My good, devoted teacher had come to meet me not only because he did not want me to walk home alone in the darkness through empty fields, but also, I instantly surmised, because he wanted to be the first to hear my impressions of the meeting in Haifa. Whether my surmise was correct I don't know, but I do know that all the way home I didn't stop talking for one moment. As we reached the small bridge over the stream, Shifroni stopped, interrupted my story of the Haifa meeting, and, with a smile in his eyes that I could just discern in the faint light rising from the stream, he said, "Now we are going to drink a toast with water from this stream! A toast to you, who have now truly assumed the yoke of fulfilling the precepts of the Law!*

*The reference was to a boy's commitment at his bar mitzvah to perform all the mitzvot, or precepts, of the Torah (six hundred thirteen in number).

The arrival at Ein-Harod of the first outside group of Working Youths, almost all of them from Jerusalem, was a major event. The proposal to take them in had come from the national secretariat of the Working Youth organization, and Ein-Harod had agreed — after some initial doubts and hesitations and, as usual, much heated debate and discussion. "What do we need it for?" demanded some of the more isolationist members. "Don't we have enough problems of our own to cope with? Is it really all that important for us to forge links with young people from outside?" But the opinion of the more public-spirited and far-sighted members prevailed. They recognized the risk in taking in young people from the poorer neighborhoods of Jerusalem and elsewhere, many of Oriental origin, all with widely different backgrounds from those of our own young people. But they felt Ein-Harod should take that risk: first, to affirm our sense of community with the workers of the country as a whole; second, and more important, to do what we could to help these groups in the distinctive ways a kibbutz, and perhaps no other society, could help.

Ein-Harod's bold undertaking was recognized as such. It was the first time a kibbutz had accepted such a group of young people, not just for additional manpower, but with the deliberate purpose of helping to reduce the social and cultural gap that separated the underprivileged young urban workers from the rest of society. Most of them had no professional skill or trade, having worked for the most part as messengers, porters, assistants to market stall keepers, or domestic helpers. So first the kibbutz would teach them a professional skill, mainly farming, and instruct the girls in the care of children. And it would extend their education by inviting them to participate in our study day and various study groups. Scarcely less important than the work and education would be their introduction to the values of kibbutz life through full participation in all its social and other communal activities.

So the first group — about twelve girls and boys aged sixteen to eighteen—came. The number may seem small, but it represented a 100 percent increase in our youth community of that age group, and their arrival immediately produced a marked change in our social life and activities. Besides our excitement at the novelty of

it, we felt our human experience being extended and deepened by
our contacts with the newcomers. They shared our living quarters — the huts or remaining tents of the adult community, no
longer the children's house; we ate together in the dining hall; we
worked together, studied together, and took our recreation together. We all made friends among them and saw a few romances
start as well. I formed a special friendship with Boaz Persov, a
shepherd. Much later I wrote a long narrative poem called "Boaz
the Shepherd My Friend," recalling the fascination Boaz's flights
of imagination and caustic observations on human nature had for
me as I sat with him tending the sheep. Boaz met a strange, tragic
end: one hot summer day, after walking about the fields, without
a hat as usual, he sat down on the edge of a well and, perhaps
overcome by sunstroke, lost his balance, fell in, and drowned.

Ein-Harod's initiative in inviting this first group of working
youth from the towns encouraged other kibbutzim to follow suit.
Besides the motive of helping to reduce the social and cultural
gap, they also had the idea of drawing the young workers of the
country to the pioneering life by giving them some firsthand experience of it. The hope, of course, was that they would remain in
the kibbutz, join other kibbutzim, or form the nucleus of a new
kibbutz. The fruits of this endeavor were the fourteen new kibbutzim established by 1941 by young workers who had learned
their new skills this way.

Ein-Harod has continued the practice it started, and there is
always a youth group, averaging twenty to thirty, living and
working here. These groups still come from the deprived
neighborhoods of the big cities as well as from development,
meaning underdeveloped, towns. They now arrive at an earlier
age, usually fourteen or fifteen; and, like our own children, attend
school until they reach eighteen, after which they go into the
army for their compulsory national service — three years for
young men, two for women. Very few return as members of Ein-
Harod or other kibbutzim, but the period they spend at the kibbutz appears to leave a lifelong impression. For example, one day
I was crossing a street in Tel Aviv against a red light when a
young traffic policeman stopped me and demanded to see my
identity card. When he saw the address Ein-Harod, he instantly
broke into a happy smile, told me he had spent twelve months

there five years ago, and oh, how he had enjoyed it, and what a lovely person Neria, who had been in charge of the group, was, and was she still there? When I told him yes, he asked me to please give her his warmest greetings — and no, he said, he wouldn't dream of taking a fine from a *chaver* of Ein-Harod.

Another time a taxi driver, taking my wife and me back from the airport on our return from a journey abroad, was surly about the number of suitcases he had to put in his trunk. He was still grumbling when he heard me mention to our taxi companion that I was from Ein-Harod. He turned around in great excitement, almost losing control of the steering wheel, shouted that he knew Ein-Harod, yes, he did; he had spent two years there in a youth group nearly thirty years ago, and his instructors had been Ya'ir and Yuval — did I know them? I told him that Yuval was my younger brother, at which his excitement rose to a high pitch, and he cried out, "So you must be Zerubavel — who wrote 'Song of the Palmach'!" After that, it was all Zerubavel and "Song of the Palmach," and how sad he was to hear that Yuval had passed away, but what a good period of his life those two years had been, and how he wished he had never left. He talked all the way to Tel Aviv. At the end of our journey, still talking, he heaved out the no longer offending suitcases, pumped my hand, assured me that he would come tomorrow to live and work at Ein-Harod for the rest of his life but his wife wasn't all that keen and the younger children were at school and couldn't be uprooted — though, he added eagerly, one of his older daughters was at that moment at a kibbutz in a youth group.

It was a familiar story, one I had heard many times before in varying forms. Each time I hear it, I think to myself: If all the people in the country who appear to be yearning to live in a kibbutz actually came, we would very soon cease to be a mere 3½ percent of the population. They don't come, but they do seem to go on yearning, more or less sincerely, and that does make a bond, which I think ought not to be minimized.

7

Mentors

THE WEEKLY STUDY DAY that played such a crucial part in my education in ideas when I was fourteen to sixteen was actually a study day for just a year or two. As soon as the sixteen-year-olds for whom it had been created reached the age of eighteen and became full members of the kibbutz, the program was transformed into an evening school for the over-eighteens. But the studies remained substantially the same, and so did our two star instructors, Lyova Levite (pronounced Levvi-*tay*) and Yitzhak Tabenkin.

The whole idea of the study day was, from the start, Levite's; he was the moving spirit behind it and took the initiative in planning the curriculum. Our studies were predominantly historical and sociological. With Levite, we studied the history of the European revolutionary movements of the nineteenth and twentieth centuries and the origin and growth of the organized workers' movements of Europe, particularly the Jewish labor organizations of Russia and Eastern Europe. His knowledge was encyclopedic, and he had a great gift for portraying the characters and personalities of the leaders of those movements. He spoke of them as if they had been his intimate friends, with full knowledge and warmth of appreciation that made them live in our imaginations, too. When he was expounding the concepts of social emancipation or describing the struggle of the workers against their brutal capitalist regimes, Levite was eloquent, bringing the ardor of imaginative participation to their suffering that could not help but kindle a responsive flame in us. Within the framework of these lectures, we read the classics of Zionist socialism, from Moses Hess to Ber Borochov and Brenner, winding up with the writings and personalities of the leaders of the workers' movements in Eretz Yisrael.

Lyova Levite was a Russian intellectual of the finest breed, and he openly cherished his origins to the end of his life. Perhaps this was the reason he never adopted a Hebrew first name but firmly remained Lyova, though most people called him by his surname anyway. One of those lucky men who get handsomer as they grow older, he had a sensitive, thoughtful face of a typically Russian-Jewish cast. But there was nothing of the Russian melancholy in Levite. In a community generally gregarious, he was exceptionally sociable. He intensely enjoyed the company of people of all ages, was always available for talk and willing to enter into any topic, mundane or intellectual, with the same generous zest. In conversation his face broke easily into a warm, radiant smile expressive of his interest and delight in his interlocutor. A born raconteur, Levite told his stories and anecdotes at a leisurely pace with many digressions, but no one ever became impatient; somehow he made the digressions as interesting and entertaining as the story itself.

He was a brilliant lecturer and public speaker, proceeding at the same easy pace at which he told stories and giving the impression of an off-the-cuff spontaneity. But this impression was deceptive; he actually thought out and prepared his lectures and speeches with the utmost care, and they were a model of lucidity and orderliness.

My earliest proof of Levite's distinctive talents came a year or so before I was a member of his lecture classes. We in the children's house would run out in the late afternoon to meet the field workers — the *fallachim* — returning from the fields. Each of us had his own fallach, and Levite was mine. We used to wait for them on the dirt track running along the quarry, and as "your" fallach approached with his pair of mules or horses, you ran forward to be swung up onto the animal he was riding. One afternoon I had a special question to ask Levite as I sat happily in front of him on the mule's back. We had just started reading newspapers seriously, and that day in 1926 our Labor paper,

Davar, had been full of the news of the British general strike. I had struggled to understand what it was all about but without much success; I didn't really know what a strike was or who exactly the working class were, or who was involved in a political struggle with whom. So I decided to ask Levite if he could tell me what this strike was all about.

By the time we reached the stables I had my answer. In simple, lucid language, and as if he were talking to a friend and equal, not to an ignorant boy, he explained the meaning of each of the key concepts that had defeated me, why the strike had been called, and why it was a historical event in the political battle of the exploited against their exploiters. Even more than the substance of Levite's exposition on the mule's back, I remember its spirit: the timbre of his voice in protest against the evils of the capitalist system and his ardent identification with its latest victims, the British working class. It was my first lesson, and one of the best I have ever had, on the meaning of the class struggle and the vision of socialism as the one means of society's deliverance from it.

To the end of his life Levite remained a unique figure at Ein-Harod and in the whole kibbutz movement. Of all that remarkable first generation, he was distinguished by his intellectual gifts, tastes, and accomplishments. Although in his lectures he generally confined himself to his fields of expertise, he was a man of wide interests, devoting almost as much time to the study of literature and literary criticism as he did to his historical and sociological studies. He knew intimately the poetry and fiction of the Russians and Germans, but he also had a deep knowledge of Yiddish and modern Hebrew literature. He was the sort of person who naturally and effortlessly read everything new as it appeared, keeping in touch with all fresh developments, and he was always ready, in his generous, unaffected way, to share his knowledge with all comers.

Levite produced scholarly works that made him a recognized authority in his field, constantly consulted by professorial experts in the country. It all started when he was invited to be editor in chief of a massive three-volume selection of Lenin's works in Hebrew translation. He supplied all the historical notes and interpretative comments, which were so richly informative that the

experts pronounced them a small encyclopedia of Leninist learning. Then came his magnum opus: his edition of the works of Ber
Borochov, the leading Marxist theoretician of the Zionist Workers' Party in Russia before the Revolution and in the United
States during the First World War. A precocious genius who died
at the age of thirty-eight, Borochov managed, in his short life, to
publish a phenomenal amount of fundamental research, especially in the area of Marxist economics and theory of society. He
used this research in his expansion and refinement of Zionist doctrine, and in effect worked out the economic foundations of Zionist socialism, which are still considered valid. Levite's work
included a scholarly and critical "apparatus" of biographical, historical, and theoretical notes, which comprised virtually a volume
by themselves and remain a definitive commentary on Borochov,
widely used by students of the subject and the period.

For Levite, Borochov was more than just a rewarding subject of
research; he was a spiritual hero. A huge photograph of Borochov
hung on the wall of Levite's hut immediately above his bed, and I
remember how struck I was the first time I saw it. When Levite
told me who it was, I still found it hard to understand why a
grown man should want to sleep night after night with a picture
of a man called Borochov behind his head.

Levite's lectures soon extended well beyond the Ein-Harod evening school. He was repeatedly invited to give courses in other
kibbutzim, in the national colleges of the kibbutz movement, in
the country's youth organizations, and in the universities. But his
teaching and scholarship by no means exhausted the sum of his
activities. He was also very active in the emissary work of the kibbutzim, and all the while — except when he was on full-time missions that took him away from Ein-Harod and for the times he
devoted himself exclusively to his research and writing — Levite
was putting in a full day's work in the kibbutz. He always worked
with the field crops, going out in the early morning in his blue
field workers' garb, always conspicuously clean and neat, to drive
his tractor for eight hours or longer. He worked with the same
zestful enjoyment he brought to his lecturing, reading, and writing — and with the same methodical precision and attention to
detail. Ein-Harod people used to point him out to visitors, calling
him our "scholar-tractorist" and saying, with justifiable pride,

"Where but in a kibbutz will you find such a man?" He was exceedingly popular with the younger generation of field workers, who loved him for his sociability and good humor, his expert instruction, and his seemingly inexhaustible stock of entertaining stories, which he recounted during rest periods in the fields with an enjoyment that matched the pleasure of listening.

I had my own reasons for being grateful for Levite's knowledge and taste in literature. From the time I was thirteen, when I published my first juvenile poems in our children's magazine, he showed warm interest in my poetic efforts and, later, a most discriminating appreciation. I always took his comments and criticisms seriously, invariably finding them illuminating and helpful. And what generous enthusiasm he accorded my poetry, in his public comments on it. Ein-Harod has always celebrated the publication of new books by its members by holding a *sicha*, "conversation" or "discussion," in which everyone is invited to participate. Most of my books of poems or stories have been honored in this way, and Levite was almost always one of the speakers. I still remember his speech in the sicha for my very first collection of poems, *Niyurim* ("Youth"), published in 1936. It was the first to have been produced by a member of Ein-Harod's second generation, and Levite expressed the general joy and excitement at the event. Here was evidence, he said, that a kibbutz was not the narrow, restrictive milieu its critics said it was, which by its perverse principles of equality destroyed individuality and creative power. The reverse was true, Levite contended, and this book proved it — anyone in a kibbutz with the spirit of poetry in him had every opportunity to give expression to it.

He did, however, have one reservation about *Niyurim.* The lyrical evocation of personal experience was fine, he said, but I had nowhere addressed myself directly to the experience of the collective life of the kibbutz. This, he intimated, was something he missed in my poems. I remember being somewhat startled and disturbed by this remark: Was he, for once, being a doctrinaire Marxist, demanding some sort of Soviet-style social realism? If he was, he was not going to get it from me — I was already pretty sure of that. But this did not prevent him from continuing to read and enjoy my poetry or from talking to me about it with his customary discernment. When, years afterward, I jestingly reminded him of his early reservation, he shook his head, laughed, and said, "Like all you poets, you remember only the thorns in the roses I threw at your feet!"

As for my poetry, I can say with confidence what I was still groping for when I published *Niyurim*. Though a direct treatment of the collective life is absent from my poetry, scarcely a line of it is not informed by the spirit of Ein-Harod, and it seems to me that a poet who writes under the inspiration of this spirit is surely evoking the essence of the life of the kibbutz.

Yitzhak Tabenkin, our second distinguished instructor, was strikingly different from Levite. If Levite was the man of inspired reason, Tabenkin was closer to the inspired Hebrew prophet. His system of ideas and convictions was profoundly coherent and, if anything, more consistent than Levite's, but his style of communication was far less orderly. His arguments tended to proceed by leaps and bounds, with many missing steps — which his listeners were presumably expected to supply for themselves. He was often repetitive, taking two steps back to move one step forward. His mind seemed to work most naturally by a process of free association, in which one work or phrase suggested the next and this in turn the one following, making the structure of his argument rhetorical rather than logical. People often found him difficult to follow and tiring to listen to, and the difficulty was compounded rather than alleviated by the passion of his every utterance. Passion — the passion of the prophet and visionary — was the keynote of his being. He didn't just think his ideas, he *lived* them with his whole soul, body, mind, imagination — everything he had. This intensity expressed itself in a style of eloquence which tended to be exhausting, and was by no means to everyone's taste.

But the combination of passion and eloquence was riveting and electrifying. You might be exhausted at the end of a Tabenkin lecture, you might have found much of it irritating, but you also felt challenged and provoked; you rarely came away unchanged. This was the essence of Tabenkin's originality and the secret of the impact he made on us: he made us think, feel, experience the ideas he flung at us with something like his own passion. His philosophical flights and prophetic afflatus were in fact a tireless straining after the largest, most wide-ranging moral impli-

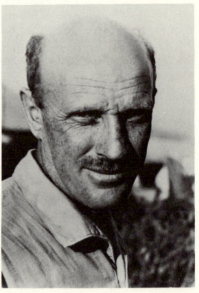

The most original, most variously gifted of our first three teachers was Moshe Carmi, who put his stamp on my whole generation at Ein-Harod.

A natural leader with tremendous personal authority and charisma, Chaim Sturman was a father figure to his comtemporaries, a hero and idol for the young.

cations of the ideas and values he believed in, which made us say later in life that he "gave them wings" as no one else did. The soaring quality of his mind and spirit wrought a change in us, making us feel we were no longer what we had been before we were exposed to it.

The ideas and values Tabenkin explored with us were fundamental. He endeavored to transmit to us a Weltanshauung that would provide a philosophical foundation for a Zionist-socialist society in Eretz Yisrael. With him we studied selected works of some of the leading Jewish thinkers of the late nineteenth and early twentieth centuries — Achad Ha'am, Micha Yosef Berdichevsky, Brenner, A. D. Gordon. Each in his own way was a rebel against tradition, questioning and probing institutionalized views, grappling with new ideas with which to replace the old. One of their preoccupations was the struggle to liberate themselves from the Orthodox Judaism in which they had been brought up and, at the same time, to extract from it those perma-

Of that remarkable first generation at Ein-Harod, Lyova Levite was perhaps the most intellectually distinguished — he could not help but kindle a responsive flame in us.

Yitzhak Tabenkin was like an inspired Hebrew prophet, electrifying in his passion and eloquence.

nent human values they hoped could form the basis for a nonreligious, humanist world view. Under Tabenkin's guidance, we participated in these exhilarating intellectual and spiritual battles as if they were our own. Tabenkin would appear for class with a newspaper tucked under his arm or, more often, the weekend literary supplement of *Davar*, which contained the long, thoughtful articles on the problems of the day. As often as not, he also carried a single fresh flower he had picked on his way. Tabenkin was personally rather sloppy: shirt and trousers crumpled, jacket trailing carelessly from one shoulder, shabby peaked worker's cap on his head. But he had a great feeling for the aesthetic in everything else, and the flower and his custom of always beginning the class by reading a poem aloud were typical expressions of the artistic side of his nature.

After reading the poem, he would proceed to an analysis of a news article he'd chosen for the day — often one that took a position contrary to his own. He seemed to need the challenge of op-

posing views to work out his own, and we saw that happening before our eyes: Tabenkin's position emerging, bit by bit, from his
exposure of the errors and flaws in the adversary's argument.
There was a concreteness and immediacy in the process that engaged our interest as no other method could have done, inviting
our active participation in working out the problem, making us
partners in our teacher's exploration and discovery.

Ein-Harod remained Tabenkin's home during the long years of
his public career. He became a leading theoretician of the kibbutz
movement and the labor movement as a whole, a powerful influence in the political life of the nation before and after the establishment of the State. He was a member of the Knesset for the
first twelve years of the State's existence, giving up his seat volun-
tarily at the end of his twelfth year to make room for younger
men. In the 1920s and early 1930s, he worked in tandem with the
other two leading Labor leaders, David Ben-Gurion and Berl
Katznelson. Afterward, they parted ways, and Tabenkin became
a passionate opponent of some of Ben-Gurion's policies. For
twenty years the Labor and kibbutz hemisphere of our political
world was virtually divided into two camps, the Ben-Gurionist
and the Tabenkinist. Tabenkin pursued a fiercely independent line in all the matters at issue between them, generally
opposed compromise, and succeeded in winning over some of the
best of the younger leaders to his "activist" approach. Yisrael
Galili and Yigal Allon were among the outstanding younger
leaders who were proud to call themselves disciples of Yitzhak
Tabenkin.

Tabenkin's activism cut across the political lines that divided
left from right. He was opposed, on the one side, to passivity
wherever it might be found and, on the other, to the chauvinistic
militancy of the Revisionist movement, forerunner of Menachem
Begin's Herut party in the Likud. Activism in essence meant *taking the initiative* — bold, imaginative, creative initiative — in Jewish self-defense, in building settlements, in rescuing Jews from
Hitler's terror, and in fighting the British Mandatory power when
it sought to prevent that rescue. From the start Tabenkin was a
fervent advocate of the Haganah and the Palmach; of the illegal
immigration that brought the persecuted Jews of Europe to Eretz
Yisrael in spite of the British coastal patrols; and, generally, of the
policy of "creating facts" by Jewish initiative and labor in every

sphere of national life without waiting for "diplomacy" to grant them permission. This policy was closely linked with another famous doctrine Tabenkin preached, that of *hagshama ishit,* literally "personal realization" or "personal embodiment," meaning that you are *personally* required, by your own labor and sacrifice, to help attain the goals of Zionism — not by giving money for someone else to do it, but by doing it yourself, body and soul.

Jewish settlement in Eretz Yisrael was the first goal, without which none of the others could be achieved. Tabenkin saw the kibbutzim as the avant-garde of the pioneer settlement movement, which would provide the leadership and inspiration for a new mass exodus of Jews from the lands of exile. Constantly, persistently, he called for this mass aliyah of the world's Jews to Eretz Yisrael. To the last ounce of his power he believed in the doctrine of *shlilat ha-gola,* the denial or repudiation of Jewish life in the Diaspora. There was no future for the Jews as Jews in the lands of the dispersion; if they stayed back, he contended, they would either be destroyed by pogroms or would cease to be Jews as a consequence of assimilation. So they mustn't wait, they must come immediately to Eretz Yisrael, the only place on earth where they could save themselves as Jews. The sense of urgency, the passion, often the despair with which he pleaded with them to come has since been regarded as a prophetic premonition of the Holocaust.

Although Jewish settlement of Eretz Yisrael was the first goal, it was not the only one. The extension of Jewish labor into areas that till then were monopolized by Arab workers was another. The goal of *kibbush avoda ivrit,* "the conquest, or triumph, of Jewish labor," would be achieved by calling on Jews to work in the quarries, at the ports, and on railways, and to build roads — all to advance the restoration of the Jewish national home in Eretz Yisrael. Tabenkin was an ardent supporter of kibbush avoda ivrit and, along with it, of another goal that bore directly on the economic life of the nation. He constantly urged the expansion of independent workers' enterprises owned or controlled by the Histadrut in agriculture, transport, banking, consumer goods, industrial products, and construction. There was a visionary side to it, of course: the hope of creating a truly socialist economy in which, through the Labor Federation, the workers themselves would own most of the means of production and public service.

But such a goal was also thoroughly practical and down to earth, and it was typical of Tabenkin to be as concerned about the practical, everyday applications of his visionary ideas as he was about the ideals behind them.

The same was true of his attitude toward the kibbutz. One day he might make a tremendous speech giving his exalted view of communal life as the zenith of hagshama ishit, as the highest, most noble embodiment of the pioneer spirit. The following day he would be intensely involved in the practical problems of the kibbutz — and not only the big, broad problems of building and developing a kibbutz, but also the minutiae, such as, in the early days of poverty, whether the kibbutz could afford to buy a cot for the first baby born at Ein-Harod or whether it must continue to sleep in a wooden box. The parents, true pioneers, were quite willing to keep the baby in the box, but Tabenkin would not hear of it; he insisted on the cot and got his way. To the end of his days, no human problem was too small to command his attention, so long as it was genuinely human, affecting the happiness or misery of others.

When you walked into his modestly furnished room at Ein-Harod, you would find Tabenkin sitting in his high-backed armchair, either intently reading or as intently engaged in conversation with someone — anyone who had come in, invited or uninvited. It might be a cabinet minister, an old friend from Kibbutz Kinneret, or a young Ein-Harod son or daughter. No matter who it was, he would shoot eager questions. To the old friend from Kinneret: "What have you been doing since I last saw you?" To the cabinet minister: "What did you think of So-and-so's speech in the Knesset last night?" To the young son or daughter: "What are you doing in the army and how do you like it?" Meanwhile, two or three of his ten grandchildren might come trooping in and receive a welcome as though he hadn't laid eyes on them for months, though he had probably seen them the day before. Beaming with delight, he would bombard them with questions and let them crawl all over him, stroke his beard, and prattle their heads off. In his last years, Tabenkin wore a long white beard, which gave him the appearance of a biblical patriarch or prophet and, to his small grandchildren, made him seem the perfect grandfather, the envy of all the children with beardless grandfathers.

I lived for something like half a century with Tabenkin's ideas and turbulent personality, and was particularly close to him during the last twenty years of his life when, as editor of the Kibbutz ha-Meuchad quarterly, I regularly revised and edited his public speeches. He wrote very little himself; he said he could develop his ideas only before an audience. But he wanted his ideas disseminated in print and was grateful for my services. He read his edited speeches with the utmost care, making revisions and improvements, leaving nothing he considered an inaccuracy or distortion of his meaning uncorrected. I came to know Tabenkin's doctrines almost as well as he did and, whether or not I agreed with them, to the end I found them as inspiringly original and impassioned as I did when I had my first taste of them at the age of fourteen.

Inwardly divided almost all his life, Tabenkin was often wildly irritable in his last years, disappointed by the false directions in which Israel seemed to him to be moving. But a child, a young person, or a poem could instantly lift him out of his gloom. Perhaps that is why, after his death, I wrote a poem called "Tabenkin Is Reading Poetry":

> He sat sunk into himself with closed eyes.
> Only the fine web of wrinkles beneath them
> was conciliatory and stormy in turn —
> and the book
> in front of him.
> Suddenly he opened his eyes
> and smiled.
> Paused a moment, as if startled, then immediately
> went on:
> "How many Tabenkins are there, d'you think?
> Here in my skull — ten!
> Each pulls at the garment of the other;
> one says — it's all mine; the other cries — it's mine!
> And each sticks to his opinion —
> and you have to decide
> which is yours!
>
> "Only when I read a poem
> are they all silenced . . .
> Come, listen with me to this grief,
> the aching compassion of a soul open
> to sky and earth and rock

which speaks to you, you,
in a voice human and warm:
'Stone among stones — I do not know
how ancient is my life
and who will come next
pushing me with his foot
to roll down the slope.' "*

The last years of Ein-Harod's first decade were marked by a momentous event in its history — the move to its permanent location. In spite of the powerful appeal of its biblical associations, the
site at Ma'ayan Harod, by Gideon's spring, was never intended to
be permanent. The fields there were inconveniently situated —
too dispersed and stretching out too far from the center of the
kibbutz — and the climate was bad; we were plagued by malaria
from the mosquitoes in the shallow parts of the stream and the
remains of the swamps. But the biggest problem with the first site
was security. The settlement was difficult to defend because it was
low lying and thus exposed to Arab attack from the Gilboa,
whereas the new site, on the slope of Kumi Hill, four kilometers
up the road toward Beit-She'an, was higher and, therefore, safer.
Chaim Sturman had made persistent efforts to acquire additional
land through the Keren Kayemet, and by 1926 he had succeeded
in purchasing the Kumi land from the Arabs. The area was
nearly 1000 acres bigger than the old site, giving Ein-Harod a
total of about 12,000 dunams, or 3000 acres.

The move was carried out in stages, from 1926 to 1931. The
first group to go were the builders, who were all members of the
kibbutz; only later, when the pace of development made it impossible for the kibbutz to supply all the workers required, was
hired labor introduced. The cowshed, stables, chicken runs, and
other farm buildings were the first to go up, and construction of
living quarters began only when all these buildings had been
completed. People moved in approximately the same order: as
soon as the cowshed had been built, the cowmen moved into temporary shacks at the new site; when the chicken run was ready,
the workers in the chicken run moved; after them, the stable peo-

*The last five lines are from a poem on Jerusalem by Lea Goldberg.

ple; and so on. The people who worked at the new location led a somewhat schizophrenic existence until the move was completed — they lived at Kumi, coming only occasionally to join their families at the Ma'ayan, which caused hardship and dissatisfaction all around. With the 1929 Arab riots, the moving process was speeded up for reasons of security and was completed by 1931, even though the living quarters were far from ready and about one third of the members again found themselves in temporary huts and tents.

The building of the houses was beset with special problems. The funds had to come from the Settlement Department of the Zionist Executive, but some of its people still did not believe that a big kibbutz could survive. Consequently, they at first refused to assign funds for building the communal children's houses, wanting us to build instead the kind of small family house that was standard on the moshavim — in case Ein-Harod could not survive as a kibbutz and had to be converted to a moshav. In the end they submitted, but the struggle caused considerable delay and much bitterness.

All the first permanent houses are still in use at Ein-Harod. They have been slightly enlarged and modernized — each unit has its own shower and toilet and a kitchenette — but they are still of great historical value. They remind visitors and our younger generation what "in the early days" was regarded as luxurious living quarters. Constructed of concrete and cement with red tiled roofs, each building consisted of a row of four or six small rooms, each with a porch facing west. The rooms measured about 18 by 10 feet, and the porches 10 by 7 feet, making a total living area of about 190 square feet. Parents with children between the ages of six and fifteen would enclose the porch to form a second room for them, separated from the main room by a curtain. There was no running water, no indoor shower or toilet, no electricity, and no cooking facilities of any kind. Each house had one outside tap that served four to six families. There were two showers and two toilets, one for men and one for women, for each group of three houses — that is, twelve to sixteen families. Not the last word in comfort and convenience perhaps, but what an improvement on the conditions at the old site, where just one communal shower house served *all* the tents and huts. And the toilets, at last, were

flush toilets, no longer the dreadful buckets that had caused
Batya Brenner's violent nausea. We used paraffin lamps for more
than a decade; electricity was not installed in the living quarters
until 1942.

The move to Kumi was by no means an unmixed joy to the
members of Ein-Harod. They had become deeply attached to the
Ma'ayan site and found it difficult to leave, because of its biblical
associations and its natural beauty, and because they were leaving
behind an intimate, irrecoverable part of their lives. The children,
in particular, loved the old site and desperately missed their familiar surroundings: the stream, the spring, the cave, their eucalyptus grove, their threshing field. They hated Kumi, which
besides being new and alien was as bare as Ma'ayan Harod had
been at the start; there were no trees, no green grass, no cooling
waters — nothing but a stony hill dotted with thorns and thistles.
They demanded to go back to the Ma'ayan, and to impress their
loathing for Kumi on their elders, they held protest demonstrations, chanting as they marched in angry procession down the
center of the kibbutz: *"Ein-Harod chamuda! Kumi smartuta!"* ("Ein-
Harod is a lovely thing! Kumi is a trashy rag!") I was too old by
then to join in children's demonstrations, but I watched them
with great sympathy.

Over the years, of course, they became reconciled and even attached to the trashy rag as it became less bare with the appearance of trees, grass, and flowers. It also helped that instead of
calling the new Ein-Harod Kumi in accordance with the custom
of naming a kibbutz after the place where it is built, we decided
to keep our old name, even though we were no longer near the
Spring of Harod. The emotional bond with the original site remained, however, and was expressed in regular pilgrimages by the
children, who loved to spend a Sabbath morning or afternoon
picnicking by the stream and having a good swim in it. And, once
a year, on the festival of Yud Chet Elul, the whole kibbutz returned to the Ma'ayan in a fleet of trucks for a tremendous picnic
of steaks and potatoes in their jackets grilled over scores of open
fires, the smoke and the aroma of the food mingling with the festive music, singing, and animated chatter, filling the ancient valley at the foot of the Gilboa with modern scent and sound.
Ma'ayan Harod was transformed into a small national park that

is a favorite scenic spot of the Emek, drawing crowds from all parts of the country on the Sabbath and other holidays.

By 1931 Ein-Harod had been in existence for ten years, and its members felt the need to take stock. Reviewing the first decade in his memoirs, Lyova Levite wrote that it had "all the ingredients and flavor of a drama, a great, living personal and communal drama."

> Human actions, a plot, suspense, a great conglomeration of dramatis personae, profound experiences, fateful decisions . . . Conflicts of the most serious kind; a combination of circumstances producing clashes of ideas, clashes of personalities, clashes of emotions . . . And the human actors in the drama tossed from side to side on the horns of a dilemma, between the feeling of being trapped, of no way out [of their desperate situation], and the fear that the chances of a change for the better were a far-off dream . . . The drama has a significance beyond that of Ein-Harod: a national, historical, social, human significance.

I think Levite's analogy is apt, and I am even inclined to say it also bore a resemblance, on its own minute scale, to the act of creation in Genesis. For Ein-Harod, too, had started "without form, and void" and had had to build something out of nothing — something totally new. There had been no models, no precedents to guide it; it had had to discover everything for itself, problems as well as solutions. And it had had to proceed by trial and error, and through stormy democratic disputes about every problem, every proposed solution, every decision — disputes that the divine process was happily, serenely, free of. Yet, somewhat like the divine act of creation, the development had been neither arbitrary nor haphazard. It had been directed and controlled by a vision, and though the vision was largely worked out as we went along, though it was constantly revised and modified, it was there all the time, from the start, and still recognizable through all the vicissitudes of those first ten years.

The great heartening achievement of those years was that a framework, a mold, had been created that promised to be permanent. "Norms of life," as Levite called them, had been established; certain basic principles of conduct, and habits and practices broadly consistent with those principles. There had been no certainty whatever at the start that the whole community would not collapse within a few years. The variety of ideologies, the absence of models, the hundreds of people coming and going — coming with a view to joining us and then not staying — created confusion close to chaos, and induced acute uncertainty about the chances of survival. But at the end of ten years the insecurity was almost gone. A sense of permanence had replaced it, the sense that we were there to stay, that we would not go under. We might survive better or worse, but we *would* survive.

8

Inner Conflicts

IN 1928, at sixteen, I became a full-time worker in the kibbutz, an event that marked the definite end of my boyhood. My job, as before, was in the kibbutz nursery, where we had just started to grow fruit tree saplings on a serious scale. A full day's work was eight to ten hours in the winter months, and up to twelve hours during the long summer. This was nothing new for me, of course, since all through my school years I had done full days of seasonal work at the time of the harvesting, grape picking, and planting of new citrus groves and orchards. But I soon discovered that it made a great difference to do it day after day instead of just from time to time, when hard work had been fun, even a relaxing, refreshing change from school. As an everyday job, it was a serious business, and in many ways a grim one as well.

To begin with, the physical exhaustion was stupefying. For the first six months or so I was simply unfit for anything else at the end of the day. With my fellow greenhorns I soon discovered that the way to combat the fatigue that threatened to turn me into a mindless peasant was to take a shower immediately after work and then go to sleep for a few hours. This gave me a second wind, starting at about nine o'clock in the evening, for intellectual and social life.

Besides the physical exhaustion, there was the monotony of the work itself to contend with. My new work with the saplings tended to be solitary most of the time, and I missed the congenial

company I'd enjoyed during my part-time stint in the plant nursery. Fortunately, I soon discovered, like countless laborers before
me, the best weapon for fighting, and indeed preempting, the periodic attacks of boredom: to become, as quickly as possible, a
professional in the job. Acquiring expertise helped to reconcile me
to the uninteresting spells because I began to regard them as part
of a cyclical process, alternating naturally with the more interesting creative phases. With time, of course, the work also became
easier, and therefore pleasanter. Once I had mastered the basic
techniques — how to drive the horse-drawn plow between the
narrow rows of saplings without damaging them; how to cut away
the superfluous shoots correctly and efficiently; how to water the
saplings without breaking down the furrows or exposing the roots
by "flood" watering — I found my mind was free to think and my
senses ever more fully open to my surroundings. The silence, the
absence of inner tension, the repetitive pattern of hoeing, watering, and snipping all contributed to a state of relaxation that
made mind and body acutely receptive: to the sounds of birds, insects, butterflies; to the scents of the different seasons; even to the
time of day. This last awareness was a necessity for few of us
owned watches; and those who did would not have dreamed of
wearing such a precious object to work.

The greatest gain for me from these years in the tree nursery
and the orchard was my intimate contact with nature. The sense
of what was happening in the partly visible, partly invisible natural world grew and developed, becoming as important in my life
as human beings and their society. Nature became a principal
source of the imagery and symbolism of my poetry, and my work
a direct stimulus to the actual composition of my poems. As I
walked behind my horse-drawn plow, I found poems shaping
themselves in my mind and growing to maturity, doubtless under
the influence of the solitude, the steady motion of the furrowing,
the inner tranquillity, and the openness of the soul to the influx of
fresh sensations. It was then that I formed the habit of composing
in motion — in buses, trains, and cars, if not walking behind a
plow — and I still find it difficult to create while sitting at my
desk.

Although my work in the nursery was solitary for long stretches
of time, some of it was also done with others, and I quickly discov-

ered that people reveal themselves more fully at work than in other situations. Then, as now, we tended to confine our personal and social lives to our own special group, and contacts with people outside our circle were generally casual and perfunctory. But at work I met people I would not otherwise have known, and I came to know them very well. Day by day, they disclosed their personalities and expressed their opinions far more spontaneously than was possible at a meeting of a committee or the General Assembly, and alas, what they often disclosed was the weaker side of their natures: their meanness, pettiness, vanity, and egotism.

By the time I turned sixteen, I was beginning to be critical of myself, critical of others, critical of the ideas and ideologies I had been taught; most of all, perhaps, I was becoming painfully aware of the gap between the ideal and the actual.

Not everyone, I discovered, was a Chaim Sturman, a Levite, a Yitzhak Tabenkin, or for that matter, a Rachel Kravtzov or Chaim Shifroni. Some members of the kibbutz were there not because they were inspired by the idea of building a better society, but simply because they had been brought there, and because they found kibbutz life the way of least resistance. Others, who had a pronounced authoritarian streak, were capable of exploiting the docility of their weaker brethren. The kibbutz framework imposed limitations on their power to exercise their egos, but unpleasant traits would surface nevertheless, inducing in me, after the initial shock of discovery, a sense of profound disappointment and depression.

I was also tormented by a deeper question. How was it possible for these small-minded characters to coexist with people of integrity and vision within a single community? And, even more baffling, how, in spite of their traits, could these people make substantial contributions to the development of the kibbutz? I discovered the answer later, and have rediscovered it, over and over again, all through my life at Ein-Harod. It is simply a fact that even people with serious shortcomings make some kind of contribution to the growth and well-being of the kibbutz; and this may be another unique feature of the kibbutz structure, and one of the secrets of its survival.

In addition to these disappointments, I began to feel the restrictive effects of the kibbutz on my personal life. Ever more con-

scious of its power to prevent, or at least seriously impede, my intellectual and spiritual development, I found I had not enough
time or energy to read, study, or think at the end of the exhausting day's work. It took real strength of mind to overcome the fatigue, and the low spirits it induced, and I felt I simply didn't have
the strength to fight this battle afresh each day. My sense of these
restrictions was intensified by my growing certainty that writing
was to have a central place in my life. I needed time and spiritual
energy to develop in that direction, and I keenly felt the frustration of not having what I needed — and the fear that I might
never have it. At the same time, I cherished my work in the orchard, wanting to devote myself to it wholly and to become an
expert in that field. But this also required time for study and
thought, and how was I to divide my meager allotment of time?

As if this were not enough, I felt the force of still another claim:
that of the kibbutz movement, of which Ein-Harod was a part.
The Kibbutz ha-Meuchad Federation had been formed in 1927
to oversee the group of kibbutzim to which we belonged. It
needed kibbutz people to organize, supervise, and guide its member kibbutzim, and I very much wanted to participate in this new
and exciting work, feeling that the federation was crucial for the
survival of the kibbutzim and that it was my duty to contribute to
its development. I felt the conflicts between my writing, my farming work, and the kibbutz movement acutely and could see no
way of resolving them. To make matters worse, the pressure to
found new kibbutzim, especially in the undeveloped parts of the
country, was tremendous, and this created yet another conflict,
for I was tempted by the excitement and the challenge of becoming a founder of a new kibbutz rather than remaining a follower
in an old one. Yet Ein-Harod was my home. It still needed people,
and its future would depend on its second generation to produce a
third, the third a fourth, and so on. In the end, I could find no decisive argument either for staying or for going.

These were some of the doubts, uncertainties, and confusions
that overcame me between the ages of sixteen and twenty-one.
The conflicts and self-questioning varied in intensity from day to
day, and on a theoretical level they were in fact never satisfactorily resolved. The one thing of which I remained certain through
all these doubts and vacillations was that I would remain in a

kibbutz, that there was no question for me of any other life. In this respect I was luckier than many young members of kibbutzim today who are going through their period of Sturm und Drang. For them the question often is whether to go on living in a kibbutz or to build a life in the outside world. This is a deeper, sharper conflict than any I experienced, and one that can lead to a lifelong state of indecision. Those who are dissatisfied with their life outside are just as often unable to reconcile themselves to life in the kibbutz, and they may go and come back, go again and come back again, in constant pursuit of an elusive contentment.

At the beginning I kept my inner conflicts and self-questioning to myself, but before long I discovered that I was not alone. Other members of my age were going through similar crises, which revealed themselves both in casual conversations and in more intimate talks with two friends, one a little older, one a little younger than I. The older one was Arieh Zakai, the younger, Moshe Tabenkin, the eldest son of Yitzhak Tabenkin, who became my closest friend at Ein-Harod.

Arieh Zakai came to Ein-Harod from a small town in Poland in 1926, when he was sixteen. He was a reserved youth, balanced and judicious in his opinions, but always interested in ideas and the lives of others. He was active in the Working Youth movement from the start, and the first of our young people to be sent on a mission to Poland. A good listener and a faithful friend, Arieh helped me most by his very reserve, by his quiet, unexcitable way of considering a question. "Yes, there is a great deal of truth in what you say," was his most usual response to any of my arguments; and this was no evasion, but a genuine expression of his thoughtful weighing of the rights and wrongs of an issue. If I unburdened myself about the restrictions and frustrations of our life in the kibbutz, his quiet, final answer was almost always, "Yes, but do you know of any life better than this?" I didn't, of course, and knew even then that I never would, so the answer really was conclusive. I found myself in later years using it again and again in disputations with the rebellious young, including my own daughters who, in the end, have been obliged to agree, sometimes grudgingly, that they, too, do not know of any life better than this one.

Arieh's more mature appreciation of the kibbutz was partly

Moshe Tabenkin and me, at age twenty. My closest friend at Ein-Harod, Moshe shared my lifelong passion for poetry and literature.

due to his being those few years older than the rest of us, but it was mainly a result of his having had a more recent experience of exile and a fresher awareness of the inspiration of building a new society. Perhaps his appreciation was also sharpened by his having come from a particularly poor family, for he never took for granted the minimal material security the kibbutz provided. His thankfulness for what he was receiving often made me ashamed of my own lapses into ingratitude, and his acute sense of the inspiring, heroic dimension of the kibbutz enterprise had the effect of reinspiring and rekindling my own sense of it in my hours of disaffection.

Moshe Tabenkin — always called by the affectionate Yiddish diminutive Moishele — could have been Arieh's polar opposite. He was a person of strong, excitable emotions; sensitive, imaginative, and intensely intellectual, with a taste for high-flying generalization. His seriousness was offset by a sense of humor that often took the form of self-irony, and he was a superb storyteller.

From his twenties onward, the range of Moishele's preoccupations constantly widened. He wrote poetry and stories and taught Hebrew literature, theory of education, kibbutz ideology, and politics, throwing himself into each activity with wholehearted enthusiasm and generosity of spirit, which kindled a like ardor in others. Unfortunately, he often succumbed to the temptation to drop the subject he was working on to pursue another he found equally irresistible, and he was to suffer acutely from this division of purpose throughout his adult life.

None of this was as yet evident in the handsome blond boy whose first poems I published as editor of our children's magazine. Though I had known him since he was a child, our real friendship began when I was nineteen and he just past fifteen, but so mature that I never felt the difference in our ages. Naturally precocious, Moishele had also had to assume heavy family responsibilities from an early age. His father was often abroad on Zionist and kibbutz missions, and his mother was often ill, harassed, and preoccupied with her communal activities. So Moshe, the eldest of the four Tabenkin children, was all too frequently obliged to take charge. He did this willingly for years, because he was simply one of the most goodhearted people I have ever known, always ready to respond to every claim made on him, incapable of refusing any call for help.

These obligations created an initial bond between us, for my father had left us on his last sad quest for medical help in Paris, and I had begun to be a substitute father to my baby brother, Yuval, who was the same age as Moshe's youngest brother. Moshe was experiencing the limitations, the narrowness of outlook, and often the downright nastiness of some kibbutz members, and because he was the son of Yitzhak Tabenkin, he was more exposed than I to direct assault. Moshe worked in the carpentry shop, whose work force at the time included a number of people who had come to Ein-Harod with little or no preparation for kibbutz life and who had a minimal understanding of the purpose and vision of the kibbutz. They resented Yitzhak Tabenkin's high idealism and the demands it made on them, and since they rarely dared to challenge Tabenkin himself, they took it out on his sixteen-year-old son. Moshe felt their attacks keenly, and with his sensitivity, he was inclined to become deeply depressed by the lack of vision, philistinism, and crude cynicism of his fellow workers. They had the effect of sharpening his uncertainties about kibbutz life, his inner debates, and his generally troubled state of mind. As my spiritual condition was similar, we had much to share, and our intimate talks often turned on the large problems raised by our common experience: the meaning of our life at Ein-Harod, how to cope with its limitations, what to do about the seemingly ineluctable gap between the ideal and its imperfect realization in the world we inhabited.

Beyond the problems of life at Ein-Harod, we were also intensely preoccupied with the larger questions turning on the national tasks of the kibbutz movement as a whole. The question of illegal immigration was one of the most pressing. In view of the cruel restrictions on Jewish immigration to Eretz Yisrael, was it not the task of the kibbutz movement to participate actively in the rescue of the suffering Jews of eastern and central Europe, even by illegal means? Then there was the allied question of the youth immigration movement, started in the early 1930s in Germany to bring youngsters aged fifteen to eighteen to Eretz Yisrael. Ought not the kibbutzim take in groups of these youngsters, give them a home, education, and vocational training? Meanwhile, we were also concerned with more strictly political problems bearing on national policy. For example, how could the kibbutzim best participate in the movement for kibbush avoda ivrit, and even more urgent, what was to be the contribution of the kibbutzim to the constantly changing defense needs of the country? Moshe and I were committed to the political activism of Yitzhak Tabenkin, Berl Katznelson, and other leaders of the Labor and kibbutz movements, and our earnest discussions and debates about these national problems was our way of expressing our commitment.

We also shared more practical activities that drew us ever closer together. Both of us were active in bringing the youngsters of Ein-Harod into the Working Youth movement and we were instructors to the boys and girls of Moshe's younger brother Yosef's age. One of our tasks was to teach Yosef's generation to become instructors to the younger children, and Moshe liked to tell the story of how memorably I failed with his little brother, one of the quickest, brightest, most precocious fourteen-year-olds in our charge. I had given Yosef an outline of sixteen "theses" to be transmitted to the younger fry, on the understanding that these would be taught over three months. At the end of his first meeting with his group of youngsters, he came to tell me, beaming with satisfaction, that he had succeeded in finishing the course. I looked at him aghast: "What do you mean, you completed the whole course in one lesson?"

"Oh," Yosef answered cheerfully, "I just read off the outline you'd given me, they wrote it all down, and we were through in half an hour!"

His quickness had brought my scheme of instruction to ruin, and since he couldn't be made to understand what he had done wrong, we just had to take him off our list of trainees.

My deepest bond with Moshe was probably our common passion for literature and our keen interest in each other's writing. We read our newest poems to each other and spent hours discussing and criticizing every line, image, rhyme, and cadence. Preferring to keep these poetry workshop sessions a secret from others, we invented a code word for communicating about them in public. "Can you come in tonight? I've got an egg for you!" he said to me, or I to him, correctly presuming that no one listening would guess the newly laid egg was a poem. The books we read were another frequent topic of discussion, and we argued heatedly about the relative merits of our favorite poets. Moshe preferred Shneour; I, Tchernichovsky, and neither succeeded in moving the other to modify his preference. But we were always at one in our admiration of Bialik, and later of Avraham Shlonsky, Shin-Shalom, Lea Goldberg, and most of all Natan Alterman. Nor was poetry all we talked about; it was novels, stories, and plays as well, and often the Bible — as literature, as philosophy, as moral and spiritual wisdom, as national history.

The details of these talks have become vague with the passage of the years, so it was a moving experience for me to read, in a collection of Moshe's letters published in 1984, a letter he wrote in 1934 on Ecclesiastes, which reproduces almost exactly what he said to me in one of our talks. I remembered it clearly and vividly from the moment I started to read.

> You question whether I have a right to hate our life in this world because there is evil and injustice in it. But I did not say that. I said the question is one of justice and the reward of the just; in other words, the question of belief in a moral providence in human life, which is an inseparable part of religion. The absence of justice in human life induces in the religious man the thought of rebellion and heresy. But in order that a man may arrive at the notion that

he is required to change the unjust arrangements of life, he must first have an awareness that there is no one else to do it for him. This is a matter that did not greatly concern the author of Ecclesiastes. He is more a philosopher, intent on exploring his own self, than a social prophet, who sees the absence of justice and moral logic in the life of society reflected in the lack of moral logic in the life of the individual. If there is no reward and punishment in the world to come, and death is naught, what meaning has life? Why be happy, why be full of ardor, why hope and do battle, if in any case "there is no knowledge or wisdom in the grave whither thou goest"? The question is not only, Why should I live? It is also how to live with the awareness of the certainty of death. Is it surprising then that in the great inner war turning on this question there should be moments when a man comes to hate life? Not only the author of Ecclesiastes struggles hard with this question. Every man who lives the life of the spirit and listens to his own soul does the same, and only a very few, only the most exceptional, emerge whole and unscathed from this battle.

Though he was only seventeen when he wrote this, it was typical of his spirit and style throughout his life: the impulse to probe the deepest questions of human existence; the elliptical argument, sometimes making it difficult to follow the sequence of thought; the aspiring imagination and eloquence that break through the ellipses; and the struggle for spiritual wholeness constantly threatened by the hovering despair.

In his middle years — when Moshe's life became increasingly taken up with his multiple activities, when he seemed to be tearing himself apart with his teaching, political work and writing, taking care of his father, loving, enjoying and worrying about his own family — these spiritual probings and grapplings tended to be articulated in his poetry. In his outward life, he was full of vitality and joie de vivre, humorous, witty, accessible to all comers, a rock of support, and often salvation, to the weak and helpless. But in his poetry, and especially in the poems he wrote shortly before his death, the hidden other self is manifest: an often divided self, still puzzled by its own being, still struggling to understand the mysteries of evil and injustice and death. In a poem I wrote in his memory, I most wanted to express my sense of this complex double self — the happy outer man ready to romp with the children at a moment's notice, and the tormented inner one haunted by nameless nightmares, often images of the Holocaust.

The epigraph is from a letter Moshe wrote on a visit to Eilat, Israel's desert port on the Red Sea.

> In this tremendous dryness, which transforms all human effort and high-flown talk into hallucination, incapable of being realized, dooming to disappointment all those who link their fate with it . . .

> Even when he became a grandfather
> they went on calling him Moishele,
> perhaps because of the light of childhood
> that shone in his eyes at the sight of children
> and certainly when he ran
> a race with his small granddaughters.
> Who will be the first to get to the bush
> at the edge of the field?
> In the evening, behind the house where once
> there was a wadi,
> he gathered together the neighborhood tots
> to hear a story and light a bonfire
> to cook potatoes in their skins.
> And he starts a story, an old story,
> which is born anew at the moist sparkle
> in the eyes of the little ones.
> At night, sunk in reverie on the edge of sleep,
> he broods.
> "Instead of the story I should have taught them
> to draw chestnuts out of the fire."
> Later, in the dense darkness,
> he wakes crying out: a weight like a mountain.
> He whispers: "Never mind, never mind,
> only a bad dream."
> He falls asleep, again pursued by the same dream:
> lost among sharp-pointed mountains
> heaped savagely one upon the other,
> helpless, and the tremendous dryness
> choking his heart.
> Suddenly the mountains are swallowed up
> and he is alone in a field of ashes
> facing a heap of children's shoes.
>
> Beyond the window rise voices of children:
> early in the morning two little urchins
> are ready for a race.

"Wait, wait, I'm coming, too!"
he calls out to them with ardor.
"See who gets there first!"*

I think Moshe's happy, sunny self probably expressed itself most fully in his stories. Ein-Harod abounded in good storytellers, but Moshe Tabenkin was regarded as the master of them all. He had the gift from his earliest years, and as it matured I realized he was a storyteller because he was, first and last, a storymaker, a storyweaver. The story was the medium of his imagination, of his mode of apprehension, as the painter's is paint and the sculptor's stone or clay. Everything he touched seemed to turn magically into golden story. Whatever he perceived, thought, fancied, heard from others, read in a book — every scrap of his experience tended instantaneously to transform itself into a story, which he told on the spot, in the heat of creation, with freedom and facility, a sense of the dramatic, and an actor's panache that made each one more an enactment than a narration.

His high school pupils, my eldest daughter among them, recall his way of transforming his experience of the literature he was teaching them into story and drama, and the impact this unusual mode of literary appreciation made on them. He loved to tell stories to children and wrote a successful series, *Uri, Guri, and Shuri,* about the adventures of three fun-loving kibbutz children. He loved to tell stories on himself, not minding that they were as self-revealing as they were entertaining. And he loved to recount a commonplace exchange with someone he had met on the path or in the dining hall, reproducing the turns of speech, accent, and personal style of his interlocutor with the natural humorist's gift for just the amount of exaggeration required to make it hilariously funny. His wit, his fancy, his high spirits, and his humanity all went into his stories, and I think he was never more fully happy than when he was telling them.

In the last fourteen years of his life, Moshe's political passion virtually drove out everything else. Immediately after the Six Day War, under the influence of Yitzhak Tabenkin's teaching, the movement called Shlemut ha-Aretz (the integrity of the land)

---

*Zerubavel Gilead, *Gachalei Retamim* ("Coals of Juniper"), Kibbutz ha-Meuchad Publishing House, Tel Aviv (1980), pages 41–42.

was founded, and Moshe was intensely active in it from its inception. Its central doctrine maintained — and still does — that Israel should in no circumstances give up the territories taken from Egypt, Syria, and Jordan during the war they had launched against Israel in June 1967. The Golan Heights, the Sinai desert, Judea and Samaria (the West Bank), and Gaza are all considered integral, inseparable parts of Eretz Yisrael, essential buffers against further attacks by the surrounding Arab states, which had been trying to destroy it from the day it was established, and gave no sign of having renounced this plan. This minimal security was to be achieved by Jewish settlement in these areas. *Not* — they were emphatic about this — by the Israeli army sitting in barracks guarding a land empty of Jews, but by tens of thousands, hundreds of thousands of Jews actually living in those places, in peaceful coexistence with their Arab neighbors exactly as they were doing in the State of Israel within the Green Line, the pre-1967 borders.

There was also a religious, quasi-mystical stream in this movement, that emphasized the God-given character of the land and the biblical-historical right of the Jewish people to it; it would be a sinful flouting of God's will and a desecration of the Name to relinquish any part of this divinely bestowed territory to the enemies of the House of Israel. Moshe, his father, and their associates, however, belonged to the secular stream of the movement, and though they fully endorsed the historic-rights doctrine, their own emphasized the elementary security needs of the State of Israel to be ensured by Jewish settlement in the new territories. It would be suicidal madness, they said, to give them up, for it was through these very territories that the Arab enemy had, three times in nineteen years — in 1948, 1956, and again in 1967 — attempted to invade and destroy the Jewish State. It would be an unforgivable crime against the whole Jewish people, present and future, to expose once more the one home they had on earth to the danger of annihilation.

I did not share Moshe's unqualified view. I certainly believed that Judea and Samaria, and the Golan Heights and Sinai as well, were integral parts of the land of Israel. Wasn't that exactly what Judea and Samaria had been in my childhood and youth, before they were annexed by Jordan in 1948 during our War of

Independence? As for the Golan, Sinai, and Gaza, I had not forgotten that for nineteen years the Syrians had lobbed their shells
into our settlements on their border from those heights, or that
the Egyptians had repeatedly tried to destroy us from Sinai and
Gaza. So I understood and profoundly sympathized with the
Shlemut ha-Aretz position that Moshe upheld. On the other
hand, I also feared the consequences for the Jewish character and
integrity of our State of attempting to absorb into it the one and a
half million Arabs in these territories. Consequently, I broadly
supported the Labor party's "territorial compromise" solution,
based on the plan proposed by Yigal Allon immediately after the
Six Day War, the Allon Plan.

But this difference of opinion did not prevent me from understanding Moshe's state of mind. I knew how passionately he believed in the truth of his idea, how he lived by it and for it day
and night, how he worked for it without respite, and how in the
end it consumed his life.

When the peace treaty with Egypt was signed in 1979, he regarded it as a fraud and a delusion — a base trick to get Sinai
back without giving us anything of substance in return. As the
time approached for the last stage of the withdrawal from Sinai,
scheduled to take place in April 1982, he became almost frantic
with anguish at the thought of what we were doing, the mad,
self-destructive thing, as he saw it, that Begin and his government
were allowing to happen. I met him on the path by the kibbutz
clinic one morning. As we stood there in the sun Moshe said, "I
tell you, Zerubavel, I feel as if it's a piece of my flesh they're giving back to the Egyptians. Each piece of Sinai they've given back,
each piece of Eretz Yisrael they're planning to give back, is a
piece cut out of my body. I can't bear it, I tell you, I can't bear
it!" He half laughed as he spoke, to show he was conscious of the
extravagance of his image. But I knew his other half was in dead
earnest, and that he was suffering as if they were indeed hacking
out lumps of his flesh.

He had had high blood pressure for years, and the doctors had
warned him that he must slow down. But he couldn't. He rushed
to address meetings of the Stop the Withdrawal movement in all
parts of the country, often traveling long, exhausting distances in
a single day. He wrote article after article, late into the night, ex-

plaining why the withdrawal would be fatal, pleading with the government to halt it. He was obsessed and he knew it, and often said so, in his humorous way, which scarcely concealed the frenzy of anguish and rage in his heart.

He died of a brain hemorrhage in May 1979, a few weeks before his sixty-second birthday. The suddenness of it was appalling; he was taken to Afula Hospital on a Sunday night and by Friday morning of that week he was dead. I was certain, and so were his family and other close friends, that the intolerable stress he had lived under in the preceding months had contributed directly to his death. A man killed by his suffering for a political idea — what a rare fate that must be. Perhaps it could happen only to a Moshe Tabenkin, in whom the political passion was the informing principle of his being. He had been my closest, most intimate friend for nearly fifty years; I had shared the most important experiences of my life with him. When he died I felt that a great part of my life had died, too.

9

Youth Aliyah

WHEN MOSHE TABENKIN and I first became friends, in the late twenties and early thirties, I had already acquired a certain expertise in my work in the tree nursery. I was doing grafting and other specialized jobs; I was reading technical literature; and I was going on professional visits to other kibbutzim and to Mikve Yisrael, then the leading agricultural college of the country, to observe and learn. At the same time, I was becoming more active in the communal life of Ein-Harod. In addition to preparing youngsters for membership in our branch of the national Working Youth movement, Moshe and I formed a Youth Circle for our age group, to study and discuss our own concerns. We considered how our generation could assume responsible tasks in the kibbutz; how we could help in the absorption of the new young immigrants from Germany who were just then arriving at Ein-Harod; and how we could meet the broader moral challenges of communal life — maintaining the principle of equality, using our leisure time effectively, and achieving self-fulfillment.

In an effort to assume responsibility — and use leisure time for the benefit of the community — two of us took charge of the *Yoman* ("Diary"), the daily news sheet. I worked with one of our master carpenters, Moshe Nagari, who had taught himself to type, and together we collected our material, going from table to table at mealtimes in quest of hot news. We also had a special "news box" attached to the bulletin board at the entrance to the

dining hall, so members could drop in news items or announce-
ments to supplement those provided by the kibbutz secretariat,
our main source of information. Then, at the end of the day, still
in work clothes, we put together the *Yoman*. I did most of the editing and layout and Moshe did the typing as I read the stuff out to
him, making sure to get it all on two stencils. Then we'd mimeo-
graph our sheet and rush to the dining hall to post one copy on
the bulletin board and place the rest on the tables, ready for the
members to read when they came in to supper.

A new wave of immigrants arrived at Ein-Harod and other kibbutzim between the years 1929 and 1939. The German, or Fifth,
Aliyah began before Hitler actually came to power, accelerated
after 1933, and reached a peak in the years before the outbreak of
the Second World War. The newcomers were generally highly
cultured young people who had received their preparation for
kibbutz life in the pioneer youth movement in Germany, and the
combination of culture and pioneering spirit made them an asset
to the kibbutzim they joined. I quickly found friends among the
group that came to Ein-Harod. By teaching Hebrew to one of
these new friends in exchange for German lessons, I learned to
read German, and as soon as I could, plunged into the second volume of *War and Peace* in German translation — thus finally completing that interrupted reading adventure. I also devoured the
publications of the so-called Vienna socialists — people like Otto
Bauer, Max Adler, and others — and, perhaps most important for
my development as a poet, I read for the first time the poetry of
Rainer Maria Rilke, Christian Morgenstern, and Stefan George,
then the most modern of the German poets.

The most stirring occurrence at Ein-Harod during the late
thirties was our participation in the great Youth Aliyah. This
movement also originated in Germany just before Hitler assumed
power, its purpose being to bring Jewish youngsters out of Germany to Eretz Yisrael. The inspiration behind it came from two
remarkable women, Recha Freier and Henrietta Szold, the first a
Zionist visionary in Germany, the second an American Zionist
leader. The people who contributed most to its practical execution in the crucial first years were the two emissaries of the Histadrut and Kibbutz ha-Meuchad in Germany, Enzo Sereni and

Eliezer Livneh, and Aharon Zisling, a leading member of Ein-Harod.

Recha Freier and Enzo Sereni conceived the idea independently and almost simultaneously in 1932. The Zionist establishment turned it down as utopian — a beautiful notion, they said, but totally impracticable. But the Histadrut and Kibbutz ha-Meuchad responded immediately when Sereni and Livneh proposed it to them, and Aharon Zisling became a central figure in drawing the kibbutzim into the enterprise, starting with our own.

Meanwhile, Hitler had risen to power, the iniquitous anti-Jewish laws had been passed, and there was a growing sense of approaching catastrophe for German Jewry. At this point Henrietta Szold entered the scene. An American representative of the Zionist Executive in Jerusalem, she became a fervent supporter of the Youth Aliyah idea and succeeded in persuading the Executive to endorse it. She then became the moving spirit behind the whole enterprise, dedicating her life to it and helping it to succeed on a scale beyond expectation.

As the Hitler terror rapidly gained momentum, Youth Aliyah turned into a rescue operation, intent on saving as many Jewish boys and girls as possible from Nazi persecution. No one could have known that we were on the verge of the Holocaust, but the leaders of the movement acted as if guided by prophetic foresight of the doom to come. The rescue work continued right up to the start of the Second World War in September 1939, bringing out some five thousand youngsters over a period of six years. The number would have been much greater if the British Mandatory government had not limited the immigration certificates it was prepared to issue for the entry of Jewish children into Eretz Yisrael. But for this restriction, designed to appease Arab opposition to Jewish immigration, Youth Aliyah might have saved many thousands more from the gas chambers and crematoriums.

During the war and immediately after, the rescue operations continued, carried out mainly by the illegal Aliyah Bet (Immigration B). Youth Aliyah now because the chief agency for absorbing and integrating the young people brought to the country by these underground means. Sometimes the children came alone, in which case Youth Aliyah took complete charge of them. When they came with their parents, Youth Aliyah made a point of sending the children straight to a kibbutz, relieving their parents of the necessity to take care of them while they were getting settled in their new land.

After the war and before the establishment of the State of Israel in 1948, the operations of Aliyah Bet were aimed at rescuing the survivors of the Nazi death camps in Hungary, Czechoslovakia, Rumania, and Bulgaria; refugee children from Russia, Poland, Rumania, and those in displaced person camps in Germany; children who had been hidden in monasteries, especially in Poland; and children from the Arab lands of persecution, Syria, Iraq, Persia, and North Africa. Youth Aliyah continued to take complete responsibility for these youngsters from the moment of their arrival in Eretz Yisrael, and the magnitude and scope of its work can be gauged from the figures. Between 1934 and 1948, some 31,000 young people were brought to Eretz Yisrael, to be educated and cared for by Youth Aliyah. Since the establishment of the State, a further 181,595 have been absorbed. Thus by 1983, the year of its fiftieth anniversary, a total of about 212,595 Jewish children had passed through the hands of Youth Aliyah — a great record and a soul-stirring tribute to the humanity, the compassion for the young, the love and care of fellow Jews that has inspired it.

Ein-Harod's contribution to the work of Youth Aliyah was minute in absolute numbers. But it was not negligible if one considers that it was made by a small rural community chronically short of manpower and living without some of the most elementary amenities of life. Between 1934 and 1948 Ein-Harod took in, educated, and cared for 588 boys and girls, the majority of whom later settled in other kibbutzim, or founded new ones with other groups. Kibbutz Alonim was the first of these new kibbutzim, followed by Hulata in the upper Galilee, Gvar-Am in the Ashkelon area, Beit-Ha'arava by the Dead Sea, and Tzuba in the Jerusalem hills. Ein-Harod has continued, almost yearly, to take in a group of young people within the framework of Youth Aliyah: in the first years of the State, from the transit camps of new immigrants from Arab lands; and in the past twenty-five years or so, from underdeveloped towns such as Kiryat Gat and Kiryat Shmona and from the poorer neighborhoods of Tiberias, Hedera, and other towns.

It was not by chance that Ein-Harod was the first kibbutz to take in a Youth Aliyah group. The sixty boys and girls who arrived from Germany in 1934 were there thanks to the devoted labors of Aharon Zisling and Reuven Cohen. In his early thirties, and already recognized as a leader of the kibbutz and the labor movement, Zisling — like so many other great people of that pioneer generation — was both a visionary and a realist. At nineteen he had been a founding member of the Histadrut; he was a member of the National Council of Eretz Yisrael, the governing body of the Jewish community before statehood. After Israel's independence, he became minister of agriculture in David Ben-Gurion's first cabinet.

One of Zisling's most important contributions to the kibbutzim was a sort of bill of rights, a codification of the rights and duties of kibbutz members. Most of these were already being observed somewhat haphazardly, but Zisling, in his *Orchot Chaim* ("Ways of Life") set them out explicitly and systematically for the first time as a set of binding rules and regulations. From the *Orchot Chaim* a kibbutz member knew exactly how many hours a day he was required to work; that pregnant women worked fewer hours; that women over fifty-five and men over sixty had their workload reduced; how many holidays members were entitled to each year; how many members could be exempted from the work force to go to school; and so forth.

Zisling also had a Solomon-like gift for finding solutions to special problems consistent with kibbutz principles. When German reparations payments to members of kibbutzim started in the 1950s, he proposed that all the money be turned over to the kibbutz, to be used exclusively for cultural and educational purposes. Ein-Harod's culture center was completed only after his death in 1961, at the age of sixty, and was appropriately named Beit Zisling (Zisling House). Another of Aharon Zisling's major achievements was Ein-Harod's art museum. The idea had come from Chaim Atar, our professional painter, but Zisling was the practical executive force behind it, tirelessly finding the funds and getting support for the museum from artists in Eretz Yisrael and abroad. He was originally inspired by the vision of a kibbutz museum that would become a center of Jewish art through the ages and, after 1939, by the further vision of a permanent home for the work of twentieth-century European Jewish artists who perished in the Holocaust. Atar's and Zisling's dream has been realized. Today the Ein-Harod museum's collections are still growing; special exhibitions are held regularly; and visitors arrive in a constant stream — groups from other kibbutzim, students, artists from abroad, tourists, and kibbutz guests. All are curious to see the first rural museum in the country, and perhaps anywhere in the world, and they are usually enchanted and inspired by what they see.

Zisling's immediate responsiveness to the idea of Youth Aliyah was typical of him. He was guided by a vision, what he called *yishuvim mechanchim,* "settlements for education." The word *mechanech* is used in the sense of the German *erziehen,* a total upbringing or nurturing. His point was that participation in kibbutz life is an education in values and human relations, which is scarcely less important, perhaps even more important, than formal schooling. Of course, he also saw in this nurturing a preparation for the pioneering life, which might help to extend the modest domain of the country's settlements.

This conception was behind his ardent support of Youth Aliyah, and the moment it was proposed to him, he established close relations with Henrietta Szold and the kibbutz emissaries in Germany. The idea must be carried out without delay, he told them, and Ein-Harod must set an example by taking in the first group of youngsters. He had to fight hard to persuade the kibbutz. As usual, a large group of quasi-isolationists argued that Ein-Harod, for purely economic reasons, could not afford to take care of them, and anyway, it wasn't Ein-Harod's responsibility, it was that of the Jewish Agency, whose job it was to deal with immigrant absorption. The economic argument was the stronger in this instance because the framework proposed for Youth Aliyah would be more costly than that for the indigenous Working Youth groups; the immigrants were to be required to work only half a day, the other half being reserved for study. And the size of the first Youth Aliyah group, about sixty boys and girls, would be five to six times that of the normal Working Youth groups Ein-Harod was already taking in — a large burden for a community the size of Ein-Harod to assume. In the end, Zisling succeeded in bringing the opposition around by his powerful, eloquent plea for his vision of the settlements as a force for transmitting the best human and Jewish values, and of Ein-Harod's mission to lead the way in this as it had done in other spheres.

Zisling was firmly supported in his stand by another leading member of Ein-Harod, Reuven Cohen. Vinya, as he was always called, had come from Russia in 1924. A trained agronomist, he quickly became a force in economic planning and organizational development. He introduced scientific rotation of crops and the mechanization of farming, and was insistent about the advantages of a mixed economy, that is, of developing a variety of agricultural and other enterprises, on the sound principle that if one fails another might succeed. He was a strong supporter of the big-and-growing kibbutz because it allowed for this kind of development.

Many at Ein-Harod found Vinya Cohen a rather dry person, immersed in economics, often at the expense of people. How mistaken they were is proved by his unqualified support of Zisling's view of Youth Aliyah. In spite of the arguments against it, Vinya pressed hard for Ein-Harod's involvement in the enterprise, insisting that it was not only a matter of economics.

I found it refreshing to have a Vinya about the place. In the midst of our soaring ideologies, here was a man whose feet were firmly planted on the economic ground of our communal life. He had a clear, cool mind that was full of common sense and practical sagacity, yet he was capable of taking the idealistic view of things with the best of them.

When the intensive arguments about taking in the first Youth Aliyah group were going on at Ein-Harod, I was in Tel Aviv on a two-year mission to Working Youth. But as national secretary of the movement, and thus a representative of the indigenous youth of the country, I was called to Ein-Harod to take part in some of the discussions and to express my opinion on various aspects of the plan. On one of these occasions I met Recha Freier, the initiator of the whole enterprise, when she came to see for herself the place proposed as a home for the first Youth Aliyah group. She made a great impression, this tall woman with stately carriage, large dark eyes, abundant dark hair, and a strong face full of character. When it was proposed that the first group, individually, become affiliated with Working Youth, I came to Ein-Harod to explain what the organization was all about and why it was important for them to join. Still later, when they were approaching the end of their two years at Ein-Harod and wanted to join some of our Working Youth who were preparing to establish a new kibbutz, I was naturally the person who brought the two groups together. They did in fact establish a new kibbutz, Alonim, and it was a landmark achievement, the first kibbutz started jointly by Youth Aliyah and Working Youth.

That first Youth Aliyah group made history, for Ein-Harod and for the country. These fifteen- and sixteen-year-olds came from all social classes, but most of them had a good educational background, with a taste for things of the mind and spirit. Dr. Hanoch Rinot escorted the young immigrants and stayed with them as instructor and mentor for their whole two-year period at Ein-Harod. In addition, the kibbutz assigned eight instructors to work with them. Shlomo Rosenberg, a founding member of Ein-Harod and another original character in that colorful first generation of members, was the overall supervisor of their work program.

A devoted lover of Franz Kafka, Rosenberg also became famous for his Rosenberg Concerts, as they were known, which became an institution after the arrival of the German immigrants, who brought with them a large number of classical music records. Rosenberg had sole and undisputed control over the one record player that Ein-Harod possessed. He held his weekly concerts on the Sabbath in the late afternoon, in the so-called music room in one of the wooden huts, with an overflow audience outside on the narrow verandah and on the lawn beyond. The concerts lasted at least an hour, and the program was always chosen by Rosenberg. He conducted these events like a priest of the Temple performing a ritual, handling the records as if they were sacred vessels. We were forbidden to utter a word while the music was being played — a good lesson in concert manners, which none of us ever forgot.

Several members of the first Youth Aliyah group, now veteran members of Kibbutz Alonim, came to Ein-Harod on its sixtieth anniversary in 1981 to recount their recollections of their stay here. Said one woman, "Ein-Harod gave us a feeling of being in a warm home, helping us to overcome our homesickness and long-

Ein-Harod celebrates its twenty-fifth anniversary in 1946 in the avenue of palms outside the dining hall.

ing for our parents. It also gave us some of its best members as our teachers and mentors. One of them was Zisling, who took part in *all* the meetings of our committees. A wonderful man. Ein-Harod very much wanted this enterprise to be a success, and for us those two years were indeed a success."

Someone else recognized Ein-Harod as the parent of Alonim. "When people say that Ein-Harod is our second home, it is not just a phrase; it really is so. Whenever I meet a member of Ein-Harod, I feel a tugging at the heart. We are a continuation of that first initiative of Ein-Harod, the first Youth Aliyah group in the country that founded a kibbutz." And then, to show how they have carried on the good work, "We, too, have taken in and educated ten youth groups within the framework of Youth Aliyah." Our guest was telling us that we were the grandparents of their ten groups, and that is just how we felt — like proud grandparents.

I had my own opportunity to enjoy the pleasures of reminiscence in 1984, when Youth Aliyah held worldwide celebrations of its fiftieth anniversary. Ein-Harod organized a special party for all the surviving members of our first group (forty-five of the original sixty came), along with the Working Youth group with whom they had jointly founded Alonim, and all the surviving instructors. My speech to them was probably the shortest I have ever made. I just wanted to mention, I said, that I had been the marriage broker who, fifty years ago, had brought the two groups together, and I was delighted to see how well the marriage had worked out. About four couples came up to me afterward to tell me that I had succeeded better than I knew. "You were certainly a successful marriage broker for *us!*" they said, with happy smiles. They told me there had been six or seven "intermarriages" between the two groups, and that within two to three years they would be celebrating their own golden jubilees.

One marriage that I did not mention to them was my own. I am grateful to remember that Youth Aliyah, with the other benefits it bestowed, brought to Eretz Yisrael the girl who was to become my wife. I was away in Poland when Susi Kellner arrived at Ein-Harod in 1938, in the third Youth Aliyah group. We met a year later, on my return, and our romance began almost immediately. Susi had already made her mark at Ein-Harod. She came from Vienna and had the great advantage of knowing Hebrew, having been educated in the Hebrew high school in Vienna, where her father was the principal. She had also been a member of the Pioneer Youth movement preparing for life in Eretz Yisrael and was an ardent, idealistic Zionist. Vivacious, full of intellectual curiosity, immensely interested in people, she was also very beautiful, with golden hair, large, vivid blue-green eyes, and an enchanting smile and laugh. To me she looked like Ingrid Bergman in her early films, and I had a distinct weakness for that kind of beauty.

When she had completed her two years at Ein-Harod, Susi went with her group to Kfar Sabba, an agricultural village near Tel Aviv, to prepare to set up a new kibbutz in the Negev desert. But instead of going to the Negev, she came back to Ein-Harod in 1941 and we were married — just before I was called to the Palmach, to start a period of national service that was to last eight years. But all that was later.

II

Beyond Ein-Harod

A Kibbutz Emissary in Tel Aviv

BEFORE I EMBARKED on my two-year mission to the Working Youth movement in Tel Aviv, I had been away from Ein-Harod for longer than a week or two only once. I was eighteen when I went to work for several months at Kibbutz Na'an, near Rehovot in the coastal plain, the first kibbutz to be founded by an indigenous group of Working Youth pioneers. After that I worked for a while as a hired laborer in a citrus grove in Rehovot — my first and only experience of earning wages from a regular employer. I was dreadfully homesick most of the time, and wrote a poem about my yearning for Ein-Harod. But the setting, curiously, was its old site at Ma'ayan Harod:

> Precious corner
> in the bosom of the mountain
> home of my childhood.
> There cypresses
> bow their heads
> from all sides
> and eucalyptuses sing in the wood.
> Here I dream and daydream:
> the willows spread their boughs
> above the streaming water
> light golden ripples roll
> roll
> and a child runs to chase the waves.

Precious corner
in the bosom of the hill
home of my childhood . . .
My yearning overwhelms me.

The poem remained a favorite among my juvenilia, but when I
reprinted it in my first collection, I left out the last line, feeling the
point had been sufficiently made without it.

In 1932, at the age of twenty, I was elected national secretary of
No'ar ha-Oved, Working Youth, and for the next two years the
center of my life shifted to Tel Aviv. I was the first member of
Ein-Harod to be sent as an emissary to the youth of Eretz Yisrael.
All through the twenties and early thirties, a constant stream of
emissaries had gone to the Jewish communities in eastern and
central Europe to exhort its youth to come to Eretz Yisrael and to
prepare them for a pioneering life here. Yitzhak Tabenkin, Lyova
Levite, Aharon Zisling, Vinya Cohen, Avraham and Yochevet
Tarshish, and others had all done their stint abroad. But mine
was to be the first mission undertaken in Eretz Yisrael, and it was
regarded as something of a breakthrough — a new venture
watched with eager interest. For me, it was a fresh challenge and
a test to be met in the spirit of Gideon's men, and I worked hard
to make my mission, like a well-tended orchard, yield a decent
harvest.

I can best indicate what our work was about by recounting two
sample case histories. I prefer to think of them as stories of young
fellow Jews saved from lives of misery, deprivation, and crime to
become creative, productive human beings.

The hero of my first story is Shlomo Tivoni, always called
Mokka, who came to Eretz Yisrael from Aden in Southern Yemen
in 1923, at the age of three. He arrived in the care of a married
sister, and for two years he lived happily with a paternal aunt in
the Yemenite quarter of Tel Aviv. Then, when he was five, his father appeared and Mokka went to live with him. From that hour
his life became a nightmare of helpless suffering. His father was
fanatically religious and determined to make little Mokka into a
rabbi, teaching him Torah, Mishnah, and Talmud, all at the age
of five. When the child didn't understand, his father beat him.
The beatings continued after Mokka was enrolled in a religious

elementary school; each time his performance at school did not meet his father's exacting standards, Mokka was flogged. The kind aunt tried to intercede, but couldn't stop the fanatical father.

Two years of this was as much as the child could bear, and at the age of seven he ran away from home, sleeping in empty packing cases on the seashore or in the stairwells of apartment buildings. He managed to earn some money by carrying bags for shoppers in the marketplace, stealing a bit from the stalls, washing the front steps of houses, or doing other small cleaning jobs. Soon he found other youngsters in the same straits and joined them, acquiring a special status among them because he proved to be particularly inventive, on their childish scale, about ways to cheat and steal.

This went on for three months. Mokka kept in touch with his aunt, sending her messages to say he was all right. In the end she extracted a promise from his father that he would not beat him if he came home again, and Mokka returned to his father's house. But he continued his street life, selling newspapers and giving his earnings to his father. He got up at four in the morning for prayers in the synagogue, stayed out all day selling newspapers and picking up any other work that came his way, and was rarely home before eight, usually falling into bed in his clothes, too exhausted to undress. Sometimes, however, when he felt fresher after supper, he would return to his newspaper beat in the evening, from force of habit and because he had nothing else to do. There he would sit with his remaining papers, automatically calling out their names even though no one was about at that hour to buy them.

One evening a passer-by stopped to look at the papers, turned them over, didn't buy any, but started to talk with the boy about this and that. He reappeared the following evening, and the evening after that, each time looking at the papers, not buying, chatting with the boy in his pleasantly hoarse voice and getting him to talk about himself, striking up a friendship. It was the first time in Mokka's eight years that a human being other than his aunt had shown him any kindness, and he was deeply moved and grateful. The stranger's visits continued, the boy's trust in him grew with each visit, and then one night the man asked him if he would like to learn to read and write in the evenings. The boy immediately said no, he didn't want to learn anything; learning was associated in his young mind with terrible beatings, and he didn't want any more of those. The man, who by this time knew all about them, promised there would be no beatings at all; the teacher would be his friend, just as he was. In the end Mokka was persuaded to come to our Working Youth club, and of course he found it wonderful, and stayed. The man with the hoarse voice who had coaxed the street child into learning to read and write was David Cohen, my first mentor at Ein-Harod, then my colleague and friend in Working Youth in Tel Aviv.

When Mokka told his father what he was doing in the evenings, there was a fearful row. The father knew all about No'ar ha-Oved and regarded its members as a bunch of atheistic Bolsheviks who would deprave the child's mind and rob him of the religion of his fathers. But again the aunt intervened, and Mokka went on to complete his elementary schooling and to become a proud member of our club. When he was about ten he got his first job, in a book bindery, where he was subjected to the usual appalling work conditions. Before long he and his fellow apprentices organized a strike and, with the support of Working Youth, succeeded in getting a reduction in their working hours. But Mokka was eventually thrown out of the bindery and, again with the help of our organization, learned the trade of tile laying. By the time he was thirteen, he had become expert at it, and was earning as much as a grown man, giving half his wages to his father.

Five years later Mokka joined Kibbutz Alonim, remaining to marry a fellow Yemenite, have children, and continue laying tiles in the new houses constantly going up. Now he works periodically in No'ar ha-Oved helping the deprived young of Tel Aviv and Haifa as he had been helped in his youth.

When Mokka went off to join a kibbutz, his distraught father observed shiva, the seven-day period of mourning for the dead. More than twenty years passed before they were reconciled, and then the father went so far as to admit that Mokka was, in fact, his best son even though he was a Bolshevik. His brothers, said the father, had done nothing with their lives, while Mokka had been a man of faith, doing what he believed in.

My second story is about Yemima, a very beautiful Yemenite

girl of about fifteen, who lived in Rishon Lezion in the Tel Aviv area, was a member of Working Youth, and worked in a razor-blade factory. Her father and elder brothers, in accordance with traditional Oriental practice, wanted to marry her off to a rich Yemenite much older than herself. She refused, threatened to commit suicide, and finally appealed for help to her Working Youth branch. There were emergency consultations with our veteran activists, David Cohen and Yisrael Galili, and it was decided that she go to a small, little-known kibbutz, where she was to pretend to undergo *hachshara,* "preparation," before joining. She adopted a new name, was cared for by a woman member who knew her real story, and stayed there for more than a year, working as if she were really preparing for life in a kibbutz.

Yemima's family searched for her, with the help of the police, but could not track her down. After a while, she wrote to let them know she was all right, but not disclosing her whereabouts. She told them she was willing to return, but only if they didn't force her to marry and allowed her to train to be a nurse. In the end they agreed, and Yemima became a nurse, married, had children, and continued to work, never forgetting that she owed her freedom and happiness to No'ar ha-Oved.

The life of a kibbutz emissary at that time was not an easy one. The movement paid our travel expenses and supplied basic office requirements, but we had no salary and no allowance at all for living expenses. So we had to work part time to earn our keep: as construction workers, office workers, and messengers. Our small, carefully hoarded earnings were just enough to pay for our meager meals and personal transportation; we went everywhere we could by bicycle, but occasionally had to take a bus or train. We had lunch at the Histadrut cafeteria — usually just soup and eggplant salad, but sometimes, when we could afford it, also a meatball or fish with vegetables. For supper we went to the cooperative dairy shop for *leben* (a kind of yogurt), potatoes, an occasional egg, and tea.

Finding a place to live was as tricky as finding regular work. We were expected to sleep with relatives or friends, and in my first six months or so in Tel Aviv I led a nomadic existence, moving from place to place every few weeks. For a time I slept on the verandah of Berl Katznelson's apartment and then on a collapsible bed in the small children's room of David Cohen's place. Finally we were allotted one rented room for all the kibbutz emissaries in Tel Aviv. Five of us shared that first room — four men and one girl — forming what we called a *communa,* an urban micro-replica of a kibbutz. Though our new accommodations were scarcely comfortable, they were at least relatively permanent, and this in itself was a luxury.

The truth is, we were too busy and on the whole too happy to mind much about our living conditions, or even to notice them. Our jobs in Working Youth were rewarding, exciting, and thoroughly engrossing, and we had the enthusiastic moral support of the whole kibbutz movement, the Histadrut, and most of the Labor leadership. So it was no wonder that we did our work with an élan that sprang from our sense that we were performing a national service widely acknowledged to be of prime importance. It also helped that the social and economic circles in which we moved in Tel Aviv were sufficiently similar to our kibbutz milieu to make us feel reasonably at home. We all belonged to the working class, that was the point: they were urban working class, we were rural working class, we all earned our living by work, and we were all poor. When almost everyone around you is poor, and many poorer than you, it is easy to reconcile yourself to being poor. And for us it was made easier by the basic attitudes we shared with our urban friends and associates — a respect for work, a taste for a simple style of life, and love of Eretz Yisrael and the desire to build and develop it, which was perhaps the deepest bond of all.

Tel Aviv, to be sure, had other socio-economic circles as well. We knew of the existence of its gilded youth: the sons and daughters of the wealthy citrus owners, businessmen, and financiers, who lived in handsome houses, went abroad to study, danced the Charleston, cared nothing about the unemployed young workers, and were indifferent or hostile to the pioneering ideals of the kibbutzim and their supporters. But we rarely encountered them and, indeed, had a wholehearted contempt for these privileged adolescents, so sure were we that there was nothing better in the world than to be what we were, doing what we were doing, and knowing that our work was appreciated by the best people in the country.

Then there was the city itself, giving its own interest and excitement to our existence. What a place it was in those early 1930s! Little Tel Aviv, as it is now somewhat nostalgically called, with its all-Jewish population of about seventy-two thousand, was marked by an easy informal atmosphere. Everybody seemed to know everybody else and people hailed one another in the street as if they were in a village rather than a town. Architecturally it was an extraordinary mixture of styles. Houses of the Turkish period — with their oriental arches, cupolas, high narrow windows, and multicolored ornamentation — mingled with the humble, plain style of the shtetl, and modern Western European architecture. There were narrow streets full of mean little shops, and there was the more elegant shopping district in and around Allenby Street, where the new German immigrants set up shop to cater to the well-to-do. The smattering of outdoor cafés, with their gaily colored umbrellas shading the tables from the Mediterranean sun and heat, evoked a Parisian air that Tel Avivians were particularly proud of. In sharp contrast to the Allenby Street opulence were the older, poorer neighborhoods of wooden shacks and even some tents, in which the new immigrants from Poland and elsewhere lived. They were shabby, but they had a certain charm and a great deal of human warmth, and it was good to see the young workers coming out into the streets to sing and dance on Friday evenings and holidays.

Against this friendly, easy social background there was much political tension, springing from the conflict between the Labor-Histadrut movement and Vladimir Jabotinsky's Revisionists, forerunners of Menachem Begin's Herut party. Even now, the memory of that tension is painful and frightening. The Revisionists were greatly influenced by the rising fascist movements of Europe, Mussolini's in particular, and their youth movement, Betar, adopted a brown shirted uniform with their antisocialist, antiworker ideology. They formed "fist groups" to break workers' strikes, aiming to undermine and if possible destroy the Histadrut, and they attacked and beat workers who resisted them. The Histadrut reacted by forming its own "workers groups" to counter the fist groups, and the two units often had violent street clashes. At the same time, the Revisionist press conducted a continuous campaign of verbal violence against the Histadrut and the Labor leadership of the Zionist Executive, especially Ben-Gurion, the chairman, and Chaim Arlosoroff, head of its political division. When Arlosoroff was murdered on a Tel Aviv beach in 1933 it was widely believed that the killing had been perpetrated by the Revisionists, who for many months had been denouncing him and explicitly calling for his death. Although the two Revisionists charged with the murder were acquitted, many people remained convinced that they were guilty.

It was in the midst of this hatred and violence that our mission to the Working Youth of Tel Aviv had to be accomplished. In June 1933 I wrote a long letter to the executive committee of the Histadrut, urging them to take positive steps to combat these poisonous antilabor influences. Meanwhile, we doubled and trebled our efforts to combat them by all the educational methods available to us.

My work as both national secretary and instructor was exceedingly varied. Its substance was educational, but administrative tasks inevitably took up a good deal of my time. Each day began with a load of correspondence to and from our branches throughout the country. Then came the committee meetings for our various activities. For example, the education committee prepared educational programs and national and regional seminars, and also organized meetings of instructors from all parts of the country, almost always attended by leaders of the Labor movement, like Yitzhak Tabenkin or Berl Katznelson. The committee for vocational problems, concerned with improving working conditions, submitted to the Histadrut some radical amendments to the law protecting the rights of young workers passed by the Mandatory government in 1927; succeeded in securing for them ten days' paid holiday each year; and persuaded the Histadrut, in cooperation with Kupat Cholim, its sick fund, and Mashbir, its chain of cooperative stores, to build a rest house especially for young workers on Mount Carmel in Haifa. I was also one of three members on the editorial board of *Ba-Ma'ale* ("Upward"), the fortnightly journal of Working Youth, and from time to time I wrote about problems of the movement and contributed poems — many of which went into my first collection, *Niyurim*.

At least once a week I journeyed to one of the branches of Working Youth in Jerusalem, Haifa, the agricultural villages, and the kibbutzim and moshavim. I reported to them what we were doing, heard what they were doing, and discussed any special problems they might have. We almost always finished our meetings with an exchange of new songs, and if the visit happened to be to a kibbutz or moshav, we often went together on a brief excursion to some interesting place in the vicinity.

Not all of my out-of-town visits were a success, however. One of my best remembered failures happened at Nahalal, the first moshav in the country, which had been Moshe Dayan's home from early childhood. I had known Dayan since our school days and came to know him better in the month I spent at Nahalal during the Mapai Seminar of 1932. We were about the same age and shared an interest in literature and poetry.

Nahalal was one of the few moshavim in which a majority of young people were positively unfriendly to the Working Youth movement, and Moshe Dayan was the leader of this majority. Historical reasons were behind their attitude. Nahalal was founded in 1921, ten days before Ein-Harod, by members of the Second Aliyah, who were between thirty-five and forty-five. From the start, then, it had had a relatively large number of school age children, and I remember being told — and this surprised me — that while Ein-Harod had just seven schoolchildren in 1923, Nahalal had around seventy. Consequently, unlike Ein-Harod, they never felt an urgent need for groups of youngsters from outside to supplement their community of children. Their own resources were sufficient for all social and cultural purposes, and by the time the children had reached their teens and early twenties, they had developed somewhat self-enclosed, isolationist attitudes, and wanted nothing to do with an organization like Working Youth. This was a marked contrast to other moshavim in the Emek, such as Merhavia, Balfouria, Tel Adashim, Kfar Chassidim, and others, which had active branches of No'ar ha-Oved and strongly supported it.

The movement, however, refused to take no for an answer from Nahalal and continued its efforts to bring them in, both because Nahalal was the first moshav and very influential in the whole moshav movement and because it had a substantial minority of young people who did want to be associated with No'ar ha-Oved. They invited me to report on our work and answer questions. I went gladly, hoping to break down the resistance of the hostile majority, or at least to give strength to the arm of the friendly minority.

A large group of young people had gathered in the hall when I arrived. I knew many of them from our school days and was on very good terms with them. Just as I was about to start my speech, Moshe Dayan rose to his feet and said, "Zerubavel, if you have come to us as a personal friend, then *ahalan wa sahalan"* — Arabic for "you are welcome" — "but if you have come as an emissary of No'ar ha-Oved, there is the door, and I ask you to get out of here!" The style, then and later, was typical of him: direct, unceremonious, and somewhat brutal. There was an immediate uproar in the hall — shouts of protest from my supporters, countershouts from the opponents — which made it impossible for me to speak and effectively broke up the planned meeting. Once the din had subsided, the two factions entered into a heated argument, obviously not for the first time, which continued to a late hour. I participated, but failed to move Dayan and his majority, and the next morning I left Nahalal feeling that this mission at least had been an unqualified failure.

It was also typical of Dayan that his ideological assault on me did not prevent him from calling me aside at the end of the evening, pressing into my hand a small sheaf of his poems and asking me to read and give him my opinion of them. I don't know whether he continued to write poetry; as far as I know he never published any. But I do know that he had a strong feeling for it and particularly admired Natan Alterman, the poet Moshe Tabenkin and I both loved and so often discussed. After he became a leading politician, Dayan still found time to lecture on Alterman, proof of how much the poet meant to him.

My work as an instructor gave me regular personal contact with a sampling of the young workers of Tel Aviv. I set aside two nights a week to meet my group of fifteen fourteen- to sixteen-year-olds at our Youth Club off King George Street. On a typical evening we debated important topical issues, including the political problems of the day, problems of kibbutz life — especially in the kibbutzim founded by Working Youth — and problems of Tel Aviv's young workers, including how to cope with the severe scarcity of employment. There were also cultural activities. For example, we set up a central fund for group visits to the theater. When we planned a theater excursion, we always read and discussed the play beforehand, and again after the performance, to get the most out of an experience no one took for granted. Sometimes we read a story together, following with a discussion that was almost always serious and animated.

An important outcome of these regular meetings was, as always, the comradeship and lasting friendships that sprang from them. My group came to Ein-Harod for their hachshara — their spiritual and physical preparation for a pioneering life. After it, most of them joined Kibbutz Ginosar on the shore of the Sea of Galilee, the famous kibbutz of which Yigal Allon was a founder; and some went to Kibbutz Alonim. Whenever I visit Ginosar or Alonim, I am hailed by my former charges now nearly forty years older — in the dining hall or while walking along a path or in somebody's house — as if I were an elder brother they particularly love and cherish. Then I think that one of the greatest achievements of the Working Youth movement was the sowing of lifelong friendships in the common soil of shared values and a shared way of life.

I have already mentioned Berl Katznelson, who, with David Ben-Gurion and Yitzhak Tabenkin, was one of the three great Labor leaders and nation builders of the pre-statehood period and, like the other two, molded the intellectual and spiritual life of my generation. He died in 1944, at the age of fifty-seven, four years before independence, and people still believe that his death was an irreparable loss to the new State. His peers, Ben-Gurion and Tabenkin, were devoted admirers, counting themselves among his pupils hardly less than did my own generation. After Berl's death Tabenkin paid tribute to his greatness in a discourse that lasted a full six hours — a record even in those days of mammoth eulogies.

Tabenkin titled his speech "An Exemplary Life" when it was published. He meant that Berl Katznelson, more than anyone else, was the paradigm of the visionary, the humanist, and the practical man indissolubly united. There was no creative enterprise of the Labor movement in which he was not deeply involved as initiator or sponsor or supporter — usually all three. He believed ardently in the workers of Eretz Yisrael as the one great hope for the future, as the only force capable of building a Zionist-socialist society for the whole Jewish people. But in order to do this, they must possess *power;* Berl had no illusions about ideals and beautiful motives being enough to build the society you wanted. So he set about helping to create a powerful nationwide workers' organization radiating from the Histadrut, which he helped to found.

During the twenties and thirties, he was one of the principal initiators of almost all the Histadrut's enterprises, transforming the Histadrut not just into a federation of trade unions, but into a creative force in the development of the nation, and establishing the "Labor hegemony" of the country. Among the leading enterprises Berl helped to create was the Histadrut's sick fund, which has since become the biggest fund of its kind in the country, the nearest thing we have to a national health service; Bank Hapoalim, which provided substantial financial aid for the building of rural settlements and urban cooperatives; and Mashbir, the Histadrut's chain of consumer goods stores.

But for Berl the humanist, culture and education were at least as important as health care, investment funds, and cheap consumer goods. The development of cultural and educational institutions by the Histadrut was an integral part of his vision of a powerful working class that exercised a decisive influence on the nation. So in 1925 he started *Davar,* the Histadrut's daily newspaper, and was its first editor. He started Am Oved (A Working People), the Histadrut's publishing firm, which is still flourishing; he sponsored *Ha-Ohel,* the Histadrut's theater; and he strongly supported the Histadrut network of schools for workers' children. And, from the start, he was an enthusiastic supporter of the Working Youth movement, believing that the education of the young was the surest means for creating the Zionist-socialist society of his vision. He believed in the proletariat, but not in the Marxist doctrine of the dictatorship of the proletariat. He didn't believe in any imposed solutions, only in the democratic-humanistic method of changing things by education and persuasion. In his vision, an educated, culturally and spiritually developed working class would lead the whole nation to become an *am oved* in the broad sense that encompasses intellectual and artistic as well as physical work.

Berl was capable of expounding this vision for four, six, even, once, twelve hours at a stretch, and we listened spellbound, unaware of the passing hours. What held us? His personality and style, which we found irresistibly engaging. Ben-Gurion, who could be formidable and a little frightening on a public platform, was always somewhat impersonal. But Berl was usually easy and relaxed, his delivery conversational, his tone and manner full of persuasive charm. He was of medium height, with curly dark hair that turned gray early, and an expressive, eager, smiling face. His black eyes sparkled with life, and in conversation they could fix you with a deep penetrating gaze. He wore a short mustache, which he played with constantly, giving it short, quick side strokes whenever he was about to say something humorous or witty or bitingly polemical. People watched for this gesture, often smiling in anticipation of the spurt of fun they knew was coming. He spoke very fast, very fluently, and very emotionally, too; he *believed* in emotion, insisting that every serious commitment of one's life involved the passions. If it didn't, it was merely abstract, cerebral, and for that kind he had nothing but contempt. This is why he felt that literature, history, and all the humanities were so important — not only for knowledge, but for the culture of the emotions, as he termed it, without which a human being was incomplete.

There was plenty to hold us besides his personality and style. He had ardor, eloquence, clarity of mind, and wisdom; he had humor, irony, and a sharp polemical wit to lighten and diversify his high seriousness. But most of all, we were held in our seats by the spectacle of a man pursuing his vision with absolute independence, free of all catch words, slogans, and conventional pieties. His searching, penetrating originality set him apart from everyone else in our experience. We will advance to a true understanding of reality, he used to say, only "by the strength of embarrassment and by rejection of plaster": by the "embarrassment" of constantly questioning and reexamining and reassessing our favorite assumptions, and by refusing to cover any flaws they might have with "plaster." In other words, we advance toward the truth we seek only by refusing to accept unexamined slogans, superficial certitudes, oversimplifications of any kind.

So our questions, he insisted, must be genuinely probing, exploring ones that honestly attempted to reexamine a matter afresh. This did not imply an intellectual or moral permissiveness

in Berl; every question was always an open one at the beginning
of an inquiry, but it was rarely open by the end. His inquiries always led to firm conclusions, and once a conclusion was reached,
Berl was adamant about its being accepted without reservation
by the other party. He could become surprisingly angry and fierce
when anyone attempted to resist or evade it. Berl had a good deal
of iron beneath the free, graceful pliability of his method and
manner. I struck the iron on several occasions, and I have not forgotten how discomfiting I found the experience.

He had a strong feeling for the symbolic value of certain acts
and practices, especially those of the Jewish tradition, and this
was perhaps of a piece with his views about the importance of the
emotional and imaginative side of life. I remember an episode
that exemplified his profound sense of his Jewish roots, as well as
his independence of mind and readiness to challenge accepted
views — in this instance, one of the conventional unconventional-
ities of my generation. The festival of Tisha Be'Av, the traditional
day of mourning for the destruction of the First and Second
Temples, is observed by pious Jews as a day of fasting, lamenta-
tion, and prayer. One of our youth groups had arranged an excursion on that day, on the assumption that it was a purely
religious festival, which their secular, nonbelieving youth were
not required to observe. They observed Pesach, Shavuot, Succot,
and other festivals because these were national festivals. But not
Tisha Be'Av, which they considered no business of theirs, a view
we all shared.

To our astonishment, Berl passionately attacked this attitude.
He, too, was nonreligious, he said, but we were entirely mistaken
in regarding Tisha Be'Av as only a religious festival. No, he insisted, it was a *national* day of mourning as well. The destruction of
the Temples was no less a tragic event in our national history than
the enslavement of Egypt we commemorate at Passover, and it
was the duty of every Jew of this generation, secular as well as religious, to observe it.

It was the first time any of our leaders had proposed this view of
Tisha Be'Av, and it made a great impression on us. As usual,
there was a great deal of heated argument, but in the end we acknowledged that Berl was right. We had been misled by the fasting and prayer elements, which made it seem like a purely
religious festival — like Yom Kippur, for example. I am glad to

say that the State of Israel has adopted Berl's view and treats Tisha Be'Av as a solemn day of mourning, to be observed by the whole nation.

Berl had an especially warm feeling for Ein-Harod, calling it his second home, and he visited us often. He particularly loved to talk to the children, drawing them out about what they were learning, reading, thinking. When I was a boy he once asked me at length about my reading, and I remember both how proud I was of his approval and how I admired him from that time. As a young man, I grew to know Berl well in Tel Aviv, starting when I slept on his verandah. I was treated as a member of the family, joining Berl and his wife for breakfast or supper from time to time. He had a seemingly insatiable interest in the Working Youth movement and wanted to know everything: what I had done that day, that week, that month; what we were planning to do, now and in the future; were there any meetings, conferences, seminars for our instructors that he could come to, to learn at first hand what we were doing? His interest was always eager, fresh, and direct, and wonderfully inspiring as a consequence.

And what a warm, ardent interest he took in my writing! Tabenkin couldn't write at all, he could only make speeches; Ben-Gurion wrote a great deal, but his style was somewhat lacking in distinction. But Berl was a master stylist who wrote with the precision, economy, and care for beauty of a literary artist. His collected writings fill twelve volumes, a substantial output for a man whose main occupation was building a country. He also wrote excellent long introductions to the collected works of other writers, including Nachman Syrkin, the distinguished Russian-born ideologist and leader of socialist Zionism. Berl's vivid, living portraits of authors were widely acclaimed, and were collected and published in a separate volume after his death.

I had my own unforgettable little experience of Berl's sense of style, as well as his irresistibly charming, civil method of persuasion. In collaboration with David Cohen, I had drawn up a kind of guide, a list of do's and don'ts — we called it the Ten Commandments — for our youngest group of Working Youth, aged ten to thirteen. I asked Berl if he would look them over and tell me what he thought.

He read them, nodding his head appreciatively as he read. "It's excellent! Really *very* good!" he said when he got to the end. "But perhaps this one could be improved if, instead of this here, you said . . ." and he suggested a change that was so obviously better that I immediately scribbled it in. "And now, this second one . . . Couldn't be better . . . And yet" — he gazed at it thoughtfully, seriously weighing the matter — "I *think* it would be just a shade stronger if you took out this adjective here . . . You've got two more before it, you see, and perhaps those two might be enough, don't you agree?" And so it went. Each of our remaining commandments were excellent, splendid; but perhaps just here, just there . . . until by the end he had in effect rewritten the whole lot, and I had agreed to every change without a murmur of protest. I thought that if this was his usual method of breaking down authors' resistance to criticism, I could well understand why people said he was a brilliant editor, and why he was so widely accepted as an arbiter of literary taste.

He loved to hear about our experiences with Working Youth, especially our success stories. One he particularly enjoyed was the story of Yossele Ikar, another street child of Jerusalem taken in by No'ar ha-Oved. I recount it here in memory of the pleasure he took in it.

Yossele Ikar was the child of an ultra-Orthodox family that lived off the traditional charity, *haluka,* of pious Jews abroad who sent regular donations for the maintenance of the religious Jewish families of Eretz Yisrael. When Yossele was about eleven, his whole family immigrated to the United States at the invitation of relatives. But on their arrival, it was discovered that Yossele's younger brother had trachoma, and he was not allowed into the country. He was shipped back to Jerusalem with Yossele as his guardian, and the two boys went to live with a grandmother who had been left behind.

Yossele was sent to a yeshiva, in Tel Aviv, but he often played truant, going off to enjoy himself on the Tel Aviv seashore. One day he was caught by the warden of the yeshiva and expelled. Like Mokka, he became a homeless street child, selling newspapers and shoelaces and stealing a bit for extra income. His vendor's beat was at a major intersection in Tel Aviv, near our Working Youth club and the headquarters of Betar. At this period of high tension between the Labor party and the Revisionists, our youth and theirs used to meet almost daily at a nearby kiosk that sold the fizzy fruit drink *gazoz,* which we all drank in large quantities. Not surprisingly, these encounters often developed into slanging matches between the two groups, with much shouting and mutual abuse.

Yossele, perceiving what was going on and seeing a chance to have some fun, decided to act as an amateur double agent, running back and forth between the two groups, telling each the nasty things the other was saying about them and adding fuel to the fire of their ideological dispute. "They said Ben-Gurion is a Bolshevik dog!" he would tell us cheerfully. Then off he'd go to the Betar group to confide just as cheerfully, "They say Jabotinsky is a chauvinist pig!" The young courier soon attracted the attention of the ever vigilant instructors, David Cohen, Yisrael Galili, and me. We asked him who he was and what he was doing, and when we learned how he was living we took him back to our one-room quarters until we could find him a permanent home.

We soon placed him in our evening school, found work for him in Tel Aviv, and finally sent him to the youth village at Ben-Shemen, which was closely associated with Working Youth. Yossele stayed there for a couple of years, going to school, learning farming, and becoming accustomed to living in a community. When he turned sixteen or seventeen, he and his group came to Ein-Harod for a year of hachshara. Then they left to become founding members of a new kibbutz in Haifa Bay, aiming to work in Haifa's port and as fishermen. In doing this, they were helping to fulfill the broader aim of *kibbush ha-yam*, "conquest of the sea," which Ben-Gurion had long been urging as a primary national goal. Yossele and his group worked as stevedores in Haifa, living in tents and huts in their kibbutz encampment. They were called the Sea Kibbutz of Working Youth and were much commended for their pioneer work.

Eventually, the whole group settled in a new kibbutz near Caesarea, on the sea, named Sdot-Yam, "field of the sea," to signify their wish to work both in the fields and on the sea. Yossele remained, married, raised a family, and lives there still. He became a central figure in building the kibbutz and at various times was elected to all its leading offices, including those of treasurer and secretary. I like to think of him as he thinks of himself: one more success of the Working Youth movement, which helped to transform the bright little street urchin into a first-class, creative builder of Kibbutz Sdot-Yam.

Mission to Poland: Episodes

I DIDN'T REALLY want to go to Poland in 1937. The Arab riots that had started in 1936 were spreading death and destruction everywhere, and I felt it was no time to be away from the country — the Haganah needed everyone who could use a gun for national defense, and Ein-Harod needed us all for intensified guard duty and other vital jobs. Besides, I was just launched on my literary career — having made a good start in Tel Aviv — and I was eager to press on with my writing. There were family duties as well. Since my father's death I had been helping my mother to bring up my brother, Yuval, now aged eight, and I was very reluctant to leave her to cope on her own for up to two years.

In the end I was persuaded to go by what I heard about the growing virulent anti-Semitism in Poland that was being encouraged by the spread of Nazism. Clearly, the need to prepare the young Jews of Poland for immigration to Eretz Yisrael was more urgent than ever, especially since legal immigration was practically impossible, and they would be faced with the complications of leaving Poland illegally. I never regretted my decision. To have been in Poland during those fateful years from 1937 to 1939; to have participated in the life of Polish Jews before they perished in the Holocaust; to have seen up close the inspired Hehalutz (Pioneer) movement of prewar Poland, from which sprang most of the ghetto fighters — those small bands of men and women who had the astounding courage to resist the Nazi forces of destruction in the ghettos of Warsaw, Vilna, Bialystok: I regard these experiences as one of the great privileges of my life. I have recalled and relived them over and over again in the years that have passed, and I can never separate in my mind the horror of their martyrs' fate from the pride and exhilaration I feel when I remember their greatness of spirit.

We journeyed to Poland by sea, through Alexandria to Marseilles, then by train to Warsaw via Paris and Berlin. My companions were Eliezer Regev of Kibbutz Givat Brenner and David Cafri of Kibbutz Na'an. Regev, a veteran emissary who had already been on a mission to Poland and was active in the illegal immigration movement, was the leader of our group. We stopped in Paris for a week, and my first encounter with Western Europe made a great impression on me. Our host and guide in Paris was Enzo Sereni, who was in Paris to raise funds for Aliyah Bet. Enzo knew Paris almost as well as his native Rome, and by the end of the week we had the happy, though doubtless delusive, feeling that we knew this fabulous city rather well ourselves.

Chaim Atar, our Ein-Harod artist, had been sent to Paris for a year or two to paint, meet fellow artists, and in general refresh his knowledge of the art world of Europe, and he became our self-appointed guide to the museums and galleries. Though he had scarcely any money for lodgings and food, Atar spent almost all he had to buy pictures at bargain prices for the Ein-Harod art museum he was already dreaming of, and he proudly showed us his acquisitions, stored in his squalid room on the Left Bank. It was a rare pleasure to accompany him to the Rodin Museum, the Louvre, and other museums, and when I revisited Paris for the first time more than thirty years later, I was surprised to find how much I remembered of what we had seen with him. This week in Paris with Sereni and Atar was the last happy, carefree one I was to have in the next nineteen months, the duration of my stay in Poland.

It was just as well that we stayed in Berlin for only two days. Whatever pleasant impressions I may have had of this other great capital of prewar Europe have been wiped out of my memory, leaving just one that can never be erased: the sight of storm troopers marching through the streets in their brown shirts and polished high leather boots, crying "Heil Hitler" as they went. The whole street seemed to freeze with fear at the sight and sound of them, and my heart froze, too, as I gazed silently at this portent of I didn't know what, but sensing that whatever it was would be terrible.

When I reached Warsaw I was almost immediately precipitated into the harrowing problems of the movement I had been charged to help and encourage. At my first meeting with the Hehalutz people, the day after my arrival, a member of the audience flung out the bitter rhetorical question, "What future, what economic or spiritual future, is there for these young Jews who have been vomited out by Poland?" And a woman, having told us that some young Zionists had been waiting as long as seven years to immigrate to Eretz Yisrael, asked in despair, "How long can one wait for aliyah? How long can one sustain one's soul only by hopes?"

In 1937 nearly a quarter of a million young Jews were without work and with no prospect of ever finding any; the economic discrimination against Jews had closed off every avenue of employment. On top of the appalling unemployment problem, the obstacles to emigration were driving Jews to despair. The United States was closing its doors. Legal immigration to Eretz Yisrael was severely restricted by the British Mandatory government. Thus there was no other way but to enter Eretz Yisrael illegally — but that was difficult and dangerous, and Aliyah Bet had only started and was not to gain its full momentum until it was too late. Too late to save the young Polish Jews not just from the demoralizing misery of unemployment, but from extermination in the Nazi death camps.

So there was widespread hopelessness and despair among those I had come to help. Yet there was also tremendous cultural vitality and a developed political consciousness in the Jewish communities of Poland, and among the fully committed Young Pioneers, a brave refusal to give up and a passionate eagerness to seize any chance for immigration to Eretz Yisrael. This duality of the spirit, the coexistence of vivid, confident hope with abysmal, sometimes abject despair, was something I encountered during all my time in Poland. As I became more involved in the life and spiritual condition of Polish Jews, I increasingly understood and sympathized with it.

My tasks were in some respects similar to those I had carried out on my mission to Working Youth in Tel Aviv. But the enlarged scale of my activities, the great distances I had to travel to get from one Young Pioneer center to another, and the extremes of the central European climate all made a qualitative difference between my earlier mission and this one. I journeyed to most of the Young Pioneer branches in the country to give lectures, conduct seminars, and join in summer camps, and I made extended visits to the *kibbutzei hachshara* (training kibbutzim), in which the young Jews who aspired to immigrate were learning to become farmers and workers and to live the communal life. I also helped to edit their monthly Hebrew and Yiddish journal and improved my Yiddish by reading and lecturing in the language.

The Jewish population of Poland in 1937 numbered more than three million, and I remember, strange as it now seems, what an exciting experience it was for me to encounter, for the first time, Jews en masse. The Jewish population of the whole of Eretz Yisrael was then a meager half million, while in Warsaw alone hundreds of thousands of Jews lived an intensely Jewish life — politically, socially, and culturally. Numerous Jewish political parties, religious and secular, were fully represented in the Polish parliament, in local government, and in the semiautonomous councils of the Jewish communities. The Zionist parties tended to form electoral blocs, to vote against the anti-Zionist socialist party, the Bund. There were Jewish trade unions, cooperatives, professional associations, mutual aid and health care societies, and even Jewish savings banks. There were Jewish schools and teacher training colleges, with teaching in Hebrew or Yiddish or Polish, many yeshivot for religious studies, and a Research Institute for Judaism, open to religious and secular students alike.

I was amazed by the number of Jewish newspapers and periodicals — 230 in 1937 — Yiddish dailies, weeklies, monthlies, quarterlies, with at least ten in Hebrew. There was a thriving Yiddish theater (one in Warsaw, one in Vilna), numerous repertory companies; and a special youth theater. Almost every town, large or small, had a Jewish choir, and many of the big towns a Jewish orchestra. Hundreds of Jewish painters, sculptors, musicians, poets, and writers formed a vital intelligentsia comparable only to that of pre-Revolution Russia.

When the Nazis occupied Poland and herded its Jews into ghettos in preparation for the Final Solution, there was a concentrated effort in all the ghettos to maintain these Jewish institutions as long as possible. Back in Eretz Yisrael, when I heard of these heroic efforts, which have since become a part of the history of the Holocaust, I was able to visualize in my mind's eye almost exactly what they were struggling to maintain, and I was thankful once again for this small chance to participate in spirit in their struggle. It also made me understand intimately the plain words of Zivia Lubetkin, a leader of the Warsaw Ghetto revolt, who survived to tell her tale in Eretz Yisrael. "Heroism? Heroes?" she once said sharply and impatiently when people were exalting her as a heroine. "Do you think the heroism was in risking your life, in facing death? If there was heroism, it was in just one thing: in remaining human beings, in not falling below the red line. In not going under as human and moral beings."

My journeys to the outlying shtetls gave me an unforgettable firsthand insight into two ubiquitous aspects of Jewish life in Poland: the poverty in which small-town Jews lived and the endemic anti-Semitism of the Poles, intensified by the spread of Nazism.

The anti-Semitism was most virulent in Warsaw and the other big cities, but we ran into it everywhere we went: suspicion and hatred of Jews and unappeased blood lust directly inspired by Nazism. On my train trips I made a point of sitting among Jews, and I had found a simple device for identifying myself as one of them. I would draw out my copy of *Davar,* which I received regularly from home, open it ostentatiously, and hold it high as I read or pretended to read it. Almost immediately I heard cries of recognition from the Jews sitting or standing around me, accompanied by enthusiastic gestures and calls to come and sit with them. I usually spent the rest of the time in pleasant animated talks with my fellow Jews.

On one occasion, however, I was particularly tired after a long, strenuous day of meetings and talks, and wanted to have a quiet journey without company. I was traveling from Baranowicz to Vilna on a railway line that ran close to the Russian border. I found a compartment occupied by only three other people: a young girl about fifteen, a man about sixty, and a younger man, all obviously Poles. I sat down next to the young girl, opposite the two men, drew out a book, and was reading quietly when the conductor came to examine our tickets. I showed him my passport.

"So you're from Palestine, are you?" he said civilly enough. "What are you doing here?"

"Oh, I'm a tourist," I answered.

The conductor made no comment and left, but the mere mention of the name Palestine was enough to set off the older man sitting opposite me. Fixing me with a suspicious, hostile look, he said to the others in Polish, which I understood, "He says he's a tourist, but with these Jews you can never tell whether they're speaking the truth. He must be a Communist spy — otherwise what is he doing in this part of the country, so near the Russian border?"

The young man just smiled, went on reading his newspaper, then got off at the next station, but the young girl looked at me covertly with round eyes as I pretended to go on reading my book as if I had understood nothing. Inwardly I was boiling with fury at my helplessness to answer; I knew just enough Polish to understand what he was saying, but not enough to speak. And I remembered that about a month before my colleague David Cafri had been arrested in the same area on suspicion of being a Communist, for no other reason than that he was a Jew from Palestine and was wearing a leather jacket. He had been released only after direct intervention from Hehalutz headquarters in Warsaw.

Meanwhile, the older man went on telling the young girl about the awfulness of the Jews. "Wherever they are, they're like leeches, sucking the blood of the Poles. They're everywhere, spreading their poison all over the world. I hope Hitler's anti-Jewish laws will soon be introduced into our country, too." As the train approached Vilna the compartment filled with people, and the elderly man announced to each group of newcomers, looking in my direction, "That's a Jew from Palestine, a Communist spy for sure." It was disgusting and humiliating to feel their glances, and for the first time in my life I knew what it was like to wear the yellow patch of the sons of the Exile.

At last we arrived at Vilna, and all the other passengers in the compartment hurried to get off the train, leaving me alone with the young girl, who was struggling to get her large heavy suitcase off the rack. I smiled at her and heaved it down. The look on her childish face clearly expressed her astonishment at seeing I was not a monster but a human being; indeed, rather more of a human being than her fellow Poles, who had not thought of helping her. Her look was some small compensation for the extreme unpleasantness of the long train ride.

At the end of 1938, less than nine months before the German invasion of Poland and about a year after my arrival, the country was preparing for a general election. There were posters everywhere, with slogans in huge red and black letters: "Jews Out! Jews to the Ghetto!" And the newspaper headlines proclaimed: "Blessed are the acts of Hitler against the Jews!" On a crowded Warsaw tram one evening there were a good many Jews, easily recognizable by their Orthodox garb. Suddenly a man started to yell: "To hell with these Jews who push in everywhere and take up every place! Hitler has forbidden Jews to ride on trams and buses. How long are we going to go on suffering them here?" The poison of Nazi hatred seemed to saturate the air, and I felt myself suffocating with sick horror as I breathed it.

On a bitterly cold evening in December 1938, I was standing at the entrance of the leading Polish theater in Warsaw, waiting for a friend who had invited me to see the play with him. As I leaned against a pillar in the portico of the theater, I noticed that an adjoining pillar displayed another of the vicious anti-Jewish slogans: "The Jew — Enemy Number One of the State!" Suddenly two trucks full of students drove into the plaza in front of the theater. One carried a band with its musical instruments; the other flaunted a huge caricature of Stalin, with the slogan "Down with the Communists! Long live the ND!" (ND stood for the National Democrats, the anti-Semitic party in power.)

The next moment, two students, one swinging a heavy stick, rushed toward me. The one without the stick came close, looked hard at my face, and cried "Polack!" Rushing past me, he pulled up in front of another young man who was standing nearby, looked at his face, and cried "Zid!" The student brought the heavy stick down hard on his head. The young man fell to the ground, his face covered with blood. I stood there stupefied, not understanding what had happened, aware only of the noise and confusion all around me. The two trucks drove off and before long an ambulance appeared.

By the time my friend arrived, some sort of order had been restored. Not knowing what had just happened, he urged me to hurry in so we wouldn't miss the beginning of the play. Then, in that moment, the meaning of the episode I had witnessed burst upon me. The Jew-hating student had thought I was a Pole; but for his mistake, I, too, might have been lying on the ground with my head cut open. I felt a sense of shame such as I had never experienced before. I said, "Sorry, I can't go in! I can't go to the theater tonight!" When I told him what had happened, he said he couldn't see the play either, and took me back to my lodgings.

In spite of this atmosphere of hatred, the poverty-stricken Polish Jews were often extraordinarily good-humored, accepting hardship as an unchangeable fact of life; complaining about it, of course, but also making it the subject of some of their best racy, colorful Yiddish jokes. I remember being horrified, and at the same time irresistibly amused, at hearing how a large proportion of the Jews of the small town of Wissotzk in Volyn province made a living. "By the fires!" I was told during my week's visit to Wissotzk.

"What fires?" I asked, completely puzzled.

"Why, the arson — don't you understand?" I didn't, and had to have it spelled out for me. Almost all the houses in the town were made of wood, and periodically, gangs of non-Jewish arsonists from the surrounding villages set fire to Jewish houses in order to plunder them. There were incidents of this kind almost every month. But, said my informant with a conspiratorial wink, when houses burn down you have to rebuild them. And building new houses provides a livelihood for the small timber traders who supply the wood, the carpenters who do the building, the house painters, the glaziers, the oven makers, the chimney makers, and so on. No, he wouldn't say the poor Jews of the town actually *wanted* the fires — but, well, those fires did help many people make a living, and they wouldn't know what to do without them!

Yes, to make a living, just a bare living — what is called in Yiddish a *parnosse* — this, I discovered, was the one overriding concern of hundreds of thousands of the poor Jews of Poland. It was symbolized in the extraordinary little scene I witnessed in

the Jewish quarter of the town of Kremenets, also in Volyn province. What I saw might have been a scene from a Yiddish play or
a painting by Chagall. I would not have remembered it but for
finding a full description of it in a letter I wrote home at the time.

The scene was enacted in a side street by two performing Jews.
One had an arm missing and was dressed in a tattered patchwork
jacket, theadbare and shiny from long use. The other had white
hair, was wearing a shabby, dirty *kapota,* the long black coat worn
by Orthodox Jews, and held a cheap violin. The one-armed man
was singing, accompanied by the other on his hoarse-voiced fiddle. A crowd composed of ragged, barefoot children, old women,
and young women with babies at their breasts had gathered.
From the windows of the wooden houses uncombed heads could
be seen peeping out at the performers: a cobbler with his hammer,
a tailor with his tape measure around his neck, a carpenter holding his plane. Everybody was listening intently, even a cat sitting
on a nearby roof.

The armless Jew sang with a strange fervor in a voice that
seemed to mix a clown's gaiety with a deep aching sadness. The
melody kept changing, and at first I didn't take in the words.
Then, as I listened more closely, I realized he was singing a Yiddish song of just two lines, which he repeated over and over without pause:

> *Oi, oi, parnosse!*
> *Gottenyu, gib parnosse!*

(Oh, oh, a living! God, our God, give us a living!)

He sang the lines to each new tune the fiddler played, each time
with a renewed fever of excitement shining in his eyes, beating out
the rhythm on his companion's back with his empty sleeve. Soon
the whole street joined in the singing — the children, the old
women, the feeding mothers, the men at the windows of thcir
workshops — all imploring the Almighty. The old women bent
down to draw a few small coins from their stockings, and there
were tears in their eyes as they croaked the endless refrain; "Oi, oi,
parnosse! Gottenyu, gib parnosse!"

Then, suddenly, the armless Jew stopped singing and his companion's fiddle fell silent. Perhaps the singer had had enough and
wanted to move on. As he started to walk away, he flung his part-

ing shot at the crowd. "Look, Jews!" he cried gaily, pointing to the cat on the roof. "There's a clever cat for you! He's fled to the roof on purpose, to get out of paying a few *groschen* for the song! Ai, ai, what a clever cat!"

In my letter home describing the episode, I gave it a name, "The Shtetl Sings," as if it were indeed a play or a picture. And I told my correspondent he would learn more about the reality of shtetl life from this scene than he would from all the descriptions and statistics I could supply.

12

Mission to Poland: People

I MET many remarkable people in Poland, and their personalities
are fresh in my memory. I have singled out five of those unforgettable men and women to represent them all. Three of them
perished in the Holocaust: two young sisters, Frumka and
Hantche Plotnitzki, and the famous author and educator Janusz
Korczak. My impressions of them at the time are intertwined
with my knowledge of what happened to them afterward — their
heroism once the Holocaust had engulfed them all, and their terrible end. So I can write of them only as they live in my memory
now, as I feel they are an indestructible part of my experience.
What they were when I knew them and what they were as heroes
and martyrs have become inseparable.

The other two, Yitzhak ("Antek") Zuckerman and his wife,
Zivia Lubetkin, were leaders of the Warsaw Ghetto revolt who
miraculously survived, came to live in Eretz Yisrael, and gave us
and the whole world an account of the fate of the Warsaw Ghetto
and the Jews of Poland that stands among the greatest records of
the Holocaust. They became founding members of Kibbutz Lochamei ha-Geta'ot (Kibbutz of the Ghetto Fighters), and remained there to the end of their lives.

The elder of the two doomed sisters, Frumka, was about
twenty-three when I met her, at my first meeting with the activists
of Hehalutz. She sat in a corner, hunched up in a shabby old coat,
listening in silence. But I noticed that she seemed to register

all the emotions evoked by what the others were saying about the hopelessness of their situation — the grief, rage, and frustration they felt at the seemingly endless wait for immigration to Eretz Yisrael, and the loss of hope and faith that the longed-for liberation would ever come.

Her sensitive face, with its high forehead, was habitually earnest, almost severe, but once she knew you it could express great tenderness. Her public speeches tended to be concise and spare; in private conversation she could be warm and expressive, pointing up the contrast between her sharp analytical mind, which could be ruthlessly penetrating, and her delicate love for her comrades and selfless readiness to help and support them in every way. These qualities, combined with her moral integrity, her total dedication to any task she undertook, and the high standards of conduct she consistently observed — and could therefore demand of others — made her a natural leader, in spite of her youth, in the Young Pioneers and in the Jewish underground resistance movement.

My second meeting with her, a few weeks later, was at the kibbutz hachshara in Bialystok. She was working in the kitchen, but when she saw me in the dining hall she came forward immediately, saying, with a warm smile, "You will be my guest, won't you, mine first of all?" As soon as she had finished work, she took me out to look at the town, which she knew well. She had many friends there, and we were stopped and greeted again and again. When we reached the park, she suddenly cried, with a strange note of ecstasy in her voice, "This is my favorite spot in town!" To my delight and surprise, she started to make snowballs and throw them joyously, like a small girl. "I'm afraid that's how smelling the earth and the trees affects me," she said as we sat on a bench watching the sparrows. "I get a little delirious. Imagine what it will be like when I get to Eretz Yisrael, to *our* fields. I think I shall go out of my mind altogether!"

After this we met many times in our joint activities in Hehalutz and in the kibbutzei hachshara. Our last meeting, shortly before my departure for Eretz Yisrael, was in a village near Pinsk, her birthplace. I had come to participate in a two-week seminar organized by Frumka for the Young Pioneers. She had done her work with unobtrusive efficiency, preparing the house the youngsters were to stay in and drawing up the program and the rules and regulations. She loved the young people and loved to kindle their hearts with her own passion and yearning for Eretz Yisrael, and they responded ardently. But she could also be very severe about any deviation from what she considered decent behavior. I witnessed one example of this when the baker in town failed to deliver the bread for which he had been paid in advance. She marched off to confront him about it, and I went with her. Though he was more than twenty years her senior, she let him have it. "You ought to be ashamed of yourself, leaving children without bread!" When he apologized, making feeble excuses about its having happened by mistake, she just rebuked him scornfully. "Why do you ask *me* to excuse you? You haven't sinned against me, you've sinned against yourself!" The bread arrived punctually each morning after that.

I had to leave early, to return to Warsaw in preparation for my return home, and Frumka accompanied me to the small country station. We embraced and I said, "Farewell, *lehitra'ot!* But not for long, Frumka. We shall meet again soon, in Eretz Yisrael!"

She looked at me gravely and said, "I have a feeling we shall not meet again. I shall not get to Eretz Yisrael."

"What nonsense!" I answered angrily. "What's the matter with you? Of course we shall meet there." Then, to lighten the heaviness in my heart, "Let's make a bet. If you get to Eretz Yisrael, you'll give me a big bar of chocolate, the kind I like. If you don't . . ."

But now the conductor was banging doors, blowing his whistle, and calling to straggling passengers to board. I got into the last carriage, found a seat, and went to the window for a final goodbye. There was Frumka, smiling, standing by the window with a bar of chocolate she had managed to buy at the little counter on the platform. She pressed it into my hand through the window, saying, "You've won your bet! I'm beginning to believe that I *will* reach Eretz Yisrael!" She drew back, waved to me, then turned her back and hurried toward the forest through which we had come to the station.

But her first intuition was right. She never escaped from Poland. I heard the story from Renya K., one of the first ghetto fighters to reach Eretz Yisrael in 1944.

It was 1942, and the systematic destruction of Polish Jewry was well advanced. The people at the Hehalutz center in Warsaw wanted Frumka to flee the country so she could tell the world what was happening. She accepted her mission and, disguised as a Christian, headed south to find a way into Slovakia and from there to escape abroad. On her way to the border, she stopped in one Jewish town after another, to see the genocide with her own eyes. "She passed through all the circles of hell," said Renya. "She wanted to saturate herself in the suffering in order to be a faithful emissary of a people drowning in blood."

In December 1942 she reached the kibbutz hachshara in Bendin, near the Slovakian border, of which Renya was a member. Though weak and broken by the terrible scenes she had witnessed, she called the members of the kibbutz and the young Jews of the town to meeting after meeting, telling and retelling what she had seen and pressing home one great lesson: that they must not die like sheep led to the slaughter; that they must prepare to defend themselves, to make war on the killers, to fight them to the finish.

Letter after letter arrived from her comrades in Warsaw, led by Zivia Lubetkin, demanding that she leave Poland immediately. It was still possible; she mustn't miss this last chance. But Frumka was adamant about staying. She couldn't save herself, no matter what the vital cause, while her fellow Jews were falling under her eyes. So she rejected all the possibilities of escape proposed to her and stayed in the Bendin kibbutz.

Almost every day at dawn she went into town, to visit the Jews incarcerated in the Bendin ghetto, to ease their suffering by giving comfort, affection, or good counsel. She kept in close touch with the emissaries of Eretz Yisrael in Constantinople, then the center of rescue operations of Jews in Nazi-occupied Europe, helping to effect the escape of as many of Bendin's Jews as possible.

Then in April 1943 came the news of the brutal destruction of the Warsaw Ghetto. Thousands of Jews had perished in the battles and the flames. Frumka's anguish was great but her resolution greater still. She and all the Jews of Bendin must now, more than ever, stand firm against the enemy. They must avenge the martyrs of the Warsaw Ghetto; they must, each and every one of them, die fighting when their hour came.

Frumka's came on August 3, 1943. Without warning, the Gestapo surrounded the Bendin ghetto and the destruction began. Frumka and six comrades grabbed their weapons and fled to their bunker. The suddenness of the attack had ruined their defense plans; there was no time to contact other members, there was time only to get to the bunker and wait for the last fight.

Frumka and a guard were the first to shoot as the Germans approached. Two SS men fell. One was killed instantly, the other was wounded and screaming in agony. There was more shooting from the bunker as the rest of the SS band bore down on it. The seven refused to surrender. The SS men threw fire bombs into the bunker, and all seven defenders perished in the flames.

Renya ended her account: "The bunker is burning, together with those inside it. The shooting has stopped. The Germans flood the bunker with water. The fire dies down. On the scorched earth of the cellar lie the half-burned bodies of the defenders. Frumka is grasping her revolver in her hand. She raises her head as if she wants to say something. One of the Germans instantly leaps on her, wrests the revolver from her hand, and kills her. This is how Frumka fell."

Hantche, who was twenty when I met her in 1938, was quite different from Frumka in appearance, character, and temperament. She was all laughter and high spirits, her personality a delicate mixture of the humorous and the poetic. The beauty of youth was in her brown eyes and chestnut hair, which she wore in braids. "The magic that was in her face, her smile, the movement of her two plaits, stirred one's heart with a strange power," someone wrote about her. She seemed to do everything with facility. She sang beautifully, she spoke well, she wrote well. She learned Hebrew quickly and effortlessly and was soon writing articles in Hebrew for the journal I helped edit. The Hebrew was full of mistakes, but the style was fluent and forceful.

When I met her in the kibbutz hachshara in Baranovicz, she was very active in the Young Pioneers and, like Frumka, showed distinct leadership qualities. Having been liberated from the traditional restrictions of the parental home, many of the girls in the movement developed great independence and strength of character, and it was no accident that a significant proportion of the leaders of the ghetto revolts were women. Hantche and I became friends at once, met often after that, and between meetings exchanged letters. The following extract from a letter written in Lodz on November 8, 1938, expresses in a typically fanciful way her feeling for Eretz Yisrael.

> I am reading Zvi Schatz [a young writer of the Second Aliyah] and thinking of Eretz Yisrael and the people I know there. I also dreamed a dream, a strange dream. It was as if I walked in mountains (in Eretz Yisrael, of course) — high, erect mountains. And now a brook zigzags at my feet. A thin narrow ribbon of water flows, streams, leaps mischievously from rocks, and falls joyously into the valley. The guide announces, "This is the Jordan!" A great pain seizes me, and a sharp envy rises up from the pain, as I recall in the same moment the great broad Wisla [Vistula]. I woke up that morning in a very bad temper.

When I got back to Eretz Yisrael in June 1939, there was still time for a brief exchange of letters before the war broke out and stopped all further communication. Hantche's last letters were as vivid as those she wrote me in Poland, but the oppressive feeling of approaching war could be felt between the lines, and there was a good deal less of the fancy, the gaiety, the élan I had come to love.

The rest of her story is told by survivors of the Warsaw Ghetto. From 1940, with typical fearlessness, she passed herself off as a non-Jew to perform the vital role of messenger for Hehalutz, crossing back and forth between the German- and Russian-occupied zones of Poland to maintain contact between the two separated parts of the movement. When the Warsaw Ghetto fighters were preparing for revolt and it was dangerous to be caught outside its walls, she acted as liaison between Warsaw and Bendin, bringing news of developments in each place and having the joy of being with her sister Frumka on her flying visits to Bendin.

Then, when the Warsaw Ghetto uprising began in April 1943, the leaders of the revolt decided that Hantche must assume the mission her sister had declined. She was to get out of the ghetto, flee abroad, and tell the world that the Jews of Poland were being systematically exterminated. And not only Polish Jewry: the Jews of all German-occupied Europe were being brought to Poland to the extermination camps of Treblinka and Auschwitz, having

Hantche (*left*) and Frumka Plotnitzki, the young sisters who never reached Eretz Yisrael

been deluded into believing that they were being sent for "resettlement." She was to warn the Jews that the transport trains would carry them to their deaths.

Hantche's end came just as she was setting out on this mission. Escorted by two young ghetto fighters, she was about to steal out of the ghetto when they were caught by a group of German guards. The guards shouted to them to halt, and the young men drew their revolvers, fired, and killed two of the Germans. Then they all started to run. One of the men managed to get away; the other was shot. Then the Germans caught Hantche, stood her up against the nearest wall, and shot her dead on the spot.

Susi and I named our middle daughter Hanna in memory of Hantche, who never reached Eretz Yisrael.

Yitzhak Zuckerman and his wife, Zivia Lubetkin, founders of the Ghetto Fighters' Organization and the principal leaders of the Warsaw Ghetto revolt, have become legendary figures in the history of the Holocaust and the story of the heroic Jewish resistance to the Nazi death machine. Yitzhak did his work outside the ghetto walls, supplying arms and intelligence data, while Zivia was inside, leading the ghetto fighters. Yitzhak said afterward that but for Zivia, there would have been no Warsaw Ghetto re-

Yitzhak Zuckerman and his wife, Zivia Lubetkin, founders of the Ghetto Fighters' Organization, are models for all time of Jewish courage, intelligence, and resourcefulness.

volt. When the ghetto was set on fire — the destroyers' only means of finally quelling the rebellion — Zivia was among the last to leave, escaping with the other survivors through the sewers and joining Yitzhak on the other side. After this, they both joined the Polish freedom fighters, forming a separate Jewish unit and fighting with them against the Germans until the end of the war. Immediately afterward, they devoted themselves to helping Young Pioneer survivors get to Eretz Yisrael through the illegal rescue movement Bricha. Finally they themselves came to live in Eretz Yisrael, Zivia arriving in 1946, Yitzhak a year later.

For me and my generation Yitzhak and Zivia were indeed heroes, models for all time of Jewish courage, intelligence, and resourcefulness, an inspiration for every effort of one's own life. But I also had the privilege of knowing them as beautifully simple and delightful people, and their union of the heroic with pure and unaffected humanity makes me think of them as two of the rarest human beings I have ever known.

I met Yitzhak soon after my arrival in Poland. There was nothing legendary about the tall, straight, handsome young man with the fine forehead and curly hair who inducted me into my work in Kovel, in the province of Volyn, when I arrived at its kibbutz

hachshara in December 1937. Aged twenty-two and a leading activist in the Hehalutz movement, Yitzhak had been born and
brought up in Vilna, a great intellectual and spiritual center of
European Jewry, and he bore the stamp of his background all his
life. He spoke and wrote beautiful Yiddish, and his command of
Hebrew was so good, so easy and lively, that he might have been
brought up in Eretz Yisrael. He loved Yiddish and Hebrew poetry with a passion, and I had an unforgettable demonstration of
that love, and of his great sense of humor and joie de vivre, on my
very first night in Kovel.

We had been at Young Pioneer meetings in the town and returned to the kibbutz hachshara on its outskirts well after midnight. Yitzhak led me to the single huge dormitory in which all
the members slept. It was full of beds, from wall to wall, covering
every square inch of the floor. I noticed two sleeping forms in each
bed. I looked inquiringly at Yitzhak, and he, guessing my
thoughts, said yes, alas, they had no choice but to sleep two in a
bed. It was their policy, he explained, to accept every Young Pioneer applying for admission to the kibbutz hachshara. Since immigration certificates to Palestine were so hard to come by, and
illegal immigration was a slow business, their stay was often a
long one; meanwhile the overcrowding was terrible. I appreciated
the reason, nevertheless I was secretly horrified — we were poor
enough in Ein-Harod, goodness knows, but I had always had my
own bed. I didn't at all relish the thought of sharing one with
someone else, particularly a complete stranger.

Yitzhak must have sensed my uneasiness, even though I was
doing my best to conceal it. "You know what?" he said, with a big
grin on his face. "I've got an idea! My regular sleeping mate is the
baker, and he'll have to get up soon, in an hour or so, to bake tomorrow's bread. So what do you say to our just waiting until he
gets up, and then the two of us can get into his bed? It will be
warm, at least, and that's something on a night like this!" I happily agreed. Sharing a bed with Yitzhak was the best I could hope
for in the circumstances, and the only question was where we
would wait and what we would do until the baker got up. Yitzhak
had the answer. "Let's wait in the reading room, right here next
to the dormitory!" We went in and lay down on two long tables
that stood side by side, wrapping ourselves in our overcoats

against the bitter cold. "And now," said Yitzhak, cheerfully, "let's have a competition. Let's see who can recite the most Hebrew poetry by heart." He began with a long passage from one of Avraham Shlonsky's book of poems, and I followed with a poem of Yehuda Karni, and that is how we spent the time waiting for the baker to get up, enjoying ourselves hugely. Yitzhak easily beat me with the volume and variety of Hebrew poetry he knew, and we became firm friends from then on.

Ten years later, when I greeted him on the day of his arrival in Eretz Yisrael in April 1947, he asked me whether I remembered our competition and, as if continuing our game, quoted two lines from the opening poem of my first collection: "Once more my heart yearns for the horizon / There beyond the hills." What a man! What a spirit! I said to myself as I listened to his brief declamation. He had lived through those cataclysmic ten years which transformed our world — the Second World War, the Holocaust, the destruction of the Warsaw Ghetto, fighting with the Polish freedom fighters, helping Jewish survivors get to Eretz Yisrael — yet remembered our literary competition. I never think of those lines from my early poem without hearing Yitzhak's rich melodious voice reciting them.

We had one of our most intimate talks in the summer of 1948, in the middle of the War of Independence. It was after one of several battles for Latrun. We had once again failed to take this strategic fortress held by the Arabs, and there had been heavy casualties. I was in a black mood when I reached Tel Aviv. There I ran into Yitzhak, and offered to take him to Kibbutz Yagur, near Haifa, which was his home. It was a two-hour journey, and on the way I told him about our unsuccessful battle, going into some detail about how and why we had failed. When I finished, he looked at me with eyes full of pain, and said, "Yes, I know these situations. Oh, yes, I know what it is to fail!" And then he told me a strange, moving story that was later included in a book called *Testimonies of Survival: Ninety-Six Personal Interviews with Members of Kibbutz Lochamei ha-Geta'ot* [Kibbutz of the Ghetto Fighters].

"Just before Passover Eve 1942 I decided to go to the public baths with Mordechai Tennenboim. We had no bathroom or shower in our lodgings, and one does sometimes have to have a shower, doesn't one? We entered the bathhouse. It was hot. I saw the Jews standing naked in the mist of steam. I felt as if I were going out of my mind. I said to Mordechai, 'I can see the bears tearing them to pieces.' That's how I lived with my sense of the destruction. I fled, and he with me. We didn't have our baths. When I saw the naked Jews, I had the hallucination I was seeing dead bodies. I got home in a state of mind verging on madness. Yes, I was on the edge of madness. Nothing mattered except one thing — to fight for your life. That was the only standard for me, whether you fought or didn't fight. And you see, we failed in this. It didn't happen. It went to pieces. We knew they were sending Jews to their deaths — and we did nothing."

His words were heart-searing, but they were also cryptic. What could he mean, I asked myself, by saying that they "did nothing"? They, the ghetto fighters, surely did everything humanly possible to save their fellow Jews, and if they failed . . . well, how could they *not* fail, pitted against a military power that had conquered all Europe? But perhaps he was not referring to the ghetto fighters. Perhaps he meant the Jews of the free world, who knew what was happening to the Jews of Europe and did nothing. I didn't ask him what he meant, I only registered the suffering, the bitterness, the brooding shadow of remembered failure in his face and voice as he spoke.

Long afterward I came to understand what he did mean. He *was* speaking of himself and the ghetto fighters. Yitzhak Zuckerman had been the first in Warsaw to read the signs correctly, guessing before anyone else that Hitler was planning the total destruction of the Jews of Poland and of all German-occupied Europe. He had thus also been the first to implore his fellow Jews to rid themselves of the illusion that they might somehow escape the fate awaiting them. They would not escape, and so they must now, immediately, create a fighting force for active resistance — for the sake of Jewish honor and Jewish history, even if without hope of finally prevailing against the Nazis. So where was the failure? They had not organized themselves soon enough. They shouldn't have waited until April 1943, when their numbers had been pitifully reduced by a long succession of death transports to the camps. They should have started earlier, when they were bigger and stronger. They might still have been defeated, but they would have fought longer, killed more Germans, perhaps saved

more Jewish lives. Why they had not started their resistance
sooner was a separate and painful story, and many people, many
forces were to blame for it. But Yitzhak Zuckerman did not exon-
erate himself; he blamed himself no less than he did others. When
I finally recognized the meaning of his remark, I understood better why he had claimed with such passion that he knew what it
was to fail.

We had many talks after that momentous one, the last ones
about two weeks before his death in 1981. But to the end his innermost personality was an unsolved riddle for me. He seemed to
have locked away in his heart many secret sources of pain and to
have gone through much bitter soul searching about the past,
suffered disappointments in his later years, and borne fears and
anxieties, sometimes acute enough to be a torment to his soul,
about the future of our people. But these are only guesses. About
a year before his death, his devoted friend Yosske Rabinowitch of
Kibbutz Na'an taped sixty hours of private talk with him. Perhaps the release of this record will throw some light on the secret
of his brave, suffering soul, the secret that gave him the strength
to meet and survive the incredible challenges of his life while remaining through them all a man of vision and a proud, free Jew.

I knew a great deal about Zivia Lubetkin long before I went to
Poland. She had made a tremendous impression on Yitzhak Tabenkin and Lyova Levite when they knew her in Warsaw as one
of the outstanding young leaders of the Hehalutz movement, and
I understood why soon after I got to Warsaw. She was not beautiful, but there was a distinctively Jewish charm in her black eyes
and hair, her olive complexion, and her fine facial lines. Her
smile — so full of intelligence, warmth, and sincerity — instantly
conquered the heart.

I often heard her speak in public and was struck afresh each
time by the directness, plainness, and baldness of her personal
style. There was no eloquence, no "pathos" in the Hebrew sense,
only clarity of vision, passionate objectivity, and total absence of
self-reference, which combined to give her speeches the force of a
bolt from heaven. They seemed to pierce the minds and hearts of
her audience, for people listened with such intensity as I have seen
few public figures command. She was only twenty-three, yet she

had the moral authority that an older and more experienced leader might envy. She had this stature in part because people knew that she — like Frumka, Yitzhak, and other leaders of the Young Pioneers — had deliberately left the Russian-occupied zone, where she had a good chance of staying alive, to return to the hell of Warsaw and the ghetto. Zivia resolved to share the fate of thousands of her fellow Jews and the hundreds of members of Hehalutz still there: to support and encourage them and, when the time came, to lead the ghetto revolt. But it was not only this heroic selflessness that accounted for the universal recognition of her moral stature. People also knew that there was no gap between what she demanded of others and what she demanded of herself. Zivia cultivated none of the airs of leadership, made no claims for herself, allowed herself no exemptions. In the kibbutz hachshara she chopped logs, worked in the kitchen, the bakery, the laundry — nothing was too menial or too hard for her. Her simplicity and integrity inspired the love and admiration of her peers, and so did her decisiveness, firm hold on reality, and power to encourage and sustain the weak. These qualities raised her to undisputed leadership of the ghetto, and ultimately to the command of the ghetto revolt.

I had many talks with Zivia, usually on lofty subjects such as the meaning of Zionism and the kibbutz, the gap between the ideal and the actual, the always intractable problem of how to realize the ideal in day-to-day life — talks rather like those I had so often with my good friend Moshe Tabenkin at Ein-Harod. Although not melancholy, Zivia was certainly serious, so I remember with particular tenderness an episode that led her to disclose with quiet humor one of the more lighthearted moments of her life. No doubt there had been few such moments in the strenuous, dedicated life to which she had been committed since girlhood.

I once invited her to accompany me on one of my monthly visits to the writer Janusz Korczak. Korczak received us with his usual warmth, asking Zivia many eager questions about her life and work in the kibbutz hachshara and the Young Pioneers movement. He went on to tell us about his last visit to Ein-Harod two years back, and how he had enjoyed getting up at dawn and going to work in the kitchen, helping the elderly women peel potatoes. Next to the kitchen was the bakery, and when he first smelled the freshly baked bread coming from the oven, he remembered, as a child, smelling the same delicious odor wafting from the bakery near his mother's house. At the same moment, he found himself breaking into a song of his childhood. He had no voice to speak of, he assured us, but he sang the long-forgotten song with great enjoyment and went on humming it right through the day.

As we were walking home after our visit Zivia suddenly told me, with a charming half smile, that she had had an experience very similar to Korczak's when she was working in the bakery of her kibbutz hachshara in Keltz. As she drew the freshly baked bread out of the oven, she used to find herself bursting into song — though she, too, was no singer. She was sure it was the smell of the bread that did it. Yes, she said firmly, it was the smell. And the lines that always rose to her lips, she added, were "There in the pleasant land of our fathers / All our hopes will be fulfilled," from a dear old Zionist ditty — the very song I had learned at the age of eight from the august Dr. Schwartzman in Benderri.

When Zivia arrived in Eretz Yisrael in 1946, thousands of people went to Kibbutz Yagur to hear her tell the story of what had happened to the Jews of the Warsaw Ghetto and the rest of Poland. She spoke for a whole day and we listened, wishing she would never stop. Not because there was anything to enjoy in the harrowing tale, but because we wanted to do homage to this great woman, who has since become a symbol of the young Jewish women ghetto fighters who defended the lives and honor of their people.

UNESCO's worldwide Year of the Child in 1981 was dedicated to the memory of Janusz Korczak, the aging Polish Jew who on August 5, 1942, accompanied the two hundred children of his Warsaw orphanage into the death train bound for the gas chambers of Treblinka. The Nazi officer in charge of the transport offered to spare Korczak's life, but he refused to leave his children. With Steffa Wilczinska, his lifelong partner, and the whole staff of the orphanage, he led the caravan of death to the camp.

This was the end of Korczak's extraordinary life, which is now known to most of the world. What is less well known is his con-

Janusz Korczak and I both loved children, movies, and markets. On August 5, 1942, he accompanied the two hundred children of his Warsaw orphanage onto a death train bound for the gas chambers of Treblinka.

nection with Eretz Yisrael and Ein-Harod. I had known Korczak's name since childhood. In the 1920s he was already a famous physician in Poland; an imaginative, boldly experimental educator, dedicated particularly to the education and care of deprived children; and a brilliant writer of stories and plays, as well as philosophical essays that were often poetic and mystical. One of his well-known children's stories, "King Matthew the First," was a favorite of our Polish-born kindergarten teacher, who used to read it to us from the Polish text, translating into Hebrew as she went along.

Korczak was a great correspondent, and his connection with Ein-Harod began with regular exchanges of letters with two of his former pupils who had settled there. On his two visits to Eretz Yisrael, in 1934 and 1936, he spent most of his time at Ein-Harod, becoming close friends with many members and beginning to view it as his second home. After his first visit he wrote his hosts, "It's amazing how one can be enriched by twenty short days like those at Ein-Harod, how much one can learn, understand, appropriate — for many days, and forever."

This feeling was reinforced by Steffa Wilczinska's connection with the kibbutz, which was workmanlike as well as human and warm. Steffa first came to Ein-Harod for several months in 1931, working in the children's houses and becoming an ardent enthusiast of communal education. She returned in 1936, and then decided in 1938 to settle here permanently. She stayed a year, working with the schoolchildren, and waiting for Korczak to decide whether he would join her. In the summer of 1939 he finally decided to come to live in Eretz Yisrael, but he couldn't find the money to make the move. Steffa went back to Warsaw to help him, and by the time they were ready to leave the war had broken out. Steffa stayed in Poland to help him care for the orphans, and they remained together through all the dark days of the ghetto and to their deaths.

Korczak's experiences at Ein-Harod and people's recollections of him form a small saga by themselves, but I will record only my own encounters with him in Poland, starting with our first meeting at his orphanage in early December 1937. Korczak received me with joyous enthusiasm, which I soon learned was the way he reacted to anything or anybody connected with Eretz Yisrael.

"Steffa has told me a great deal about you," he began. Then, without further preamble, he asked eagerly, "What are your plans? What are you going to do here? Tell me, tell me everything!" Among other things, I told him that I was going to edit the monthly journal of the Young Pioneers, and I asked if he would contribute to it regularly. He said he would, but only on one condition: each month I was to visit him at his home for at least four hours. In the first two hours or so I was to tell him — *"in detail,* you understand," he said with great emphasis — everything that had been happening in Eretz Yisrael and at Ein-Harod in particular. After that, I was to tell him the plan for the next issue of the journal, to guide him in deciding on a suitable topic. For the last hour or so we would just talk — the talk of two friends, about anything that came into our heads. Then a few days later I was to come back to pick up his contribution.

It worked out exactly like that. In nearly nineteen months, I missed only one meeting, when I couldn't avoid being away from Warsaw. I consider these visits with Korczak as among the great events of my life, and I think that he appreciated them as much as I did, for he'd often say, "It's a great blessing when an old man like me can find a common language with a young person like you." At sixty he thought of himself as an old man, and although everyone, including his elder sister, referred to him respectfully as "the Doctor," it seemed to me he carried his years very lightly. We discovered several common passions: we both loved children, cinema, and markets, and we shared an endless curiosity about people. Our long talks almost always took place in the apartment he shared with his sister, Anna, not far from the noisy center of downtown Warsaw. His small room was simply furnished, with a big, rather shabby table on which a Polish Bible had a conspicuous place, an old wooden sofa against the wall; a wooden cupboard; a bookcase stuffed with books and pamphlets, and just one picture, of his mother.

Just as we had planned, we always started with my news of Eretz Yisrael and Ein-Harod. He had an excellent memory, for people in particular, and always questioned me about individuals he remembered. The Arab riots that had started before I left were continuing, and the new tower-and-stockade settlements were being built as fast as possible. Korczak had a small map of Eretz

Yisrael, on which he marked the new settlements as they went up. He always asked me to describe each in detail — its climate, its views, the people who had settled there. Then we would go on to our favorite topic, children. He loved to hear my anecdotes about Ein-Harod's children, and he told his own in return. He was inclined to generalize, and often soared into fascinating psychological and moral reflections on the episodes we had exchanged.

In the afternoon we would go out for a walk, usually with the cinema as our destination. Korczak insisted on our seeing each film twice: once to watch the film, the second time to watch the children's reaction to it. Walking home, he would describe in wonderful detail what he fancied to have been the inner dramas of the children's responses to the film — how their imaginations worked on what they saw, transmuting it into something better and more beautiful than the commonplace reality; or, alternatively, creating in imagination a world of the grotesque and monstrous. The Walt Disney Mickey Mouse cartoons, he said, particularly invited the second kind of transformation, and he hated them for exposing children to frightening figures that expanded into nightmares in their imaginations.

We were both very fond of markets, and Warsaw, like other large European cities, was full of them. Korczak had friends in each of the markets we visited: butchers, greengrocers, and porters who hailed him warmly when they caught sight of him, their faces lighting up with pleasure. On one occasion the eminent doctor agreed to enter into a competition with one of his butcher friends, to see which of them could produce the largest number of curses without repeating himself. The Polish language evidently has a rich store of curses, and I could tell they were both doing very well, judging by the shouts of mirth from the bystanders watching the performance. The butcher won in the end, with a highly original threat: "I will swallow you and chew you up so that nothing remains of you, not even the smallest scrap of a turd!" Korczak never minded this sort of coarseness when it was a component of that racy, inventive earthiness he most valued and enjoyed in the speech of the common people.

At our last meeting in June 1939, less than three months before the outbreak of the war, Korczak told me about the two books he most wanted to write. He had been working on the first book for ten years, he said, and opened his cupboard to take out bundle after bundle of notebooks, the raw material of his book. "It will be the book of my life. In two volumes. Each volume the after-midnight conversations of a father and his son. The first night the father talks; the second night, the son. The talks are held in Eretz Yisrael, where the son lives. The father is a doctor. He loved his son all his life, but never found a way of communicating with him; nor the son with the father. Now, in the first frank exchange between them, each tells the other of his spiritual suffering up to this moment. The son was born in the plains, his wife in the mountains of the Caucasus. They met in Eretz Yisrael and they have a small daughter. From crossing the plains with the mountains, a distinguished breed will be born." Korczak firmly believed in the genetic theory of the interbreeding of opposites: here, the potential blessing of crossing plain with mountain. The reason he had never married, he once told me, was genetic: his father had been confined to a mental institution from the time Korczak was a small child, and he had a deadly fear of passing on his father's mental disease to his children.

The other book he wanted to write, *King David the Second*, was to be for children. He said he knew he could write both books only in Eretz Yisrael, and the *King David* only in Jerusalem. So he would go on repeating the traditional prayer of the Jew in exile, "Next year in Jerusalem!" until the dream came true.

My last sight of Korczak was at the station, when he came with Steffa to say good-bye to me. As a parting gift he gave me the Introduction to the book about the father and son. It was a beautiful gesture, and when I got back to Eretz Yisrael, we had it translated into Hebrew and published it under the title "The Religion of the Child." In all I have read of what has been written about Korczak since his death, I have never seen any mention of these two books, which he never lived to write.

By a strange, poignant coincidence, I received a last letter from Korczak at Ein-Harod on September 1, 1939, the very day of the outbreak of World War II. It had been written a week before the German invasion of Poland.

August 22, 1939

My very dear Zerubavel,

   After the [First World] war, we [the orphanage] received American, Swiss, Dutch, and other gifts. I wrote to the English consul, among others, asking him for dust cloths. No reply. After eight months a short notice asked us to pick up a chestful of dust cloths that lasted for ten years.

I asked the Polish consul in Jerusalem to present the children of Eretz Yisrael with a dozen squirrels, lovely creatures. He didn't get the point.

I have read that there are squirrels in India; here they're reddish, there gray. I am sure that if the children write to the English authorities (I don't know to whom), they will certainly send Indian squirrels by airplane. Trees without squirrels are sad and motionless. My idea about a kite game didn't work out (this is important, too); perhaps it will yet. If the adults think the time is not suitable, that it is not the right thing to do, they're wrong. In my story "King David II" there will be a ministry of games and entertainment; the politics of children need to be different. Let the petition for squirrels also be signed by several English soldiers.

You'll see, it will do you good. It seems to me you ought to come again. You should learn to construct kites (at the institute of manual work) and make Bengal lights. It's important.

Nothing new here. The children are in the country. I stayed with them throughout July. I don't want you to answer me if we're going to meet again. Perhaps (if the adults permit) I should write them a letter about the squirrels. Talk to Moshe, Shoshanna, etc. Cordial greetings to our mutual friends, the Simchonis, Gur-Ariye, Mia.

Shalom,
Korczak

The mention of kites in the third paragraph referred to the many talks we had about children's games. I had mentioned that flying kites was a favorite pastime at Ein-Harod, and Korczak had immediately taken up the idea, asking me questions about the direction of the winds there and philosophizing about it in his typical way: "Children living by rivers play at boats. Your children, living with winds, ought to play at kites. Every children's game ought to be competitive. It's not enough just to fly a kite; we have to invent special kite games that will arouse the spirit of competition." Then, together, we tried to imagine suitable kite games with appropriate rules.

Of the two long poems I wrote about Korczak, one is about the kites and its epigraph is taken from his letter.

Korczak's Kites
My idea about a kite game didn't work out . . . ; perhaps it will yet.

An orange snake pursues a red
and above them rises a green one —
No, it's not enough just to stir the imagination
or to inspire daring and ecstasy.
Please understand:
without breathless suspense
there is no children's game . . .

The light of the cigarette flickered between his lips
and he stopped and asked:
Which way do the winds blow in your parts
in the morning? in the evening?
And does the wind usually come from the sea?
Ah, that's good, that's very good! Imagine
how a kite would flutter in the wind
and a fine thread in a child's fist tremble
and glisten gold and blue, deep blue,
like the blue I saw above the Gilboa
when I came to visit you . . .

When I was four or five
I also sent a kite into the sky
and the string broke. My kite
was torn away
and swallowed among the clouds.
Tears filled my eyes
and through my tears I saw
angels' wings
embracing my kite.
Now I am old, as you know. But when bitterness rises
I close my eyes and see before me
white wings among the clouds.

The cigarette went out. We were both silent
in the darkness.

13

The Palmach Years, 1941–1947

FOUNDED IN 1941, the Palmach was designed to be the striking force of the Haganah, permanently mobilized and ready for action in any part of the country or beyond its borders at the call of the high command of the Haganah. Its name is an acronym of the Hebrew words *plugot machatz*, "striking companies"; its symbol was a sword flanked by two sheaves of corn.

From 1941 to 1945, the Palmach fought against the allies and sympathizers of the Axis powers in the Middle East, often in clandestine cooperation with the British army in Egypt and Palestine. After the war, it fought against the British Mandatory power, helping to bring about the end of British rule in Eretz Yisrael and the establishment of an independent, sovereign Jewish State. In Israel's War of Independence the Palmach was the first fully mobilized and seasoned combat force to be thrown into battle against the invading armies of the five Arab states. It won some of the great victories that ensured the survival and continuation of the Jewish State, and it became a legend in its own time. Today it stands as a symbol of the heroic struggle for independence of the restored Jewish nation in Eretz Yisrael.

The Palmach's connection with the kibbutzim was established almost immediately. Most of its fighters and field commanders were young men and women who came from the kibbutzim; and when the Palmach ran out of funds to maintain and develop itself as a fighting force, the Haganah responded to Yitzhak Tabenkin's suggestion that it become a working and fighting force combined.

The kibbutzim had supported the Palmach from the start, so it was a natural enough move for the Palmach to establish all its illegal training bases in the kibbutzim, and to earn its keep by part-time work in them. A normal month in a Palmach fighter's life was divided into an average of fourteen and a half full days' work in the kibbutz, eight and a half days' military training, and seven and a half days' leave. On the whole, the scheme worked perfectly, and the Palmach was able to cover 80 percent of its maintenance costs, receiving the remaining 20 percent, for arms, training, and the pay of its full-time commanders, from the Haganah. As part of the kibbutz work force the fighters had the cover they needed for their illegal military training, and the fields, woods, and orchards provided excellent hiding places for illegal arms caches.

In addition to its military usefulness, the Palmach's intimate relations with the kibbutzim also profoundly influenced its values, code of conduct, and whole way of life as a fighting force. The Palmach, in turn, was a powerful element in the development of the Israel Defense Forces (IDF), which sprang directly from the Haganah to become the army of the State of Israel. It is no accident that in the history of the State's existence a high proportion of the IDF officers have been graduates of the Palmach, who received their first battle and command experience in the struggle against the British or in the War of Independence. Thus, the Palmach's distinctive spirit and style passed into the IDF through the Haganah, and is still felt today.

I became a member of the Palmach the year it was founded and continued without a break until it was dissolved eight years later. After about a year of part-time training in woods and forests, concealed from the eyes of the British, I advanced to full-time mobilization in June 1942 into *Pluga Aleph* (Company Λ), based in Kibbutz Kfar Giladi, the northernmost kibbutz of the country. I soon became education officer of Company A and a year later I was appointed to direct all the illegal Palmach publications, including its monthly magazine. I took part in the weekly meetings of the general staff and, besides editing, advised on all literary matters, helped the commander and deputy commander formulate their orders of the day, and edited their reports, analyses, and addresses to the troops.

The detailed story of the Palmach is contained in the seventy-six issues of *Alon ha-Palmach*, of which I was sole editor from 1943 to 1946. The magazine was later supplemented by *Sefer ha-Palmach*, a massive two-volume publication of official records, eyewitness reports, letters, diaries, poems, and stories about the actions of the Palmach, with maps, photographs, and lists of the fallen, which I collected and edited over a period of nearly three years. These thick volumes preserve not only the actions but also the spirit, the tone, and the moral atmosphere of that brave and anxious time. As I read through them for the first time in forty years, I found the record surprisingly vivid and complete.

Back with startling force came the savagery of the Arab riots, which made planned Jewish self-defense a top priority. Back, too, came memories of late-night reconnaissance trips, to scout hostile Arab villages judged to be strategically important to acquire first-hand knowledge of their layout and to make detailed maps for future use. I recalled the long marches designed to teach us to know every inch of the country, especially those parts in which Jews were forbidden to settle by order of Whitehall. There was instruction in sabotage and night fighting, and naval training that would enable us to cope with illegal Jewish immigration by sea. The Palmach's rescue operations are recorded in full: the overland rescue of Jews from the Arab lands of persecution; the rescue by sea and land of Jews fleeing from Hitler's Europe; and the tragic rescue attempted by a small group of Haganah and Palmach parachutists who were dropped by the British into Nazi-occupied Europe behind the German lines, caught by the Gestapo, and executed.

After 1945, when the struggle for liberation from British Mandatory rule began, the record tells of new Palmach initiatives: the sabotage action of the famous Night of the Bridges, when all but one of the bridges into Jordan, Lebanon, and Syria were destroyed; and the renewed intelligence-gathering activities in the surrounding Arab lands, which were remarkable, even by Palmach standards, for their imagination, daring, and the high risk of death. Most important of all the efforts launched after the war was that of the illegal immigration movement. Palmach people participated at every stage of these exceedingly complicated rescue operations, beginning by crossing European borders to get the refugees to the secret places on the Mediterranean coast or the

Black Sea where the illegal ships awaited them. Fearlessly, they piloted the ships to the shores of Eretz Yisrael where they then had to evade the British naval blockade, smuggle the immigrants safely ashore, and spirit them away to the country's interior. The penalty for failure was the reincarceration of the refugees in the new British detention camps in Cyprus.

On the immigrant ships, the Palmach people were captains, crew, radio operators, medical orderlies, and nurses. If caught by pursuing British destroyers at sea or by the British army on shore, they would mix with the immigrants so that they, too, would be taken to the Cyprus camps, where they would then help the immigrants to organize and, if possible, to escape. From August 1945 to May 1948 sixty-five Aliyah Bet ships brought seventy thousand people to Eretz Yisrael. After the establishment of the State of Israel in May 1948, they were joined by thousands who had been caught by the British and detained in Cyprus.

The legend of the Palmach was created by the great store of tales and anecdotes told and retold by its members, both during their fighting years and long after. Most of the tales were probably authentic, some doubtless apocryphal, but all vividly evoked the life and spirit of the Palmach, as did the famous Palmach songs, whose newly minted Hebrew words were often combined, somewhat incongruously, with traditional Russian and Yiddish melodies. Still sung at every national festival, these were the songs we first sang around our campfires in the remote forests of the Galilee or the Carmel after a hard day's training or a grueling march, in the irrecoverable spirit of comradeship and youth that was the special stamp of the Palmach.

A number of novels, stories, plays, and poems about the Palmach's exploits, way of life, and typical personalities further enriched the Palmach legend: Moshe Shamir's novel *Hu Halach Be Sadot* ("He Walked in the Fields"), later turned into a successful play; Natan Shacham's collection of stories *Dagan ve-Oferet* ("Corn and Lead"), some of which he adapted into plays; and Matti Megged's book of stories *Ha-Migdal ha-Lavan* ("The White Tower"). Chaim Guri, who was known as the Poet of the Palmach for his book of poems *Pirchei Esh* ("Flowers of Fire"), wrote beautiful memorial verses to fallen comrades. O. Hillel's collection of poems *Eretz ha-Tzohorai'm* ("Land of Noon"), set in the Negev, where he had served and fought, was particularly original and Israeli in spirit. And Moshe Tabenkin and I made our own contributions to the Palmach literature. The creative writers of the 1940s as a whole are called the Palmach Generation, although authors like S. Izhar, M. Tabib, and Aharon Megged and such outstanding poets as Amir Gilboa and Abba Kovner were not actually members of the Palmach, and the well-known poet Yehuda Amichai did not even start to write until after the War of Independence.

There was a lighter side to life in the Palmach, embodied by our celebrated mobile theater, the *Tchizbatron* — a compound of the Arabic word *tchizbat,* "a tall story," and the Hebrew *te'atron,* "theater"; thus, "Theater of the Tall Story." The first army entertainment unit of modern Israel, it specialized in humorous and satirical sketches, often hilariously funny, performed by our star comedian, Shaike Ophir. Haim Hefer, who founded the Tchizbatron and wrote most of its material — as well as most of the famous Palmach lyrics — still composes popular songs, writes a regular column of political and social satire in one of the daily newspapers, and received the Israel Prize for his lifelong contribution to the gaiety of the nation. Some of the Palmach's chief performers, including the incomparable Shaike, are current favorite national entertainers: a fair indication of the extreme youth of the Palmach members — commanders, troops, writers, showmen — everybody who had a part in making the legend.

My service began with a short training course in the forest near Kibbutz Alonim. Working hard to make up for all the military training I had missed during my time in Poland, I learned to shoot at a target with live ammunition, to throw grenades, to master the arts of night fighting and reconnaissance. One young instructor, a former pupil of mine in the Working Youth, was particularly kind to me in a nerve-racking moment, when I was about to throw my first grenade under his supervision. Sensing my apprehension as I held the grenade, ready to pull out the safety pin, he patted me on the shoulder and said with a reassuring smile, "Zerubavel, it's the same as making a speech. The first time you're very nervous. Later you get used to it, don't you? Well, don't you worry, you'll get used to this, too!" I did, of course, and rather more painlessly than I got used to making speeches.

We celebrated the end of our training with a farewell party. On that last day I was completing my course in the use of a machine gun when the commander called me aside and said he would exempt me from all further exercises that day if I would compose a poem for the party that night. I refused to miss the exercises, but promised to write something during my two-hour guard duty just before the party. The song I brought was the *Song of the Palmach* (*Shir ha-Palmach*), which soon became the Palmach anthem, sung on all occasions: on marches, at gatherings and rallies, sitting around our campfires, at weddings, and even at the gravesides of fallen comrades. Still sung at all national celebrations, it has also been recorded by Jewish choirs in the United States and elsewhere, and it reached a world audience when it was sung in the film *Exodus*. Each time it is sung anywhere in the world my kibbutz gets a royalty fee, and I enjoy the thought of continuing to make this modest contribution to Ein-Harod's income.

During my first year in the Palmach, as a member of the regional Gilboa Company commanded by Nachum Sarig of Kibbutz Beit Hashita, I spent six days a month in military training and the rest of my time at Ein-Harod, again working in the orchard. In June 1942 I joined the newly mobilized Pluga Aleph, stationed in the north with headquarters at Kibbutz Kfar Giladi. At this point I had to pass a course for NCOs that had been established as the Palmach's basic training course for leadership in the field: for the exercise of independent initiative, resourcefulness, decision making, and so forth. Our night reconnaissance assignment was to go forth in a group of two or three on an undetected visit to an Arab village, and return with some decisive proof that we had been there. My partner, an instructor ten years my junior, was a particularly quick and athletic young man named Aharon ("Aharonchik") Spektor from Kibbutz Hulata.

The Arab village we chose to penetrate was Abel, at the biblical site of Avel Beit-Mo'acha, not far from our base. It was the harvest season, and we knew that the Arab villagers protected their wheat stacks by sleeping on top of them, always with a pitcher of water by their side. Aharonchik decided that we would climb up one of the stacks, silently remove the pitcher of water from beside the sleeping Arab, and carry it back *with* the water as proof of having accomplished our mission. He purposely chose the harvest field to avoid the dogs of the village, whose barking would give us away if we got too close to them.

As we approached the field the dogs did start to bark, having caught our scent even at that distance. Following the rules we had been taught, we immediately lay down on the ground on our stomachs, and stayed down, completely silent, until the dogs calmed down. Then we crawled forward on our stomachs until we reached one of the stacks, where we lay for a while, scarcely breathing, till we were sure the Arab was fast asleep. Slowly, cautiously, we climbed up the side of the stack, taking the utmost care not to shake it. I maneuvered myself within arm's length of the pitcher, held my breath, stretched out my hand, and seized it. I held it aloft as we climbed down the side of the stack and then crawled back to the edge of the field, again silently. The dogs barked when we rose and started to walk, but it didn't matter; we had accomplished our mission. It was my first experience of our training program's individual stealth tactic, and Aharonchik was satisfied with my debut.

I was less successful in another training episode with Aharonchik, at Kibbutz Negba, then the southernmost kibbutz. We had been hurried to the "southern front" because the news had reached the country that Rommel was approaching Egypt, and though our little guerrilla force was scarcely expected to stop his advance, we were sent to carry out sabotage actions behind the German lines if and when the Germans reached the country. Our field training included fence jumping, wall climbing, finding cover in rocks, bushes, caves, and so on — and jumping from heights. For practice, Aharonchik took us to an abandoned hut, told us to climb on to the roof, one at a time, and jump to the ground, a distance of about ten feet. He went first and, being the athlete he was, did the jump easily. But his trainees — all except one — showed a distinct reluctance to follow his lead. I was the exception. Feeling it my duty as officer for education and culture to set an example, I climbed up and jumped. Alas, my jump was less expert than Aharonchik's, and my attempt to set an example resulted in a broken leg and hand that put me into plaster for several weeks.

However, there was one compensation: I was sent home to recuperate, and as our home leaves were infrequent, this was a rare privilege. Bedridden and surrounded by stacks of books from the kibbutz library, I compiled a selection of stories and poems of Jewish heroism through the ages, from biblical times to that time.

It was the first of its kind in Hebrew, and although the publishers gave it the rather banal title *Heritage of Heroism,* it was widely used in the Palmach for readings around campfires and on festive occasions. It even became a modest best-seller, going into many editions and selling more than thirty thousand copies by 1945. It also became a favorite gift for boys on their bar mitzvahs; the unfortunate son of a good friend of mine received *ten* copies for his celebration. I don't suppose that could happen today, but it could in that simpler, more naively idealistic time, when the uplift of tales of Jewish heroism tended to be enjoyed without ironic reservations.

By the time I participated in the famous action of the Palmach known as the Night of the Bridges, I was a member of the general staff of the Palmach and, like all officers, went along at my own request.

The official bulletin issued by Palmach headquarters the following morning, June 19, 1946, started as follows:

> On the night of June 17–18, 1946, our forces attacked along the length of the borders of western Eretz Yisrael in order to destroy the road and railway bridges to the neighboring countries. Eleven bridges were attacked. Of these, ten were completely destroyed or severely damaged and one remained intact.

My unit destroyed the Sheik Hussein Bridge, spanning the Jordan River from a point near Beit-She'an. Our group — composed of a reconnaissance scout, two saboteurs, seven men to cover the saboteurs, and a commander — slept at Kibbutz Maoz Chaim that night. At about 2:00 A.M. we set off behind our scout, carrying our ammunition, which had been hidden at Maoz Chaim. (We called our secret arms caches *sliks* from the Hebrew word *le-salek,* "to conceal.") As one of the cover people, I was instructed to lie on the ground facing west toward the road to Beit-She'an, where there was a British police station. At exactly the appointed time, we heard the bridge explode. The shooting started immediately: from the Jordanian guards on the other side of the bridge, from the Palestine border police on our side. We waited for our two saboteurs to emerge safely from among the flying bullets, then started to withdraw according to plan.

Instead of going straight back to Maoz Chaim, we made a wide circle of more than three kilometers, most of the time running through plowed fields (which we sprinkled liberally with pepper to confuse the police dogs that might be sent after us) and wading through fish ponds to cover our tracks, all the while holding our weapons above our heads to prevent them from getting wet. We reached Maoz Chaim at dawn, put our weapons back into their slik, had hot coffee and sandwiches, and then, dressed in normal work clothes, we boarded the first bus to Afula, as if we were innocent workers going off to work.

The Palmach's bulletin on the Night of the Bridges ended: "These wide-ranging actions, covering all the borders of the country, demanded meticulous planning and perfect coordination . . . The coordination was well handled, and the operation as a whole successful."

As a whole, yes; but we paid a heavy price for the one failure, at the Keziv Bridges over the Achziv River, not far from Nahariya. When our men were within a few dozen yards of the target, they were spotted by the enemy, who immediately opened up heavy fire, killing one man. Then, as some of our men were evacuating Arab villagers who lived near the bridges, an enemy flare struck the main explosive charge as it was being placed under the railway bridge. There was a tremendous explosion, and thirteen of our men, including the commander of the operation, were killed.

The Palmach had reason to be proud of having observed its ethical code, avoidance, as far as possible, of loss of life, in this action as in all others; it justified the Palmach bulletin's claim that "wherever possible villagers or policemen were evacuated from the danger zone, or warned in good time." But the loss of the fourteen was a heavy blow, the largest number we had lost in a single action. Two of them were good friends of mine, gifted young men and among the most promising of the young Palmach leaders. We felt that our war of liberation from British rule had really started.

As I mentioned earlier, illegal immigration was another great national service undertaken by the Palmach, and to this end we formed a naval unit, *Palyam,* whose main task was to escort the illegal immigrant ships from the European ports of embarkation through the British blockade to the shores of Eretz Yisrael, guid-

ing them according to instructions to secluded spots on the coast-
line.

Once an immigrant ship had been brought into the harbor, the
Palmach rescue units took over, carrying the immigrants ashore
in small boats and quickly dispatching them to kibbutzim or moshavim or agricultural villages — always, of course, with the cooperation of the settlements. One of the first rescue operations I
participated in began on the night of November 23, 1945, when
an immigrant ship came in to shore below Kibbutz Sh'fayim, not
far from Tel Aviv. Many sand dunes and bushes provided cover,
and all the approach roads and wadis were guarded by Palmach
units, ready to ambush any British police or army patrols that
might suddenly appear to interfere. I was in the unit appointed to
bring the immigrants ashore. The Palmach commander on the
shore communicated by radio with his counterpart on the ship,
while the rest of us lay still in our hiding places, awaiting our
orders.

I remember the exhilaration that seized us all as we saw the
small cargo boat emerge from the darkness, swaying on the waves
like an empty nutshell. My intense emotion seemed to shut out
the sound of the sea. As the Palmach people started lowering
group after group of immigrants into lifeboats, we waded into the
sea to meet them and help them ashore, carrying children, the elderly, the sick, and the weak in our arms. As soon as we had emptied a boat of its human load, it returned to the ship to fetch
another. We worked in silence, with tremendous inner excitement, sensing the refugees' bewilderment and pain, but also seeing tremulous joy in their eyes. Words were inadequate to express
our emotions, and we embraced and kissed without speaking.

A small boy, of six or seven, with big eyes, clung to my neck in
dumb silence as I carried him through the water. I stroked him
and whispered tender words in his ear, but nothing could rouse
him from his state of shock — he just gazed at me, his eyes frozen.
When we reached the shore, a young girl from the first-aid team
put a slice of orange into his mouth, and the cool sweetness
seemed to breathe life into him at last. His eyes lit up, a smile flit-
ted across his face, and when I put him down he bent to the earth
whispering, "Eretz Yisrael, Eretz Yisrael!"

Most of the new arrivals — about two hundred in all — were
safely unloaded when a British destroyer appeared and drew up

alongside the boat. Immigrants continued to leap into the small boats, and we hurried them ashore. Mercifully the British did not yet shoot at the boats (though they were to start doing this soon afterward). They arrested the immigrants and Palyam people who remained on the ship, while we watched from the shore in silent fury. But we knew we were David pitted against Goliath, and we were happy enough with our small victory.

My stray encounter with the British police on a street in Tel Aviv proved to me the efficiency of the Haganah's intelligence service, SHAI, which General Evelyn Barker, commander of the British Army in Palestine, once grudgingly acknowledged to be a perfect intelligence system.

I was walking peacefully along Shenkin Street, carrying, between the double walls of my big briefcase, a bundle of the most recent issue of our illegal *Alon ha-Palmach,* when I was stopped by a group of British police who were searching for members of the Jewish underground. With others they had stopped, I was made to stand against a wall with hands upraised while they first conducted a body search and then went through my briefcase. They didn't think of the double walls, found nothing, and released me. Although these searches were common enough, I was astonished to learn, just an hour later, when I walked into the office of Yisrael Galili, a member of the high command of the Haganah, that he had already heard about my little adventure. How did he know? I asked. Our intelligence people, who made it their business to be wherever there was a British police patrol, had witnessed the whole episode — knowing who I was, they were ready to do some quick rescue work if necessary. They didn't have to that time, but it was good to know they were watching over me.

By the summer of 1946 the struggle against the British had intensified, and "Black Sabbath" of June 29, 1946, was the British reply to our Night of the Bridges ten days earlier. First, they arrested and incarcerated in Latrun all the members of the Zionist Executive except Ben-Gurion, who was out of the country. Then, for once outwitting our SHAI, British intelligence tracked down the location of Palmach headquarters at Kibbutz Misra and found a list of the names of all the Palmach members in the country. They immediately called out their paratroopers — whom we called anemones because they wore red berets — an elite force of thousands of men, tanks, Bren carriers, trucks, and jeeps and ordered them to surround all the kibbutzim in which there were Palmach bases. The troops were to search and arrest everyone on the list.

Ein-Harod, known as a hotbed of Palmach activity, was one of the first kibbutzim to be surrounded on that memorable Black Sabbath. Many Ein-Harod Palmach members, including me, happened to be at home that Saturday. We knew that the British had uncovered our Palmach headquarters, so we were not entirely surprised when, at about 1:30 A.M., our guards reported unusual movements of British forces on the main road from Haifa to the Emek. By 4:30 they had surrounded Ein-Harod with tanks and hundreds of troops. They set up a barbed-wire screening pen alongside the main road, and the British commander demanded that all the men aged sixteen to forty come there to identify themselves. He gave our mukhtar exactly four minutes to bring them in.

At the end of the four minutes, the tanks and carriers burst into the kibbutz, followed by the paratroopers. They beat the two guards at the gate and other members with their rifle butts and pulled them into the pen. The area commander of the Haganah had ordered us not to shoot, and to offer only passive resistance, which is what the British had to contend with all that day. When the troops reached the lawn in front of the dining hall, they found most of the men, women, and children sitting there, holding hands and singing. A heavy tank was brought up to disperse them; when they refused to move, the commander ordered the tank to run at them. One woman would have been crushed had we not pulled her aside just in time. The troops then fell upon the crowd, hitting out with their rifles and fists, pushing and pulling people toward the screening pen, badly injuring many.

My wife, Susi, eight months pregnant with our second daughter, was out in the chicken coop, feeding the chickens, when a group of paratroopers burst in and started shoving her out to the pen with their bayonets. She resisted and was badly bruised by the assault.

By about 9:30 they had herded everyone into the pen — old men and women and children, as well as the rest of us. We had continued our passive resistance, refusing to go, crying out in chorus, "Nazis! Nazis!" In the pen we refused to identify ourselves. When asked our names, we answered, "A Jew of Eretz Yisrael"; when they demanded to see our identity cards, we said, "No identity cards." Those of us in the Haganah and Palmach had burned ours as soon as we saw the troops approaching.

In the end they released the women, the very young, and the very old, but they arrested and piled into their trucks more than three hundred members of the kibbutz. They refused to allow the wounded of the kibbutz to be taken to the hospital in Afula, so the kibbutz doctor had to cope with them on his own. When members of neighboring kibbutzim tried to come to our rescue during the attack, the troops shot at them, and two men of Kibbutz Tel Amal were killed. In the attack on Tel Yosef, our nearest neighbor, they burst into the cowshed and killed Chaim Harodi, a member of our Company A who was doing cowman's duty on that free Sabbath at home.

At midday they took us off, first to the British detention camp at Atlit, and from there to Rafiah in the Gaza Strip.

Yes, it was a black day all right. Yet even at the time we felt that they were not all brutes. When we called them Nazis, most of them just laughed, evidently not caring a hoot. But a few, it seemed, did care, and they appeared not to like what they were doing.

More than twenty years later, I discovered by sheer chance just how uneasy these few were. In 1968 I spent a month at Exeter in England, to improve my English at an international summer school for foreign students. One of the instructors, a former army man, became quite excited when he heard I was from Kibbutz Ein-Harod in Israel. "I was there once, you know," he said, with a curious expression on his face.

"Oh, really? When?" I asked, wondering whether I had been there and what business he might have had at Ein-Harod.

"Oh, it was in 1946, the summer of 1946," he answered, his odd expression more marked.

A light broke, and I asked, "It wouldn't have been the twenty-ninth of June, would it?"

"Yes," he answered, shaking his head grimly. "It was that Saturday, June twenty-ninth. Ah, that was a bad time — a bad time!"

That's all he said, but the way he said it was enough to persuade me that he was one of the British soldiers who had not liked what they were doing that day. We became good friends and talked often about that last bad period of the British Mandate.

The sequel to Black Sabbath was imprisonment for us all. We were kept at Atlit for about three days, for preliminary interrogation. In a letter we wrote from Atlit, which was smuggled out to Ein-Harod and published in our *Yoman,* we gave a full account of the unpleasantness of those three days with our interrogators. Shouting and pushing, they took us, one by one, into the interrogation room, demanded we identify ourselves, and took our fingerprints. Three of the younger men were taken into a separate room, where they were beaten and tortured. The British, to impress on us what was happening, made sure we could hear their screams. Desperately thirsty, we asked for water. When it was brought in a can by an Arab orderly, the interrogator seized it and poured it all onto the floor. Knowing how hungry we were, he ordered omelets and fresh bread to be brought, then dashed them to the floor, saying, "You'll get no food or water until you tell us your real names." We hated him for his petty sadism, and refused to the end to answer any of his questions.

From Atlit we were taken to the huge British army camp at Rafiah. There, 1642 members of the Haganah were held prisoner by British soldiers. We were kept in the regional groups in which we had been captured, not knowing how long our incarceration would last. Fortunately, a tremendous outcry arose from the Jewish governing bodies in Eretz Yisrael and the World Zionist Executive in London, and great pressure was brought to bear on the Mandatory government to release us. In the end they did, but slowly, group by group, continuing the war of nerves. Most of the members of Ein-Harod, including me, were released at the end of six weeks, but others were confined for 130 days. Yisrael Galili admirably summed up the Black Sabbath in *Alon ha-Palmach*: "The aim of the attack of the British authorities was to break the Haganah, confiscate the arms of the Jews, destroy the elected leadership of the Zionist movement, and demolish the Jewish settlements of the country. But they did not succeed in achieving any of these aims."

At the request of the high command of the Haganah, I completed a special project during the last two years before the War of Independence: a six-hundred-page book of testimony, documents, and other records of the undercover actions carried out by the Haganah for the Allies outside Palestine during World War II. *Magen Baseter* ("Hidden Shield") described in detail actions of sabotage, espionage, special military missions carried out for the British in the Middle East (for which the British did not wish to be known as sponsors), and operations against the Nazis in Europe to liberate Allied prisoners of war and rescue Jews.

One of the sabotage efforts resulted in tragic failure. A commando unit of twenty-three Haganah men and one British liaison officer was sent to blow up the oil refineries in Tripoli, under Vichy French rule. The mission was never carried out, and the entire group of twenty-four vanished, meeting a fate that remains a mystery. This was the heaviest casualty toll the Haganah had sustained in a single action, and it fell to me to visit the twenty-three bereaved Jewish families to collect material about the men they had lost. It was my first experience of a harrowing duty in the interests of history and commemoration, but it was one I would repeat many times in the years that followed.

The most famous of the actions against the Nazis in Europe was that of a group of thirty-two British-trained paratroopers of the Haganah, including three young women, who were sent by the British to try to liberate Allied prisoners of war in Hungary, Austria, Rumania, Slovakia, and Italy. The group also intended to seize this chance to save Jews from the mass graves and gas chambers. Some succeeded, especially in Slovakia, where they helped to form anti-Nazi partisan groups. But seven, among them Enzo Sereni and Hannah Szenesh, were caught by the Nazis and killed.

Enzo Sereni was the brave Italian Jew who had been our guide in Paris. Early in the war, Enzo distinguished himself in military intelligence work for the Allies in Egypt and by his valuable anti-Nazi broadcasts in Italian. When the British sent him on a military mission to Iraq, he contrived to organize young Iraqi Jews for pioneer immigration to Eretz Yisrael. In 1944 he volunteered for the paratroop force the British planned to parachute into German-occupied northern Italy. Dropped by mistake near a German fortification, he was immediately caught, sent to Dachau, and killed. He was forty-four.

Hannah Szenesh came to Eretz Yisrael from Hungary in 1939 to become a member of Kibbutz Sdot Yam near Caesarea. She had written poetry and stories from an early age, and continued to write, now in Hebrew, in Eretz Yisrael. In 1943, at twenty-two, she volunteered for paratroop action in her native Hungary, hoping like the rest to liberate prisoners of war and rescue Jews. In March 1944 she and three men were dropped into Yugoslavia to cross into Hungary. She got to Hungary, but she was quickly caught by the Gestapo, imprisoned and tortured, tried by a military court, and executed on November 7, 1944.

Hannah Szenesh has become an enduring symbol of the heroes and martyrs of the Eretz Yisrael underground in World War II, and her story has been told and retold, most memorably in Marie Syrkin's *Blessed Is the Match*. The title is taken from the opening line of one of Hannah's poems, which poignantly expresses her idealistic spirit and readiness for a sacrificial death:

> Blessed is the match that is consumed in kindling flame,
> Blessed is the flame that burns in the secret fastness of the heart,
> Blessed is the heart with strength to stop its beating for honor's
>   sake,
> Blessed is that match which is consumed in kindling flame.

My own work on "Hidden Shield" taught me some important lessons — above all, to take pride in the greatness of the Jewish spirit. I also learned lessons that were to prove of great value in my subsequent literary undertakings: for example, the art of eliciting a life story from someone with no gift for narration; that a personality may reveal itself in personal, intimate letters in a way it never does in day-to-day encounters; and that simple people who never conceived of themselves as heroes could nevertheless act heroically, making history by their heroism.

The book almost became a casualty of the war the Arabs were conducting against our incipient Jewish State for nearly six months before the State of Israel was established. It had been printed and was waiting to be bound in the *Palestine Post* (now the *Jerusalem Post*) printing house in Jerusalem when a massive bomb destroyed the building, and the book along with it. Fortunately, the plates survived, the book was reprinted, and it appeared in April 1948. Because the Haganah and Palmach were still illegal, no names appeared in the first edition. Only in the second and third editions was it possible to disclose the names of the heroes and heroines who did their work behind the hidden shield.

14

Yitzhak Sadeh

THE EARLY YEARS of the Palmach were dominated by the towering figure of its founder and first commander Yitzhak Sadeh, always known as the Old Man. Fifty-one when he founded the Palmach, Sadeh had come to Eretz Yisrael in 1920 from Russia, where he had been a champion wrestler and an officer in the Russian army. In Eretz Yisrael, he worked as a master quarryman and at half a dozen other jobs, wrote and published stories, and became a leading commander of the Haganah and the idol of the young fighters of the Palmach. Yigal Allon, his most talented and beloved protégé, who succeeded him in 1945 as commander of the Palmach, put his finger on some of his personal characteristics and historic achievements when he described Sadeh as "that bespectacled, warm, crumpled, ordinary-looking bon-vivant-cum-poet, that great lover of country, of women, and of the implacable logic of history, who symbolized most vividly the fighting spirit of the underground, and discovered and taught war to a group of teenagers destined, within only a few years, to lead the Army of Israel."

Yes, he taught us war, by methods he invented himself or was the first to introduce. He was a compendium of firsts: the first to insist on active defense — taking the initiative, preempting the enemy's action, instead of passively waiting for attack; the first to teach us to fight in small units of two to four and to fight at night, "making the night our friend," as he used to say. He was the first to introduce the use of explosives, having learned the art of blast-

ing as a quarrier, the first to teach us ambushing, sniping, and
other skills of guerrilla warfare. The first also to teach us to fight
in big formations in the valleys and mountains, he expanded the
size of the Palmach's fighting units until it reached battalion size
and ultimately, in the War of Independence, brigade size. He introduced antitank warfare, although our only antitank weapon
was the very primitive "Molotov cocktail." He initiated air warfare in embryonic form and naval warfare, by founding the Palyam. He insisted on having Palmach women in combat units,
and was among the first to introduce the mixed task force, combining tanks and artillery with infantry, which later proved its
value in the War of Independence. And he vigorously fostered the
most original of the strategic and tactical doctrines of the Haganah, later adopted and developed by the Israel Defense
Forces — the famous "indirect" method of attack, derived from
Liddell Hart's unconventional theories of warfare and adapted to
our special conditions and needs. Yigal Allon was to put these
doctrines to the practical test with memorable success in his campaigns in the War of Independence. Sadeh himself commanded
some of the most decisive battles in the first stages of the war and,
as commander of the IDF's first tank brigade, played a vital part
in the conquest of the Negev.

It was an extraordinary military career by any standard, and
Yigal Allon could justly speak of his mentor as "a military genius
of world caliber, one of the greatest commanders in Jewish history, the father of modern warfare." But more than military genius made Yitzhak Sadeh the force that built the Palmach and
molded our lives; it was also his humanity, his wisdom, his sense
of moral values, his visionary grasp of the history and destiny of
his people. He was a father, brother, and commander rolled into
one. And for some, like me, his humanist's love of poetry and his
old-fashioned belief in its moral value, its power to inspire and
fortify the soul, had a further irresistible appeal.

I became well acquainted with him when I was put in charge of
the underground publications of the Palmach, and thus came
under his direct command. Our first meeting made such a strong
impression on me that I recorded it immediately afterward.

I had come to talk about my new job and hear his views about
our illegal monthly magazine, *Alon ha-Palmach*. Palmach headquarters were in Kibbutz Alonim, among the trees of the wood

surrounding Alonim, at some distance from the kibbutz itself. I found Yitzhak sitting under a large spreading oak tree, his back against the trunk. As usual, he sat cross-legged in the oriental style, and his big bald head reflected the play of light and shadow in the leaves above. He congratulated me on being punctual, and said, "Well, sit down and tell me what you've brought me in that little satchel of yours." His voice was warm and friendly, immediately putting me at ease.

I outlined the plan I had prepared for *Alon ha-Palmach*, explaining that the name would not appear on the cover; instead, there would be a blank space and each reader would imagine the name there and read it silently — as in the Jewish underground against the Nazis, when the members carried a flagpole without a flag and stood at attention by the bare pole, imagining the blue and white flag with the golden Star of David in the center. The idea appealed to him: "That's what I like — thinking out a thing first before you act!" he said. Then, as if struck by a fresh thought: "Certainly we must be businesslike in what we do. But I don't like the kind of efficiency that boasts of being businesslike and practical and professional. In our enterprise, which is to train our young people for defense and fighting, we mustn't use Prussian methods — the methods of the barracks, which are so attractive to those for whom this is the ideal of military competence. No, my friend, we don't yet have a nation like all the other nations, and we don't have an army like other armies. And there is no one except ourselves who will carry a Jewish gun to save us and liberate us — even though we have to carry these guns under cover of darkness!"

In the same ruminative way, intensely concentrated yet relaxed, he went on to talk of the uniqueness of every nation and the corresponding distinctiveness of its army, of heroism, of poetry, and of the special character of the Palmach.

He laughed as he said, "In my time I've seen Russian partisans and White and Red troops, I know the German army and the Russian army, and I can tell you that all cats are not gray at night! Each is different from the other, and we are different, too." Passing his hand over his bald crown, he paused, then went on. "People say that heroism is always heroism. But the question is, What is the basis of the heroism? And how do we discover it in ourselves? To show courage you don't have to be a hero; only a maniac is never afraid. But a man who knows why he is doing what he is doing, and is wholeheartedly ready to do it, also knows how to conquer fear. And that's how he becomes a hero."

"Are you saying," I broke in, "that the concept of heroism is not really a military concept, but, well, a human one?"

"Yes, yes, exactly!" he answered, and I detected a gleam of affection in the look he gave me through his glasses. "Wherever you find someone sacrificing himself for others, there you have heroism. And that's what we want to develop in the Palmach — the inner strength, the spiritual strength, of our people. Cynics call this having a tender conscience, being conscience stricken, and so forth — you know the kind of talk. But we know that this is man's preeminence, as it says in Ecclesiastes: his conscience, his moral superiority, *is* his preeminence. And this is what can make us brave when necessary." Then he suddenly reverted to the first topic of our talk. "Yes, that's good — the unseen name on the cover of *Alon ha-Palmach*. Yours is a sound intuition — and true to the spirit of our formation!"*

An invisible warbler started to sing in the thicket of the oak above our heads. The branches quivered, and I inhaled the clean smell of leaves saturated with sun and sea wind. An interval of silence fell upon our talk without our feeling it.

Then Yitzhak said quietly, "Well, have you written any new poems lately?"

I laughed, and asked, "Am I under your direct command for this, too?"

He smiled broadly. "Even if you're not, you mustn't think you're exempt from writing poetry just because you're in harness in the Palmach! I tell you, poetry is of the first importance to us. And precisely *not* the poetry that speaks in soldiers' language, as if it were coming out of a trumpet on parade, the way it's always been. No, Pushkin didn't write poems to rouse his countrymen to war. But his poetry molded human beings, and that's poetry after my own heart. You smell it, you don't just hear it. You taste the words, you don't just understand them. That is how Pushkin wrote in *Yevgeny Onegin*." He quoted four lines of the poem in Shlonsky's Hebrew translation and went on, "*Chabibi,* my friend,

*For security reasons, we always referred to the Palmach as *ha-chativa,* "the formation," the abridged form of *ha-chativa ha-meguyesset,* "the mobilized formation."

poetry is like good wine: it unites comrades, it lifts up the soul, and it inspires soul-searching. And these things, most of all, are what we need in the Palmach. I tell you, if we don't cultivate the spirit of comradeship that's beyond words and orders — that's in the blood, as the fellows say — we won't have the human beings we want: neither a fighting power nor a creative power. And we have to work for this comradeship every day, every hour. For the moment may come when you and I face the enemy alone. Just we two, and the life of each depends on the other. That's all, and that's the whole secret of our strength — that we know it, and live by it."

Then, without transition, "And now, let's go and have lunch! It's Wednesday, and we have meat for lunch every Wednesday. Mind you don't stint yourself. Help yourself liberally, take a good generous portion, don't be shy!" In one sweeping movement he leaped from his seat, stood erect, put his hand on my shoulder, and pulled me after him.

His gusto for meat at lunch, and for all other sensuous pleasures was typical of him, as was his love of fun and something I have to call wittiness in action — the way his extraordinary presence of mind and resourcefulness in emergency situations often expressed themselves. I was a passive partner in one cherished demonstration of his witty presence of mind which, for art's sake, I call Yitzhak Sadeh and the *Lustknabe*.

We had attended an evening meeting in Haifa and were spending the night in a modest hotel often used by visiting kibbutz members. As usual, we shared a room to save money. We were in our pajamas when we heard a car draw up below the window and a voice say in English, "Up you go, boys!" Within minutes footsteps approached our door. "It's British police coming to search!" Yitzhak hissed. Then, without hesitation, he said, "Quick, take off your pajamas, throw them on the floor, and lie on the bed!" As I obeyed, there was a peremptory knock on the door. In the same moment, Yitzhak stripped off his pajamas, threw them down by his bed, and, stark naked, strode to the door. He flung it wide open, glared at the two British policemen standing there, and snapped, "What do you want?" They took one look at Yitzhak's huge naked form, looked past him at me, small, naked, and doubtless tense, on the bed, and mumbled apologetically, "Oh, sorry, sir! So sorry, sir!" And they retreated without another word. When the door was safely closed again, Yitzhak said, with a chuckle, "Trust an Englishman to understand!" I gazed at him in speechless admiration.

This was Yitzhak Sadeh in one mood. In another, he was the tender compassionate Jew, comforting a Jewish "sister" — just off an illegal immigrant ship — who had been forced into whoredom in the Nazi concentration camp she had survived. As commander of the Palmach, and of our anti-British resistance movement, he made a point to be on the seashore whenever possible, helping to bring the illegal immigrants to safety. He often made a summary of the "lessons" to be drawn from these experiences, many of which were published under the pseudonym Yud Noded (Y. Wanderer), in a special column reserved for him in one of our weeklies. This particular lesson, published in his book *Misaviv la-Medura,* he called "My Sister on the Shore."

> It is dark. My sister stands before me on the wet sand. Dirty, ripped clothes, tangled hair, bare feet, head cast down. She stands, sobbing hard. I know: tattooed on her body, "For Officers Only."
>
> My sister sobs and speaks. "Why am I here? Why did they bring me here? Do I deserve to have healthy young men risk their lives for me? . . . There is no place for me in this world. I shouldn't be alive."
>
> I embrace my sister, clasp her shoulders, and say to her, "There *is* a place for you in the world, my sister — one single special place. Here, in this land, our land, you shall live. Here we give you our love. You are black and comely, my sister. You are black, because you are branded with suffering. But your comeliness is more to me than all other comeliness, and sacred beyond all other sacredness.
>
> Darkness. My sister stands on the wet sand. Dirty, ripped clothes, tangled hair . . .

The night I participated in the landing of illegal immigrants, the revolving searchlight of the British destroyer suddenly revealed Yitzhak standing on the shore, drawn up to his full height, holding two toddlers in his arms, his face radiant. A few days later he published a brief note in his column: "Listen, all you young people! When the hour comes, throw yourselves onto the scales, forcefully, courageously. It will have its effect. It will change the balance." No one knew better than Yitzhak Sadeh how to throw himself onto the scales with all his strength, and he changed the balance like no one else of his generation.

15

The Palmach in the War of Independence

EVERY WAR is hard and bitter, but the War of Independence, from 1947 to 1949, was the most devastating in our history. Those too young to remember it recall the horrors of the Yom Kippur War of October 1973 and the Lebanon War of 1982. But our losses in the War of Independence were even greater. At its end we counted 6470 dead, a third of them civilians, out of a total Jewish population of 650,000 — a loss proportionately greater than that sustained in World War II by the United States, Great Britain, and France combined.

The State of Israel was founded on May 14, 1948. One day later, it was invaded by Arab armies from Transjordan, Syria, Lebanon, Iraq, and Egypt, reinforcing the local Palestinian Arab forces who had been waging war against us since November 1947. Our weaponry was pitifully inadequate to meet the assault, and we fought the first crucial stages of the war with only a handful of rifles and machine guns, a few homemade mortars and Molotov cocktails, and nine light aircraft, which we used for reconnaissance and communications, for evacuating the wounded, and occasionally for shooting and throwing grenades.

For sixteen long months we fought in a narrow strip of land along the Mediterranean, with our noses virtually touching those of the Jordanians in Jerusalem, and in the narrow ten-kilometer "waist" of the country between Netanya, just north of Tel Aviv, and Kalkilya in Jordan. If we nevertheless survived our first ordeal by fire and won our War of Independence, we did so because

our fighters had the courage and tenacity that came from knowing they were fighting for the very existence of their homeland —
to save their families, their friends, and all the Jews of Israel from
being massacred if they lost.

As the only fully mobilized force of the Haganah, the Palmach
was thrown straight into the first battles of the war, charged with
carrying out the defensive and offensive operations required to
hold crucial positions while the Haganah was readying its reserves. In June 1948, when the Palmach was sworn into the new
national army of the month-old State of Israel, it stood at three-
brigade strength, with 6262 fighters, 1062 of whom were women.
In the north the Yiftach Brigade, under the command of Yigal
Allon, ensured our retention of the Galilee, including Safed. In
the Jerusalem Corridor the Harel Brigade, commanded first by
Yitzhak Rabin and then by Yosef Tabenkin, overcame many failures and setbacks before finally lifting the siege of Jerusalem. In
the south the Negev Brigade, commanded by Nachum Sarig,
helped to save the small, scattered Jewish settlements of the
Negev from being overrun, and to hinder the Egyptian army's
northward advance toward Tel Aviv, before the Yo'av and Horev
campaigns finally liberated the whole Negev from the invaders.
Nearly one quarter of the 4470 Jewish fighters killed in the war
were members of the Palmach.

Like all the officers of the general staff of the Palmach, I was not
attached to a combat unit and did not fight in any of the battles
of the War of Independence. However, as the Palmach's officer for information and education, I traveled constantly from
one battlefront to another, was often in forward headquarters
during battles, and was present at many GS planning sessions
for the Palmach campaigns. Of all the events I witnessed, the
two that truly stand out in my memory are the crucial battle of
Malkieh in the Yiftach campaign, led by Yigal Allon, and a
small, human episode at Abu Ghosh in the Jerusalem Corridor
during one of the worst periods of the Harel Brigade's fight for
Latrun.

My account of the Malkieh battle, published in *Pirkei Palmach*
under the title "Forty-eight Hours of Malkieh," was compiled
from my talks with three field commanders, all of whom became

well-known generals in the Israel Defense Forces: Dan Laner, battalion commander at Malkieh; Rehavam (Gandhi) Ze'evi, platoon commander; and Yeshayahu Gavish, another platoon commander, who was wounded in the battle.

Malkieh, an Arab village on the Lebanese border, had been occupied by the Lebanese army in preparation for the invasion of Galilee on May 15, 1948. They had brought in troops and heavy armor, and were just waiting for D-Day and zero hour to go into action. Yigal Allon planned to surprise them by attacking the Lebanese forces forty-eight hours earlier, on the night of May 13. But, owing to a reconnaisance error, our men arrived too late and had to launch their attack on the night of the fourteenth instead, just as the enemy was ready to invade. The commanders' description of the action highlights the typical features of a key battle in the War of Independence: the lack of arms and equipment; the absence of communications and logistic support; the ferocious fire power of the enemy; the mounting casualties; the men's despair; the commanders' efforts to rally them; and the final spurt of hope, energy, and courage that made them go on firing with what they had until the enemy broke and the victory was theirs.

> Our task was to throw everything we had into that battle. We had no armor, not enough arms or ammunition, not enough cartridge belts or other personal equipment. Some of the men had no boots and were wearing sandals . . . We had made an exhausting march on zigzagging paths in the mountains, carrying our provisions and equipment on our backs. There was no regular communication with our far-off base. Some of our fighters, with no arms at all, were waiting for "loot" to drop into our hands from the fallen enemy.
>
> "We have only one way open to us: to be brave and bold enough to block the path of the invader with our bodies," or something like that, is what the commander had said to us. We knew he had complete confidence in us because he spoke to us so frankly, without concealment or pretense; and the knowledge of the truth of the situation braced us. Each of us heaved his load of equipment, water, and food onto his back, and we marched, silent and bent, into the night . . .
>
> We seized the hill dominating the approaches to the village, and started to fortify our position. In the same hour — the sun had already risen and driven off the shadows — fire was opened on us

from the Lebanese side of the border. From west and north the armor of the invaders approached, spitting fire. Under cover of the malignant fire, hundreds of enemy troops poured forward. Here it was, the invasion, the threatening danger that had been charging the air all these last days. And here was the enemy: column upon column, fully marshaled; units fanning out in all directions; armored vehicles in front of them; and behind them, close by, a secure hinterland . . .

We had been ordered to hold these fortified heights at any cost. The advantage was all on the enemy's side: in the number of his fighters, in arms, in territory, in his closeness to his hinterland . . .

The fire, dense and ferocious, came from three directions. Our men were wounded, one after the other. We had meant to spend the day fortifying our positions and to start a fresh attack that night. But the enemy was concentrating all his forces to dislodge us. The bombardment was heavy and continuous. We tried to extricate our wounded, but every move we made brought intensified fire from the enemy . . .

The crisis reached its peak at midday. The enemy fire had not diminished. We were tormented by thirst. The number of our wounded was mounting all the time. And worst of all was the growing apathy of the men, which is worse than fear, because it springs from fatigue and induces fatalistic passivity. We knew what we had to do: we must try immediately to restore the men's self-confidence and strengthen the weakness of the spirit. We gave a quarter of a cup of water and half a bar of chocolate to each man. Then we crawled about among the men, gave them ammunition, shot and sniped at the enemy with Bren gun and rifle to set an example . . .

In a flash, they seemed to recover their initiative and to understand that they were fighting a defensive action. They started to hit the enemy, and their spirits rose. Their courage, their valor, their care for the wounded, their confidence in themselves, returned. They seemed to be saying to themselves, We are no longer dust and ashes confronting the armor and columns of the invaders. They are only Arab soldiers, and not particularly brave: when one of them is wounded, his comrades bolt. And, yes, when you have a gun in your hand, and can see the enemy through its sight, why, you are stronger than he. They hit the enemy again and again, and saw them fall. We saw scores of enemy dead rolling before our eyes. Our bullets had done their work. The invasion had been halted!

*   *   *

Abu Ghosh is the Christian Arab village that from the start was friendly to the Jews, and remains so to this day. About ten kilometers west of Jerusalem on the road to Tel Aviv, Abu Ghosh stands directly below the monastery that was the headquarters of the Harel Brigade, commanded by Yosef Tabenkin. The narrow winding road in the valley of Shar-Ha'gai leading up to Jerusalem had been closed by the Arabs, who controlled the hills on both sides and were shooting down into the valley. The Harel's desperately difficult task was to open the road by dislodging the Arabs from their hilltop positions.

The number of young Palmach fighters assigned to the Harel to carry out the mission was hopelessly small, and their arms and ammunition minimal. They had been fighting night after night without respite, and there had been heavy casualties almost every day; it was not surprising that the young soldiers were increasingly haunted by the thought that death was inescapable, if not today, then tomorrow.

This was the prevailing mood in the Abu Ghosh unit when I arrived with Yigal Allon early in June 1948. In fact, the situation was about to take a radical turn for the better. Yigal and I had come to Abu Ghosh by an alternative route called the Jeep Pass, which was soon to become famous as the Burma Road, a back road that would enable our forces to break the siege of Jerusalem. Ammunition and provisions were being brought in along the Jeep Pass even though it was not yet a road, and the Harel commanders knew that the turning point was approaching. But the young fighters could not feel it and were bracing themselves for yet another assault on the key position of Latrun. Several previous attempts had failed, each time at the cost of many dead, and soldiers saw the same fate awaiting them: more and more deaths, with nothing to show for them and no final victory in sight. They were saying grimly, "There's a bullet with his name written on it waiting for each of us."

Many of the young Palmach fighters had girlfriends among the female soldiers at headquarters, and the comfort of body and spirit that the girls provided helped the men to sustain their almost daily ordeals in battle. One afternoon I came upon a young soldier, still in his teens, leaning against a pillar in a passage of the monastery, crying quietly. When I asked what was wrong, he raised his head and looked at me with eyes full of pain and doubt. "I can't bear it any longer," he said in a low voice. "I have to go out to an action tonight. All the other fellows are there in the dormitory, in bed with their girls. My girl wanted me to do the same. She said, 'You may not come back from tonight's action. We may never have another chance to be together. Let's seize the chance now — it may be the only one we ever have!' But I couldn't. I couldn't lie with her, for the first time, with all those other people around us. I couldn't do it. So I got up and fled, and here I am."

He survived that night, but was killed in a later Harel battle. I cannot forget the look in that young soldier's eyes, which reflected the special suffering reserved for the most sensitive young souls in a war they had no choice but to fight.

Under the command of Yigal Allon, who had become commander of the southern front in the IDF, the Yo'av campaign liberated the Negev from the Egyptians, starting with the battle at Hirbat-Mehaz. Like Malkieh in the north, this was another crucial battle in the War of Independence. A strategic position near an Arab village of the same name, Hirbat-Mehaz was being held by a single Palmach platoon of thirty men when the Egyptians launched an all-out attack that should have dislodged the defenders within hours. The field commanders described the battle in *Pirkei Palmach*:

> It was our first face-to-face encounter with the Egyptians, who came in waves of hundreds upon hundreds of troops against our single platoon with their heavy mortars, their massive artillery, and their airplanes bombing us. We had not one airplane. We fought battle after battle for a week. One day they drove us out, with many casualties; the next day or the next, we drove them out, with more casualties. They brought in more and more artillery, mortars, Bren carriers, Spitfires, and a battalion of infantrymen against our platoon of thirty men. Only our dead and wounded were being replaced; otherwise we had no reinforcements . . .
>
> They fought for a week but could not defeat us. In the end they broke and fled, leaving their dead behind on the battlefield; leaving their arms and burning vehicles, running with their last breath . . .
>
> It was a great test for us, and for them. Our secret weapon was

our tenacity. It shattered the armor of the invaders, undermined the morale of their soldiers, and confused the calculations of their high command. It was the best possible "softening up" for the Yo'av campaign.

This tenacity has remained our chief secret weapon—and we put it to good use again years later in the deadly surprise attack of the Yom Kippur War of October 1973. In the first fateful hours of the war in the Golan Heights, we were outnumbered four to one, six to one, and in some places ten or twelve to one by the hundreds of Syrian tanks that poured across the border. Yet we held back the Syrians and prevented them from overrunning the country — as they could easily have done if their tenacity had matched ours, if they had been as ready, as the commander at Malkieh said, to block the path of the invader with their bodies. No doubt our Arab enemies *would* have had that kind of tenacity if they had been fighting as we were, to defend homes, families, our national existence. But the Arabs were only fighting an abstraction they called the Zionist entity, and it is hardly surprising that when it came to a choice, they broke and fled rather than stay and die.

Our willingness to sacrifice our lives when necessary has counted for a great deal in saving us from destruction ever since the War of Independence. But our leadership has counted, too, and no leader counted for more in that decisive war and for many years than Yigal Allon.

Yigal was twenty-seven when he became commander of the Palmach, and thirty when he was appointed commander of the southern front in the War of Independence. He was one of the youngest commanders in an army generally remarkable for its extreme youth. Strikingly handsome, he had a charismatic charm irresistible to women, and just as powerfully attractive to men. His charm sprang from deep within him, though it was often expressed simply enough — in his warm, firm handshake, in the affectionate, appreciative smile in his eyes, in the way he put his arm round your shoulder as he talked to you, in the steady, attentive gaze with which he listened. His humor and high spirits contributed to his personal magnetism. He loved to recount stories, anecdotes, jokes, witty sayings, wise sayings, anything he had enjoyed, and he was never at a loss for the lighthearted quip that spices the talk of friends. Whole-hearted in everything he did, he

Palmach founder Yitzhak Sadeh (*left*) was, according to his most brilliant protégé, Yigal Allon (*right*), "a military genius of world caliber, one of the greatest commanders in Jewish history, the father of modern warfare." Allon became commander of the Palmach at twenty-seven and was a national hero by the age of thirty.

joined energetically in singing the Palmach *pizmonim* around our campfires, and on hot nights at Kibbutz Ginosar he danced the hora for hours, never minding the sweat that poured down his handsome face.

But beneath his ease and informality was the authority of the born leader — the courage, self-discipline, power of mind, moral sensibility, boldness of imagination, and precision of judgment, that inspired total confidence. One knew, as one of Yigal's commanders put it, that "he would never fail to reach the mark."

I often marveled at the naturalness of his authority. Yigal never had to work for it; he seemed to breathe it forth as effortlessly as he walked or talked, and he exercised it so lightly that it was almost unfelt, even while it was acting most powerfully. This was of a piece with another of his rare qualities — perhaps rarest of all in a military leader — his delicacy of feeling about people. There was an inborn civility and consideration in his approach and attitude to people — in the way he asked them to do the hard, painful things he wanted them to do — that infused an extraordinary grace of spirit into the power of his personality. He could get angry or impatient, of course, and he could be caustic about people's stupidities or dishonesties or perversities. But his anger never seemed to affect his basic respect for another person as a human being, and I found in this a nobleness of spirit I came to admire in him perhaps above all his other rare qualities.

The first time I saw him command a large action was at the opening battle of the Yiftach campaign at Malkieh, for the defense of Galilee. At his invitation, I joined him for a few days at the beginning of the campaign. In his headquarters at Rosh Pinna, near Safed, I observed firsthand his marvelous sense of timing, his resourcefulness in adapting his tactics to the changing conditions of the battle, and his gift for finding solutions — surprising, unconventional solutions — to problems as they arose. He received bad news from the battlefront gravely, but without succumbing to depression or despair, and he had the strength of mind to stick to his battle plan, refusing, for example, to send more men and arms as reinforcements to the battlefront because he would not reduce his reserves to the danger point, knowing they had to be kept back for the decisive blow he'd planned.

I heard him talk to the soldiers before they went out to battle, inspiring them with confidence in their power to accomplish their task, then sharing their grief when they returned without their fallen comrades. He listened intently to the reports of field commanders of all ranks, and he weighed each criticism and suggestion from the commanders and troops with the utmost care. And below the listening and talking and arguing, heard and felt like hidden music, there was always the sense of comradeship, of an intimate human bond between the commander and his men that made each soldier feel he was a cherished friend of Yigal Allon and could count on his love and care, now and forever.

And he could. Yigal proved his loyalty to old friends and comrades again and again in the years to come. He was occasionally criticized for it by political adversaries, who called us the Palmach Mafia, sometimes in jest, often more than half seriously. But no one denied that old members of the Palmach were not the only beneficiaries of Yigal Allon's loyalty. He was loyal to everyone he loved, admired, felt indebted to, or felt he owed allegiance to: from Yitzhak Sadeh, his military mentor, to each of the prime ministers in whose cabinets he served — David Ben-Gurion, Levi Eshkol, Golda Meir, Yitzhak Rabin — though he often had radi-

cal differences of opinion with them. In the self-interested ethos of
the world of politics, his loyalty was sometimes taken advantage
of and, as a consequence, he lost many political prizes. But he
never lost hold of his own code of honor. When he died suddenly,
at the age of sixty-one, thousands mourned for a prince of Israel
without peer who had gone from the land.

He was a national hero at the age of thirty, was idolized and
feted for years after the War of Independence, and spent the remaining thirty years of his life in the public eye. Through it all, he
retained intact his love of his people and the three ruling passions
of his life: his love of the land, his lifelong affection for the Arabs
of Eretz Yisrael, and his passion for writing and authorship.

Yigal Allon's knowledge and love of his country matured as he
did. On our many journeys together I felt that every hill, valley,
and stream, every road and path, and every tiny settlement was
imprinted in his mind, making maps superfluous. He loved the
natural beauty of the land, but he was also well aware of the necessity to develop it and had a deeply informed passion for planning that development. "This is where we need settlements," he
would say as we gazed across an empty valley or at a treeless
mountainside. "This is where we need a highway ... Here's the
place for a ring road." Somehow, the look in his eyes seemed to
combine the ardor of the visionary with the sharp practicality of a
master construction worker.

As a cabinet minister in successive Labor governments for sixteen years, Yigal contributed enormously to the physical development of the country, in the interests of both settlement and
defense, in accordance with the Allon Plan, Yigal's proposed solution to the problem created by the conquest of Judea and Samaria in the Six Day War. The Allon Plan proceeded on the
assumption that the State of Israel could not absorb the more
than a million Arab inhabitants of these territories without fatally
undermining its Jewish character. Consequently, it rejected an-
nexation as a solution and instead proposed a territorial compromise by which Jordan, in return for a full peace treaty with Israel,
would be ceded the most heavily Arab-populated parts of Judea
and Samaria, leaving under Israel sovereignty an undivided Jerusalem as Israel's capital, certain security areas around Jerusalem,
and the Jordan Valley, with the Jordan River as the new natural

Palmach men on a long march in the Judean desert, coming down
from Masada, 1943

border between Israel and Jordan. There was to be a corridor,
under joint Israel-Jordan sovereignty, from around Jericho across
the Allenby Bridge, to link the west and east banks of the Jordan.

It was never formally accepted by the Labor governments in
which Yigal served, but the plan largely guided Israel's settlement
and other development policies as a direct result of Yigal's constant pressure for its de facto implementation. He vigorously encouraged the line of new settlements established in the Jordan
Valley and the Golan Heights immediately after the Six Day
War, the Gush Etzion and other settlements around Jerusalem,
and Jewish settlements within Judea and Samaria in areas where
there were no Arab inhabitants, like Kiryat Arba near Hebron.
He also initiated a network of roads and highways designed to
ensure the security of the borders proposed by the Allon Plan.
Since his death people have said that he put his seal everywhere,
and if they were less aware of it during his lifetime, it was only
because he implemented his visionary building with a minimum

of fanfare, content to let his works speak for themselves.

Before and after his term as minister of education, Yigal took a keen interest in the development of the universities and initiated important new institutions, including our first Open University and the Council for Higher Education, the supervisory organization of the country's universities. At the other end of the educational ladder, he introduced compulsory kindergarten education and insisted on "integration" of children from lower- and middle-class neighborhoods in the new junior high schools. He worked hard to reunite the two kibbutz federations that had been ideologically divided since the early 1950s, and shortly before his death he succeeded in bringing about the United Kibbutz Movement (Takam). Throughout his public career he continued to be a major force — though, again, mainly unpublicized — in the defense developments of the country. In a provocative article he published in February 1967, four months before the Six Day War, Yigal set out his ideas and predictions about any future war we might be forced to fight with our intransigent Arab neighbors. Reading it again after the Six Day War, I realized that it was an exact blueprint of what was actually done by the IDF in that victorious war. He laughed when I taxed him with his prophetic powers, saying it wasn't prophecy, only his contribution to the top-secret deliberations of the Prime Minister's Security Council, of which he had been a member ever since he first became a cabinet minister in 1961.

Yigal's relations with the Arabs, particularly the local Arabs of Galilee, were very much like those of our Ein-Harod hero, Chaim Sturman. He knew Arabic well, believed ardently in the possibility of peaceful Jewish-Arab coexistence in this country, and did what he could to advance it. Every year he invited a large contingent of local Arabs and Jews to a festive get-together at his kibbutz, Ginosar, at which the friendly talk and good will flowed as freely as the fruit juice and the good Arab coffee. I attended these gatherings a few times and was always impressed by the mutual affection and regard between Yigal and his Arab friends.

Their love and admiration was expressed most memorably in a small but touching incident on the day of his funeral at Ginosar, attended by some thirty thousand people from all parts of the country. It was a wet winter's day, and rain poured down ceaselessly on the sea of umbrellas. More Arab *kefiyas* were under the umbrellas than anyone could remember having seen at a Jew's funeral. Among them were those of a whole Arab clan, who had arrived early in the day, announcing that they had come to dig the grave of their beloved friend Yigal Allon. It must be dug with their own hands, they insisted, and not by machines — and they accomplished their task in pouring rain, refusing all offers of help.

I can still hear Yigal's voice saying, firmly, with a peculiar ardor, "I *love* writing!" He said it to me again and again, in the forty years I knew him, and it gave me fresh pleasure each time I heard it. The first time he said it also marked the beginning of our long friendship. Toward the end of 1939 I edited a book on the kibbutzim founded by Working Youth, which included Ginosar. I had read a speech Yigal had made about Ginosar that greatly appealed to me: it had a spirit and style that showed the distinct promise of an immature but real writer. When I told Yigal I wanted to publish it, he was exuberant — it was probably his first time in print. He was just twenty-one, I nearly twenty-seven, and the difference in age and my editing experience conferred on me the status of an authority on the subject of writing. I said to him, jestingly, "I'm going to make an author of you; see if I don't!" I was touched to see how pleased and proud he looked, and by the vehemence with which he said, "I love writing!"

I faithfully carried out my promise to help Yigal become a writer. When he became deputy commander, then commander, of the Palmach, I helped him to draft his orders of the day, reports, and other communications, but he learned quickly and was soon doing them alone. Before long, he was also writing many of the leading articles for *Alon ha-Palmach*. He dictated them to me, I edited them, and we signed them Gali, a name that neatly incorporated my underground code name, Gal (from Glass), into his code name, Gali (an acronym of Yigal in Hebrew). We frequently worked in his room in Tel Aviv, which I sometimes shared with him; for security's sake, he had chosen to live in the busiest, noisiest part of Tel Aviv, correctly surmising that the location would reduce the likelihood of unpleasant surprise visits from British security people.

This was the beginning of a lifelong collaboration that continued until the week before his death. I was struck from the start by his gift for expression and his sensitivity to nuances of meaning and the weight and timbre of words. His style, at its best, was simple, direct, lucid; he said what he wanted to say plainly, and his writing took its force from that plainness. With few exceptions, Palmach leaders were not noted for their gifts of authorship, so when ten years after the War of Independence, Yigal announced that he wanted to write a book on the Haganah, nobody believed he could do it. But he surprised them all, and *Masach shel Chol*, "Curtain of Sand," became the first full account of the strategy, tactics, and broad defense policies developed by the Haganah and continued by the IDF. After that, he wrote, in English, *The Making of Israel's Army* and *Shield of David*, and, again in Hebrew, his autobiographical *Beit-Avi*, translated into English as *My Father's House*.

From the time I became editor of *Mibifnim*, the Kibbutz ha-Meuchad quarterly, he contributed to it frequently on a wide range of topics, including national and kibbutz problems and defense and foreign affairs issues. He was always eager to respond to my requests for a contribution — Yigal was no prima donna, he just loved to write. And so it went on to the very week before his death, when we met to discuss the interview I wanted from him about the United Kibbutz Movement, which he had been instrumental in establishing.

But Yigal didn't live to give me the interview nor to write the books he most wanted to write. One was an ambitious historical work, *A History of the Yishuv* in three volumes. What he most loved writing was history. He had acquired the taste for it and a good deal of the skill in the short years he had spent at Oxford, after the War of Independence, doing postgraduate study in history and winning high praise from his tutors. He was prevented from completing a doctoral dissertation on problems in the modern history of the Middle East by his appointment to Ben-Gurion's cabinet in 1961. To work on the history of the Jewish community in Eretz Yisrael from its beginnings to the founding of the State was a project close to his heart. He had a firsthand knowledge of its final phase; he had done some research on its earlier periods and was longing to do more (his wife used to say he was never happier than when he was sitting in a library or archive surrounded by piles of books and documents); and, most of all, he felt deeply, and rejoiced in, his own rootedness in that ancient community of Jews. It would doubtless have been an excellent, living history, which perhaps only he could have written.

He also wanted to write a history of the War of Independence, which he was of course peculiarly qualified to write, and a history of his kibbutz. He had often told people what a revolutionary event it had been for him to join Working Youth at his famous agricultural school, Kaduri, in founding this new kibbutz on the shores of the Sea of Galilee. He was deeply attached to Ginosar, had shared intimately in its early struggles for existence, and he wanted to place on record this and other phases of its stormy history. These, too, would have been books that bore the stamp of his special knowledge and vision.

And this would have been most true of the book about the Palmach he wanted to write. It might have been called *A Personal Record of People I Knew in the Palmach*. He spoke to me about it again and again: how he had known the leaders and men of the Palmach in "the hour of truth," when they stood face to face with the imminent danger of death; and how they revealed themselves, and humanity as a whole — the good and the bad, the noble and ignoble, all in one — in those irreversible hours. It would have been a unique book, and perhaps a great one. When I remember the quiet passion of excitement with which Yigal spoke of it, I miss the book and yearn for it, along with the brilliant noble leader and friend who never lived to write it.

16

Arabs

REMEMBERING YIGAL ALLON, his annual Arab-Jewish gatherings at Ginosar, and the history of the Allon Plan has led me to reflect on my own attitude toward the Arabs of Eretz Yisrael. I think now that it took shape almost imperceptibly under the influences of Chaim Sturman and Moshe Carmi in the years of my boyhood and early youth; and though it was reinforced as I developed by a better understanding of the political problems of Jewish-Arab relations in this land, the basic conception has remained unchanged.

"We have to live with them," said Chaim Sturman, and, in his own way, Moshe Carmi said the same thing. This was the axiomatic truth behind the attitudes they transmitted to us. We took it for granted that the Arabs of Eretz Yisrael were our neighbors and always would be. The idea that they ought to be driven out or "evacuated," by persuasion or force, did not enter our heads. Nor was there any question of seizing Arab land. We knew that the land we settled had been bought for hard cash from its effendi owners, and, although we were not legally obliged to do so, we often paid compensation to the effendis' serf-like tenants for the loss of their means of livelihood. We aimed for friendly coexistence and had no doubt that this was possible through good will on both sides. We believed this, even though we knew that the overwhelming majority of the Arab leadership didn't want to hear of coexistence; they just wanted the Jews to get out of "their" land.

Our response to this Arab claim was clear and firm: our presence in Eretz Yisrael was not dependent on Arab consent, and never would be. We had belonged to this land for more than two thousand years, it was the only homeland we had, and our moral right to be here was as unquestionable as the fact of the ancient, unbroken bond of the Jewish people with the land of the Bible. The visible changes in the land around Gideon's spring in the space of a few years seemed to us a further decisive proof of our right to be here: the marshes had been transformed into arable land, trees had been planted, the earth was being conserved rather than exploited — all accomplished by the labor of the Jewish pioneers.

In those days of reclamation and building, we were particularly conscious of the way the Arabs had ruined the land, reducing great parts of it to marshy or stony wasteland. On our excursions with Moshe Carmi in the Galilee, in Samaria around Sebastia and Nablus, in Judea, and, of course, in the vicinity of Ein-Harod, we were appalled by the backwardness of Arab farming methods and work habits. They watered their fields by opening irrigation canals, often flooding the land and carrying away the top soil; they never applied enough fertilizer to the soil; and their tools seemed incredibly primitive to us. We would watch, amazed, as they turned the earth with a rough nail plow made of two wooden handles and a shaft with a single, thin iron blade like a huge nail. It was drawn by a donkey, or a donkey and an ox, and even sometimes a woman harnessed in to help the animals.

As young farmers ourselves, we were particularly horrified by these sights, which tourists often found picturesque and romantic. It was the same when we walked around the Arab villages, seeing the evidence of ignorance and poverty everywhere: the filth, the mean hutlike houses, the perpetual clumps of dusty cacti beside and behind the houses, the almost total absence of trees and flowers. A depressing spectacle, it might well have induced in youngsters a sense of alienation, and scorn and contempt for those who lived in such degradation.

But Moshe Carmi, like Chaim Sturman, never ceased to impress on us that the Arabs were human beings like us and deserved to be treated with respect and consideration. He always made a point of showing us the good, attractive aspects of the

Arab villagers' lives and behavior — from which, he insisted, we had much to learn: their hospitality to guests; the friendliness and natural courtesy of the ordinary peasant we encountered in the fields; and their intimate knowledge of their environment and their attachment to it. When we had unpleasant experiences with stone-throwing Arab children, the adults standing around generally did not intervene, but sometimes the mukhtar of the village would come out to scold them and invite us into the special room reserved for guests to rest in, the *maddafi,* which was a feature of almost every Arab village.

In retrospect, it is tempting to view the years of my boyhood as a relatively idyllic period of Jewish-Arab relations in Eretz Yisrael, when the borders were open and a Jew could travel freely to Egypt, Lebanon, Syria, and beyond, when Arab landowners were happy to sell land for good money to the pioneering Jews, when Chaim Sturman counted Arabs among his best friends, when Arab notables of the Emek came, like any Jew from Haifa or Tel Aviv or Jerusalem, as guests to our big celebrations.

But even in the brief, comparatively tranquil years between the Arab riots in 1921 and those of 1929, the political and religious incitement of the Arab population against the Jews continued unabated. The Mufti of Jerusalem, Haj Amin el Husseini, the archenemy of the Jews and head of the country's Supreme Arab Council, was spreading his anti-Jewish, anti-Zionist propaganda — not only in Eretz Yisrael but in all Moslem countries — in an effort to unite the whole Moslem world in monolithic hostility toward Jews and the Zionist movement. He became a fervent supporter of Hitler and the Nazis in the 1930s, was welcomed to Germany by Hitler himself during World War II, and made a point of visiting the death camps to observe for himself the spectacle of the extermination of the Jewish people. In Eretz Yisrael before the war, he took an active part in the 1929 riots that led to the massacre of the Jews of Hebron and Safed, directed the riots of 1936, and conducted a successful terrorist campaign against moderate Arabs as well as Jews. It was even said that his terrorist gangs killed more Arabs than Jews. The Mufti was materially assisted in these activities by the pro-Arab bias of the Mandatory government in Palestine and by the fatal appeasement policies of the British government in London.

So there was, in fact, no idyllic period in our political relations with the Arabs in the twenty-five years before the establishment of the State. I cannot forget that the Arabs killed sixteen Jews in Jaffa in one day during the riots of 1936, following a rumor spread by their ringleaders that Jews had murdered Arabs. Nor that, incited by their local mosque leaders on orders from the Mufti and the Supreme Arab Council, the Arabs uprooted the young trees in our orchards and set fire to our crops; and that, when we tried to put out the fire, they shot at us from the Gilboa. They shot at our produce trucks going to market, but the Mandatory authorities did nothing to stop the violence and allowed us no arms with which to defend ourselves.

We defended ourselves as best we could — with an all-night guard in sandbagged positions and trenches around the perimeter of the kibbutz, shooting back with hunting rifles and illegal Haganah arms. Every member of the kibbutz between the ages of fifteen and sixty was trained in the use of arms, and we all did several hours' guard duty every night, in groups of two or four. It was not easy after a full day's work, but we did it, and in the end defeated the Arabs' attempt to make life impossible for us by their war of attrition. But it was terrible to live through: to hear of the daily murders of Jews in all parts of the country — in the marketplaces, in the streets, in their houses; and to know that it all sprang from a savage, senseless hostility fed by the Jew-hating Moslem and Christian leadership of the Arabs.

The establishment of the State of Israel led to greatly improved relations with the quarter million friendly Arabs who chose not to flee during the War of Independence and remained to become citizens of the State. But this gain has been offset by the ever more bitter, ever more implacable hostility of the surrounding Arab states. Our military victories in the succession of wars forced upon us by these states have made things worse, not better, and since the Six Day War Jewish-Arab relations have become increasingly complex and intractable.

I am sure there is no simple solution to these problems. But I am also sure that to recognize that we have to live with our Arab neighbors, and behave rationally and humanely toward them, as Chaim Sturman did, remains the basic guide to a solution. This means that we have to give our Arab citizens full civil rights and social benefits on a par with those enjoyed by our Jewish citizens. They already have full political rights and vote in national and municipal elections; they may form their own Arab parties; they have seven Arab representatives in the Knesset; they have equality before the law; receive the same health care and many of the same social benefits as Jewish citizens. But their schools, housing, municipal services, and other amenities are generally greatly inferior; their employment opportunities are by no means equal to those of our Jewish citizens, and they are deprived of certain social benefits because they don't serve in the Israeli army, as every Jew does. The issue of army service has been one of the most difficult, because all the surrounding Arab states, except Egypt, are in a state of war with us, and we cannot risk the possible introduction of a fifth column into the army. Nor can we expect Israeli Arabs to fight and kill fellow Arabs in any new war our hostile neighbors may force on us. It seems, therefore, that as long as there is no peace with the surrounding Arab states, there can be no army service for our Arab citizens. This is a serious inequality in Israel, affecting not only economic benefits but also social and human relations between our Jewish and Arab citizens.

The Arab inhabitants of Judea, Samaria, and Gaza present a different and still more intractable problem. As they live in formally occupied territories administered by a military government, Israeli law and practice may not be extended to them. The Arabs of these territories do have certain rights of Israeli citizens, including the right to appeal to the Israeli Supreme Court in disputes with the military government over land ownership and other civil matters. Wages and employment conditions for those who work across the Green Line are generally the same as those of Israeli workers, and they receive some health care and other benefits. But many Israelis are deeply disturbed about our ruling over the Arab population as though they are at best second-class citizens, and about the periodic outbursts of violence that are the inevitable consequence of such a situation.

I see no solution to the problem other than the "territorial compromise" proposed by the Allon Plan. This would return the heavily Arab-populated parts of Judea and Samaria to Jordanian rule, on the condition that Jordan enters into a full contractual peace with Israel and agrees to the demilitarization of the West

Bank as part of that agreement. Then, not only would the question of civil rights for the Arabs of these territories be settled, but so would the long-standing problem of the Palestinian refugees who still live in refugee camps in the West Bank. Once peace has been made, Jordan would no longer consider it necessary to keep the refugees in camps as a propaganda weapon against Israel, and might well resettle them in the many sparsely populated parts of Jordan, putting an end to a human tragedy created, and sustained for more than thirty years, by Arab hatred of the Jewish presence in Eretz Yisrael.

Meanwhile, as we wait for Jordan to make the momentous move from war to peace, we can do nothing but strive to behave rationally and humanely toward the Arabs of Judea and Samaria, in the spirit of Chaim Sturman, Moshe Carmi, and the other great early advocates of peaceful coexistence.

17

Susi

MY ALL-DEMANDING, all-absorbing life in the Palmach left little time for family. I got home to Ein-Harod about one weekend a month, and though there were occasionally extra days off, depending on the security situation, I saw very little of my wife Susi in those years.

Susi was only eighteen and I was twenty-eight when we married, but her remarkable maturity, even at sixteen, when I first met her, kept our age difference from ever being an issue. Our courtship was brief and sporadic — typical in wartime. During the two years she spent at Kfar Sabba before returning to Ein-Harod, I visited her whenever I could, always bringing a small gift. Once, when she was still living in a tent and I knew that they had run out of oil for their lamps, I surprised her with a bottle of paraffin oil instead of a bunch of flowers — and she was delighted with the originality of the gift and its utility. We married in 1940 and spent all of three intensely happy days at Kinneret, the Lake of Galilee. A champion swimmer, Susi swam in the lake for long stretches of each day while I, content to remain onshore, composed in my head a cycle of poems that I published soon afterward. When my unit was stationed at Kibbutz Negba in the south and home leave had been indefinitely canceled, Susi decided that if I couldn't come to her, she would come to me. Her visit made me the envy of all my comrades, who teased me about my good fortune. "What a lucky fellow. We can't get home, but he gets his home leave right here on the spot!"

Susi's independence of mind and dedicated attitude toward her work soon won her the admiration and respect of everyone at Ein-Harod. Her permanent job was in the vegetable garden, where the work force always included a good number of our schoolchildren doing their part-time stint of kibbutz work. With her gift for organization, Susi was particularly good at working with the children, who came to love her and to enjoy the work because of her.

Susi believed ardently in the pioneer ideal of self-realization through work, that every kind of work is equally important and honorable, and that giving all of yourself to your work is both a duty to the community and the most assured way of finding your true self. Certainly there were times when she missed the intellectual stimulation of the studies she had loved. She could easily have continued her schooling if she had consented to be a teacher, but she didn't want to teach; she wanted to do creative physical work. Her Zionist conviction that this was the way to ensure the renewal of our people in our own land led her to acquire a thoroughly professional knowledge of her work, and to perform it day after day with never flagging interest and enthusiasm — and without any air of martyrdom about having sacrificed study for physical labor. There was a beautiful single-heartedness, a wholeness and integrity, about her attitude, in this as in other things, that I loved in her and never ceased to admire.

But she did not find the life of the kibbutz wholly beyond reproach. There was plenty to criticize, as she discovered during her first stay at Ein-Harod, when she was learning the art of vegetable growing. Only fifteen at the time, she had been badly overworked by the kibbutz taskmaster, who expected the greenhorn teenagers to work like experienced grown-ups. After our marriage, she got a liberal taste of what appears to be a built-in weakness of kibbutz society: the initial suspicion and hostility toward a newcomer. She was dubbed "the daughter of the professor" because her father, Dr. Victor Kellner, was a master at the prestigious Herzliya Gymnasia and one of the teachers of its outstanding first graduation class, which included Moshe Carmi. Some didn't like her intellectual aspirations, others resented her distinguished connections, and still others were simply jealous of her all-around abilities. Of course, she was finally accepted and made many close friends, but that first period was a hard and lonely one for her.

She could not help but notice, too, that the principle of equality, so sacred to the kibbutz philosophy, was by no means upheld by all. She herself, firmly believing that one's actions should match one's principles, had immediately on her arrival at Ein-Harod handed over all her books and the box full of good clothes she had brought with her. Afterward, she was both annoyed and amused to see that some women members who worked in the clothing store room had appropriated a good deal more than a fair share of clothes she had denied herself for equality's sake.

Susi was critical of some, deeper, aspects of the kibbutz as well. Although passionately interested in ideas, she disliked long ideological speeches full of catchwords and slogans — and the fact that she was usually in substantial agreement with the content did not make her less impatient with the cant. When there were attitudes and doctrines she positively rejected, she let me know about it with characteristic vehemence. One was our attitude to the Soviet Union and its regime. In the early 1940s our kibbutz federation was still broadly sympathetic to the Soviets, but Susi insisted we were idealizing them, seeing them through rose-tinted spectacles, exalting a New Soviet Man who didn't exist. She believed in socialism, too, but she did not believe in the existing socialist parties of Europe, and she was particularly severe about Vienna's Social Democracy in the early years of Hitler's rise to power. She had lived through the Anschluss, had seen the Nazis marching into Vienna and the Social Democrats hanging swastikas over their red flags. She never forgot this example of socialism's cowardly hypocrisy, and would get angry every year when we put out red flags for our Red Vienna Day, commemorating the struggle of the Social Democrats against the early manifestations of Nazism in Vienna.

Yes, she was a great believer, but never a blind believer, and she was just as clear-sighted about people — severely critical of meanness, pettiness, selfishness; scornful of evasions of duty, half-heartedness, or dragging of feet in the performance of one's appointed tasks. It was not surprising that her moral sensibility, her high standards of conduct, and her intense commitment to everything she undertook created an inner tension that did not make her life easy. People felt it, and some were uncomfortable with it. But I liked and admired her for just these qualities and never minded the vehemence that sometimes disturbed others.

Left: Susi, age twenty-seven. *Right,* my brother, Yuval

The deepest, most enduring friendship of Susi's life was with Elisheva Becker, whom she had known since their childhood in Vienna. They had gone to school together, had come to Ein-Harod in the same Youth Aliyah group, and had gone together to Kfar Sabba to prepare to set up a new kibbutz in the Negev. Both endured the hardest separation of their lives when Susi came back to Ein-Harod to marry me and Ellie married Hanoch Ilan and went with him to the Negev to found Gvar Am, more than four hours away from Ein-Harod. They sustained their friendship through long affectionate letters, at least one a week, met whenever they could, shared every joy and sorrow, every new interest and preoccupation of the succeeding years, and remained inseparable in spirit to the end.

My brother, Yuval, eleven when Susi came to live at Ein-Harod, was another special friend. He was not an easy child: very independent, imaginative, and original, but somewhat stubborn, with some eccentric habits, and not readily responsive to people. But Susi succeeded in winning his affection, and he became greatly attached to her. My mother, beginning to age, was often plaintive and impatient with her young son, and since I was scarcely at home during these ten years, I was most grateful for Susi's loving care of Yuval.

She was the same, however, with many people, at Ein-Harod and outside. Always available to give active help to anyone, everyone, in need, she stood out even in a community in which mutual aid was a basic principle of existence. In her readiness and power to guide, advise, comfort, and sustain the weak and the strong alike in times of trouble, Susi was the female counterpart of our best friend, Moshe Tabenkin. Ruth Zakkai, the young, somewhat high-strung wife of my friend Arieh Zakkai, never forgot that Susi stood by and helped her through her worst periods of confusion and depression. Re'uma Sturman, Moshe's wife, and Yael Tabenkin, Yosef's wife, were both strong, brave women, but not so strong as not to be grateful to Susi for the support she gave them in their times of greatest need: Re'uma after Moshe's death, Yael when, in spite of herself, she missed Yosef's help with their young children during his prolonged absences in the Palmach. Susi was a leading spirit in forming the circle of Palmach Wives, who met regularly to compare notes and lament together, half humorously, half seriously.

But not only her active, practical help drew people to Susi. There was something in her marvelous vitality and ardor, the faith that flashed from her beautiful eyes, her smile and her laugh, that seemed to fill a void in the lives of others. She animated the chronically low-spirited or depleted, somehow managing to raise the pitch and tempo of their emotional lives, introducing a joy and radiance into their souls that lingered like a fragrance long after their first meeting with her, even if they never saw her again.

It could happen on a first encounter, sometimes without a word being spoken: the magic seemed capable of working instantaneously. I treasure the recollection of a small episode in the apartment of our good friends Ruth and Natan Nevo, when we were staying with them on one of our periodic visits to Jerusalem. They had a guest, a distinguished young academic from the United States, who was not staying with them but constantly dropped in and out. Susi was resting one afternoon in the Nevos' living room, on a couch under the long west window, when the guest came in and, not knowing anyone was in the living room, flung the door open. He stood for a long moment in the doorway, staring at Susi, then quickly closed the door and, according to Ruth's report, rushed at her to ask, "Who is that lovely woman? I've never seen such beautiful eyes! They're enormous — huge beautiful green eyes! Who is she? Who is she?" Allowing for the exaggeration of a susceptible young academic, I knew his reaction was typical enough; her beautiful expressive eyes could affect people because they immediately felt the spirit and force of character behind them.

Characteristically, Susi treated her family as she did her friends, with loyalty and love, the same desire to help, the same enjoyment of their companionship, and the same impatience, anger, even scorn, when they seemed to fall below her standards of character and conduct. She adored her mother, Emmi, who was the paragon of a mother for such a daughter. A vital, free, unconventional spirit, Emmi exuded love of life, generosity of mind, humor, and high spirits. After separating from her husband she had come to live at Kibbutz Hephtzibah, not far from Ein-Harod, so mother and daughter were able to keep in close touch. This meant a great deal to Susi, for she seemed to get from Emmi what she herself gave to other people: a great dose of revitalizing, regenerating energy when body and spirit most needed it, and love and care that knew no limits. It was typical of Emmi, for example, to come marching into Ein-Harod on the very day of the Black Sabbath of June 1946, after Susi had been manhandled in the chicken coop. Emmi came bearing an old, gaily colored peasant dress — on the sound assumption, as she explained, that nothing better raises the spirits of a woman than a new garment. Susi wore the dress for years, long after Emmi's early death, at the age of fifty-three, in 1950.

Susi's relations with her father, on the other hand, were never good. She disliked Victor's self-centeredness, his love of showing off his knowledge, his sharp, censorious tongue, and his tendency to care more for books than for people. When he came to visit her at Ein-Harod, the atmosphere was often uncomfortably charged, and although I did what I could to defuse it, I was not always successful. Susi was nevertheless a good, dutiful daughter, constantly worrying about Victor's physical welfare, sometimes taking a day off from work to go to Tel Aviv to clean his one-room flat and mend his shirts. Her father, although he loved her dearly, seemed to lack the power to express his love normally and naturally. Aware of this, as Susi wasn't, or perhaps didn't want to be, I felt much compassion for him and visited him regularly in Tel Aviv. When he was over eighty and fell ill, I brought him to Ein-Harod, and with my daughters took care of him for two years, until his death in 1970.

Susi's standards of human conduct were high and firm, but they were not rigid, and she was most ready to overlook the flaws and failings of her own family. She may have found her father's egocentricity and lack of simple humanity too much for her nerves, but she remained devoted to her brother, Michael, even though he chose to live in England instead of Eretz Yisrael, married a non-Jewish Scotswoman, brought up his only son as a non-Jew, and generally wanted to have as little as possible to do with Zionism or Israel. Though deeply committed to the life and values Michael repudiated, Susi nevertheless maintained close ties with him, twice visiting him in England, and becoming great friends with her sister-in-law and her clever, charming English nephew.

Susi was also on excellent terms with her parents' extensive circle of friends in Jerusalem, who treated her as a daughter. All these scholars, writers, journalists, and editors were passionately Zionist. Colorful and often somewhat eccentric, they conducted their lives in Jerusalem in much the same style as they had done in their native Prague or Vienna. The group included Hugo Bergman, first professor of philosophy at the Hebrew University and its first rector; Robert Weltsch, journalist and famous editor of the Berlin Jewish newspaper *Jüdische Rundschau,* who had the courage to expose the atrocities of the Hitler regime from the start and right up to 1938; his cousin Felix Weltsch, philosopher and political writer; and Sigmund Katznelson, owner of *Jüdischer Verlag,* the well-known pre-Hitler Jewish publishing house in Germany. Susi was particularly fond of Sigmund's wife, Lise Katznelson, sister of Robert Weltsch and one of her mother's oldest friends, who had known Franz Kafka well and had fascinating recollections of him. On our summer visits to Jerusalem, we always went to see her, and each time I enjoyed the charming animated Lise and the pleasure she and Susi took in one another.

The greatest, deepest joy of Susi's life, however, was motherhood. Like Emmi, she loved children, particularly babies, and

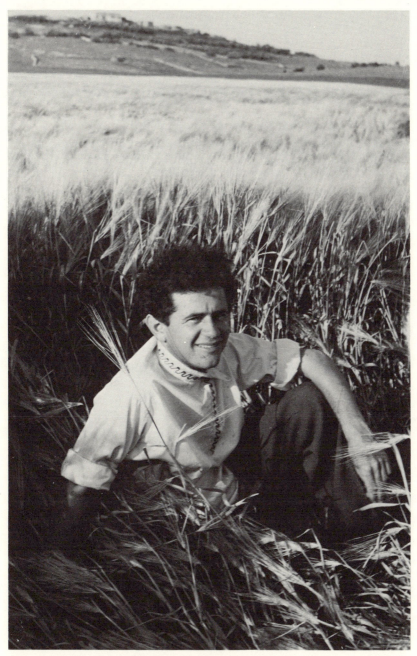

At home in the fields of Ein-Harod, age thirty-two

could not wait to have her first child. She was nineteen when our eldest daughter, Tirza, was born, soon to be followed by Hanni and Eyla. For Susi, motherhood was the consummation of love in marriage, and from the time of Tirza's birth, the center of her life became the love, care, and enjoyment of her girls.

I found, somewhat unexpectedly, that fatherhood affected me similarly. I had always loved children, but, as every father knows, having one's own child is something different and special, and I surrendered myself to the joys of fatherhood with abandonment. On my home leaves from the Palmach, I used to spend hours out of doors just sitting by Tirza's cot, gazing and gazing at her through the mosquito netting, seeming never to have gazed enough. I once observed another young father sitting by his baby's mosquito-netted cot, reading a newspaper, and I remember thinking to myself, How *can* he? Reading a newspaper when he could be gazing at his baby! What he's missing, the *fool*! I was unable to conceive how one could prefer anything in the world to just sitting and watching one's baby.

I was most fascinated and moved by the thought of the infant's total dependence, and by the beautiful completeness of this tiny creature and the ever changing expressions chasing across her face, all under a fixed, unblinking stare. I began to compose new and different poetry, all about the experience of Tirza, and of her mother as the cherished bearer of the precious gift. I wrote a lullaby for Tirza called "Numi, Numi" ("Slumber, Slumber"), which became a national favorite, and a rhymed cycle of poems, *Bat-Tzchok* ("Smile"), in which the opening poem rejoices in mother and child together.

> A golden smiling sparkle
> illuminates our daughter's eyes.
> Joyous, joyous,
> like a field of ripened corn.
>
> A tiny golden sparkle —
> How it stirs a tumult in my heart!
> Like the sparkle of an earlier time
> in your eyes
> which stirred my field
> and all my sheaves bowed down
> before you.

* * *

With my daughters: Tirza (*left*), Hanni, and Eyla, 1954

The Palmach years came to an end at last. I was formally demo-
bilized and sent home in the spring of 1949. But almost immediately I was called away again to collect and edit the documentary
material for *The Book of the Palmach* — eventually a two-volume
book of more than 2000 pages — which was composed of eyewitness accounts, letters, diaries, stories, poems, and official records
and reports on the actions of the Palmach in the eight years of its
existence. From 1950 to 1953 I traveled all over the country gathering the material, and again Susi was left on her own most of the
week, to take care, unaided, of Tirza, aged seven in 1950, Hanni,
four, and Eyla, born in 1950. She bore it with fortitude, believing
with her typical fervor that what I was doing had to be done and
that no one was better suited to the task. When the book was finished and I was offered two years of study at the Hebrew University of Jerusalem, she urged me to go. She said I mustn't miss this
chance on any account, and once again I was an absent husband
and father. I wrote her daily letters from Jerusalem, came home
most weekends, and, of course, spent my four to five months' va-
cation at home.

Meanwhile, she carried on her tasks at Ein-Harod with undiminished energy and zest. Though the children were the center of
her life, she seemed to find time for everything else as well: to do a
full day's work in the vegetable garden; to participate actively in
various committees; to take her turn at the arduous jobs of kibbutz secretary and work organizer; to help those who needed help;

to read books, listen to music, write long letters to Ellie, hear my flood of Jerusalem tales when I came home; and stay in touch with scores of friends in Ein-Harod, in neighboring kibbutzim, and elsewhere. She loved to read aloud poems of her favorite German and Hebrew poets, and I loved to listen. We had many reading sessions in the years of our life together, and I can still hear her clear, ardent voice reciting poems of Eduard Moericke or Karl Kraus or Rilke; or reading me a favorite chapter of the Bible, usually from Jeremiah or the Song of Songs. She was always the first to hear my newest poems, even before my old friend and fellow poet Moshe Tabenkin, and I also read her any new poem I came across and liked.

In the autumn of 1958, when she was thirty-six, Susi suddenly began to feel severe pains in her back. She ignored them at first, thinking they were caused by muscular strain or chill, or something else that would pass on its own. But they became worse. She had to stop work and began to see doctors who, after a series of misdiagnoses, discovered she had cancer of the spine. In the six years that followed she had three operations, each bringing a remission, but no cure. After her first operation, she was able to work again, but soon the good periods came to an end, and there was nothing but agonizing pain. We went to England, hoping that the top cancer surgeons at London's Maida Vale Hospital might be able to help, but they could do nothing and refused to operate, presumably because they knew it would be to no avail.

During her illness, Susi spent long periods in Tel Hashomer Hospital, where Dr. Haim Sheba, its founder and director and a pioneer builder of Israel's medical services, and Dr. Eliyahu Gillon, chief medical officer of the IDF, spared no effort to help her. All who knew her in the hospital loved her and said they had never known a terminally ill patient so full of vitality and joy in life. It was the same while Susi was home — when she was not prostrate with pain, she loved to have visitors, and as our small living room filled up with friends in the evening, her animated talk and laughter seemed to turn the visit into a party.

But her greatest joys were the two grandchildren she lived to see. At the age of eighteen Tirza married Abbi Peled and in the last three years of Susi's life gave her a grandson, Ori, and a granddaughter, Ayelet. Just thirty-eight when Ori was born, Susi was the youngest grandmother in the Emek — and she boasted of it to all comers. No matter how bad she felt, she managed to slip over to the babies' house to be with her grandchildren, to help bathe them, feed them, and cuddle them, thus reliving the delight she had taken in her own three daughters when they were babies. It was perhaps the greatest fulfillment of her life.

During these years my own mother was sinking slowly, suffering from several painful ailments of advancing age and in need of constant care. I did what I could to make her last years as comfortable as possible. She died in January 1964 when she was seventy-seven. Her last illness had been so painful that she no longer wanted to live. But I could be glad only for her, not for myself. I sadly missed her, never forgetting that I owed my life at Ein-Harod to her brave, enterprising act of forty years back.

Almost exactly a year after my mother's death, Susi was brought to Ichilov Hospital in Tel Aviv for a third operation, which we hoped would give her a further respite. She died under anesthetic on January 2, 1965. She was forty-two.

We mourned her for years. My daughters live to this day with the memory of a mother who was lovely in herself and their best, wisest, most beloved guide and friend. And I, who had loved and rejoiced in her for twenty-five years, felt the shield of my life had gone.

> Like a shield you covered my life.
> Don't say to me now,
> Go, wander like a bird!
> My soul thirsts
> for your water brooks,
> beloved.

I wrote poems in remembrance of her for years. "The Bell" and "Praise" were two of the earliest.

The Bell

> Rings. Rings.
> And no one comes in.
> Your voice and your light
> surround me.

Rings. Rings.
And the silence runs wild
in my heart.

Fool!
Rings. Rings.
Stricken by light
haunted by shade.

Praise

1

The whole earth, the whole earth
is full of you:
flashes of light and the echo
of your voice
and a wind in the standing corn.

Joy of the earth,
I whisper,
joy of the earth.

And small grasses
in the dust
praise the Lord.

2

An unseen cloud
in a circle of the festive sky.
And yet perhaps it is seen —
an inexhaustible goatskin of
tears —
from which voracious birds
flee
for their lives.*

*From *Pomegranate Tree in Jerusalem,* Kibbutz ha-Meuchad Publishing House, Tel Aviv, pp. 36, 38.

III

In the State of Israel

———————— ﬡ ————————

18

A Vocation Renewed

WHEN I RETURNED to Ein-Harod after the War of Independence,
the kibbutz was still mourning its dead. Two hundred of its five
hundred fifty members had been called to fight. Of these, fifty
were in the Palmach at the start of the war and the number increased as youngsters of seventeen and eighteen began to join. It
had been our first experience of what happens in a kibbutz when
a full-scale war breaks out, and the pattern was to be repeated in
the Sinai Campaign of 1956, the Six Day War of 1967, the Yom
Kippur War of 1973, and the Lebanon War of 1982.

The first upheaval is, of course, the sudden loss of more than a
third of our work force, which is a serious matter for an economically autonomous community chronically short of manpower.
Nevertheless, because we are a cooperative, mutual-aid community in which every worker is ready to stand in for every other,
work schedules can be reorganized rapidly and fairly smoothly.
Men over fifty-five and women who normally work in the service
sectors — kitchen, children's houses, school, administration —
take the place of mobilized men and women; older women replace
younger ones in the services; children from fourteen to seventeen
leave school and join the work force, everyone works extra
hours — and the economic life of the kibbutz somehow goes on.

Local defense also takes time and manpower. In the War of Independence, air-raid shelters had to be improvised and trenches
dug. Permanent shelters now crisscross the kibbutz, but everyone

must stand double and treble the hours of guard duty because fewer numbers are available for the shifts. The kibbutz also shelters children and their mothers evacuated from kibbutzim near the battlefronts, and, of course, the atmosphere is heavy with the tension and anxiety of the mothers and wives of the men at the front. When news of the dead and wounded starts to come in, more and more after-work hours tend to be spent with the bereaved and, when possible, the wounded.

Ein-Harod lost seven of its sons in the War of Independence, and each was a deeply personal loss — in times of war, more than ever, the kibbutz becomes one big extended family, and every young man killed is your son or your brother.

In Zisling House we have set aside a memorial room for our dead, in which the history of every member who has passed away is recorded. The young men who fell in battle have their own special corner, each with his own tall black box file containing the story of his life and deeds, photographs, and other memorabilia. There are now twenty-eight of these black boxes.

The end of the War of Independence marked the beginning of a new phase of my life. After prolonged inner debate and many talks with Susi, Moshe Tabenkin, and other good friends, I finally decided on my life's task. I wanted to devote myself to advancing the literary interests and aspirations of the kibbutzim, by recording and commemorating kibbutz life myself, and by helping to develop means for encouraging and fostering literary self-expression. Therefore, I accepted the invitation of the Kibbutz ha-Meuchad Publishing House to join its editorial board and to edit its quarterly journal *Mibifnim* ("From Within"). My work on the editorial board would give me the best opportunity to spot new literary talent, especially in poetry, and ensure its publication; and the editorship of *Mibifnim* would allow me to encourage the expression of fresh ideas in politics, economics, sociology, and education, as well as in literature and literary criticism. I would pursue my own literary career as part of the broader task, though it would not necessarily be confined to this framework.

Remembering Gideon's men and the idea of vocation and test, I thought of this as a vocation renewed rather than a completely new one, for I was in effect recommitting myself to a task I had been committed to all along. The difference was that I would pursue it consciously and as a full-time occupation, instead of half consciously and sporadically because of all the other occupations with which I had previously had to combine it. Nearly thirty years after I embarked on my renewed vocation, I am glad to say it has worked out well on the whole.

Before I finally got to *Mibifnim* and the editorial board, however, I had five years of further preparation for my rededication, including the three spent compiling the *Book of the Palmach*. Personal interviews with senior commanders, junior commanders, plain soldiers, and various observers; checking and counterchecking official records; reading and selecting letters, diaries, poems, sketches — usually of the fallen, whose families submitted them to me — all provided me with knowledge of the history, structure, and actions of the Palmach and tremendous insight into the minds and hearts of the human beings who created them. In spite of its bulk and high price, the book sold about 100,000 copies in six years, and went into eleven printings, proof of the general public's warm interest in the Palmach at that time. I don't imagine that many who bought it read all the way through its two thousand pages, but each time I walk into the homes of families who bought it, I greatly enjoy just seeing the book on their shelves.

Before I joined the publishing house the Kibbutz ha-Meuchad Federation sent me to study at the Hebrew University of Jerusalem for two years. Famous Rabbi Akiva is said to have claimed with pride that he began his education after the age of forty, and I felt pride in having at least this in common with him. I was not the only former Palmachnik making up for the loss of the normal years of higher education. Yigal Allon had already done his stint at the Hebrew University and gone on to St. Antony's, Oxford. Moshe Carmel, commander of the northern front in the War of Independence, and a cabinet minister in several Labor governments, had studied history and philosophy. Chaim Guri, poet of the Palmach; Haim Hefer, founder and director of the Palmach's *Tchizbatron;* David (Dado) Elazar, destined to be chief of staff in the Yom Kippur War; Gabriel Cohen, a professor of history at Tel Aviv University — were all former Palmach members who were at the Hebrew University at about the same time I was. For me, much of the interest and value of those years was in getting to know these younger members of the Palmach, and of the army, who were among the future leading research scholars, writers, and political leaders of the State. We formed what other countries call the ex-servicemen generation of students, were generally favorites of our professors and lecturers, and greatly enjoyed ourselves.

I studied general history, Hebrew literature, and elementary English and attended any other courses I fancied. I heard the great Gershom Sholem on Kabbala, Yitzhak Baer on Jewish history, and Avigdor Cherikover on the history of ancient Rome. Most of my professors were distinguished lecturers and research scholars, and I felt I was getting very good value for my kibbutz movement's money. The only bad moment I remember from these golden years I owe to Professor Joshua Prawer, who lectured on the Crusades and the Latin Kingdom of Jerusalem. On a cold winter's day, I, like most of the other old Palmachniks, was wearing our standard muddy-green knitted stocking cap, and feeling very pleased that I had it to keep my head, ears, neck, and chin warm, leaving only my eyes and nose exposed to the biting cold of the Jerusalem winter. When Prawer saw me in it, he looked at me with distaste and said, in a voice almost as biting as the surrounding air, "I wish you'd stop wearing that thing on your head. It makes you look like a butcher. It may have been the right thing in the Palmach, but it's definitely not the right thing *here!*" I was greatly taken aback by his unexpected assault on my favorite headgear. But on reflection I decided that Prawer was right, that the time had come to discard some of my old Palmach habits. I never again wore that stocking cap at the university — and Prawer became more than ever a good friend.

My English studies were at the humblest proficiency level, so I didn't attend any of the department's high-powered courses in English literature. But I became very friendly with two of my English teachers: Robert Friend, an excellent American poet who became a master translator of modern Hebrew poetry into English; and Hillel (Bill) Daleski, now a leading professor in the department. The author of many first-rate books on the English novel, Bill taught me to drink whiskey like an Anglo-Saxon — a skill I have never lost — and has remained a close friend. Through Robert Friend I met Ruth Nevo, today a distinguished

Shakespeare scholar and professor at the Hebrew University; and through Ruth I met the woman who was to become my second wife, Dorothea Krook. So my connection with the English Department at the Hebrew University is a special and long-standing one, dating back to my English courses from 1953 to 1955. About ten years later, I returned to the English Department to hear Ruth Nevo's fascinating lectures on Yeats and Eliot, which became a landmark in my literary development; since that time English literature and criticism have come to occupy an ever more important place in my life.

When my studies in Jerusalem ended, I was ready for my job in the publishing house. At the request of Kibbutz ha-Meuchad and with the consent of Ein-Harod, I have remained there ever since. My routine has never varied in all these years: I spend two or three days a week in Tel Aviv and four or five, including the Sabbath, at Ein-Harod. Though it is common for members of kibbutzim who work in Tel Aviv to spend the whole week there, going home only for the Sabbath, I deliberately chose to divide my week because I did not want to be physically cut off from my home. I had had enough of that, and so had Susi and the girls.

In Tel Aviv I attend the weekly meeting of the editorial board, meet with authors and contributors to *Mibifnim*, and supervise the production and distribution of the journal — which means having periodic rows with printers who lag behind schedule, and sometimes with the Kibbutz ha-Meuchad treasurer about delays in producing the promised budget. At Ein-Harod I do most of my reading and editing of manuscripts, and whatever writing I can find time for. Like most members of kibbutzim who have been "mobilized" to work outside the kibbutz, I have continued to perform all the appointed tasks of the kibbutz: kitchen and dining hall service on Sabbaths and festivals, guard duty, seasonal work in the orchards, and, every couple of years, a stint of three consecutive months in the kitchen and dining hall — with the grudging consent of the editorial board in Tel Aviv. I have also been an active member of our various committees and have periodically edited our weekly *Yoman* and many other Ein-Harod publications.

In my years with the Kibbutz ha-Meuchad Publishing House, I have seen it become one of the half-dozen leading publishers in the country. Although we never confined ourselves to publishing only kibbutz authors, we have particularly widened our scope in the last twenty years or so, publishing such leading Israeli poets and fiction writers as Aharon Appelfeld, A. B. Yehoshua, Aharon Megged, Natan Alterman, Abba Kovner, Amir Gilboa, Natan Zach, and Dan Pagis. Our list now includes works of academic research, scholarly editions of Hebrew classics, translations of important works of literature, criticism, philosophy, history, and sociology from most European languages, and, most recently, translations of Hebrew works into English. A good part of the translating is done by members of our editorial board. Like the country as a whole, our senior staff abounds in masters of many languages: several people can translate from Russian, Yiddish, and German; at least one translates from Latin, Spanish, and Italian; still another from French and English. What we cannot do ourselves we farm out, sometimes to members of kibbutzim.

I have observed this development with some pride, feeling it to be no small achievement for a publishing enterprise staffed almost entirely by members of the Kibbutz ha-Meuchad federation, whose total population is twenty-five thousand. Meanwhile, our raison d'être has remained intact: to ensure that no kibbutz author of merit shall remain unpublished, while kibbutz authors without merit are turned down as firmly as they would be by any commercial publisher; and to ensure that the collected writings of leading theoreticians, scholars, and creative writers of the kibbutz movement shall be preserved. The writings of Yitzhak Tabenkin, Yitzhak Sadeh, Yigal Allon, Moshe Tabenkin, and a dozen or so others have been preserved in this way, usually at the cost of many years of editorial labor.

My fellow members of the editorial board are for the most part gifted people, possessed of a wide range of knowledge and expertise, ardently interested in what they are doing, and disposed to live and work together in harmony. There is no dearth of argument and dispute at our meetings, and there have been occasional clashes of personality. But on the whole the prevailing good will and good humor, and the generally civilized behavior of our people make them a very congenial little society. Our deeper bond is the sense that we are engaged in a cooperative effort to create something worthwhile and lasting. Without being solemn about it, my colleagues share the sense of vocation that first led me into the work: the idea of helping to advance the intellectual and spiritual side of the life of the kibbutzim, and of the country as a whole. Like all publishers, we dislike losing money and do our best not to. But we all know that ours is not primarily a commercial venture, but something better and more interesting, a fact that has contributed most to my sense of well-being in my professional life.

Mibifnim divides its space between politics and letters, regularly publishing poetry, fiction, and literary criticism along with studies in politics, economics, sociology, and education. Moshe Breslavsky of Kibbutz Na'an, the editor who preceded me, had made a point of encouraging young Israeli writers, and first published in *Mibifnim* some of the best known of the Palmach generation, including Chaim Guri, Aharon Megged, and Alexander and Yonat Sened. I have continued that tradition, regularly publishing new young kibbutz poets, and encouraging them to go on writing. Naturally, articles that analyze and document the problems of the kibbutzim in all spheres of life have a dominant place in the pages of *Mibifnim,* but though I give priority to contributions from members of kibbutzim, I am always happy to publish suitable articles by nonkibbutz people as well, and have had some very good work from them. One of the longest-lived journals in the country, *Mibifnim* started life as a stenciled publication in 1923 and has appeared in print continuously since 1931. Certainly its forty-six volumes provide a fair index to the development of the kibbutzim from their earliest beginnings, and its last thirty-six volumes to the development of the State as well.

Among the great benefits I have derived from my work is the opportunity it has given me to know so many of our country's poets, novelists, story writers, and playwrights, as well as its journalists, scholars, translators, and fellow editors. These contacts have given me valuable firsthand knowledge of the creative life of the nation and the general condition of its culture, greatly enriching my personal life, too. Although I had previously known the writers of the Palmach generation, I have come to know them, especially Chaim Guri, Aharon Megged, Amir Gilboa, Abba Kovner, and Avner Treinin, a good deal better since I undertook publishing and editing.

Of the older generation of poets, I became well acquainted with

Avraham Shlonsky, Natan Alterman, Lea Goldberg, and Shimon Halkin. The first three are no longer alive, but Halkin, at eighty-five, continues to write and translate poetry with scarcely diminished vigor. I see him whenever I am in Jerusalem, and am freshly amazed each time at his poetic energy. The other octogenarian permanently on my Jerusalem visiting list is Dov Sadan, whom I have known since I was twenty and who encouraged and supported my poetic efforts from the start. As editor of the literary supplement of *Davar,* he published my first poems and stories in the early 1930s, and since then has read everything I write with unflagging interest and critical acumen. A phenomenon from that first great generation of the country's scholars and men of letters, Dov Sadan became a professor of Yiddish language and literature at the Hebrew University, and has published more than fifty books and hundreds of articles and essays on a staggering range of subjects that includes literary criticism, literary theory, philology and linguistics, the history of literature and language, and folklore and folk humor. He is also a tireless translator from Yiddish, German, and Polish and a prolific letter writer. He has handed over to the Hebrew University archives some thirty thousand letters from his correspondents, along with a few of his own letters, and he will doubtless have many more to add before he is gathered to the bosom of Abraham. Someday I shall add my own batch of Sadan letters to this vast collection.

He has a prodigious memory, not only for everything he has ever read, but also for all the people he has known and the events he has lived through. He can recount meetings, conversations, and events of thirty or forty or fifty years ago so clearly and vividly that they could have happened last week. He is frankly what we call a monologist: his talk flows in a steady stream, admitting no interruption, and it is sometimes difficult to get one's own innings. But most of his friends don't particularly care: they can hear themselves talk whenever they want to, they say, but they can only hear Dov Sadan talk on his own special conditions, and they are generally happy to grant them. His literary style is as individual as his conversation — baroque, richly ornamented, and full of intricate flourishes. But the flourishes and ornaments are his own thoroughly Hebrew inventions, deeply rooted in Hebrew sources thousands of years old. His style is not to everyone's liking, but even those who don't care for it admit its originality —

there is nothing quite like it anywhere else in modern Hebrew letters. In spite of this antique element, Sadan's writing can be sharp and caustic enough to satisfy the most advanced contemporary taste. Sadan's conversation is the same — often wittily, delightfully malicious, particularly about the great people he has known, another reason he never lacks an entranced audience for his discourses on a Sabbath morning.

Like other writers of his generation, Sadan does not separate his literary preoccupations from his involvement in the political scene and the spiritual and cultural problems of the country. He takes very clear, very firm political positions and has written extensively on the most pressing political problems of the time. But, though he broadly supports the Labor camp, he has never formally been a member of any party, and when he was a member of Parliament in the Labor party list in the mid-1960s he sat in the Knesset as an independent, nonparty member. The independence was typical of him: no one could tell him what to think or how to vote on any issue, and the idea of surrendering his individual judgment to a party whip was unthinkable to him.

I was by no means the only young writer to enjoy Dov Sadan's generous interest and help; he has encouraged dozens of young writers in the past fifty years, and has recently devoted himself particularly to the needs of refugee writers from Soviet Russia, Argentina, and other lands of persecution. He helps them get settled and find employment, and — most important — does everything in his power to promote them as writers in their new country, translating their works from Yiddish, German, or Polish into Hebrew, often without payment, and in other ways publicizing the merits of those whose gifts he believes in.

Dov Sadan has been my consultant in chief ever since I became editor of *Mibifnim*. Besides publishing anything he is willing to give me for the journal, I have gone to him for advice on scores of problems — literary, political, human, and kibbutz problems. His knowledge and insight encompass them all, and his clear-sightedness and sagacity have never let me down. On each of his birthdays I wish him, with special fervor, the traditional blessing of Jews: "May you live to be a hundred and twenty!" knowing that many others in this country find him as indispensable to their lives as I do.

* * *

Of all the creative writers I have known, master novelist and story writer Haim Hazaz stands alone. By general agreement, he ranks with Nobel Prize winner Shmuel Yosef Agnon as one of the two greatest Hebrew novelists of the past sixty years. A gigantic creative power, he seems to me truly a *builder* of modern Hebrew literature, comparable to the great builders of the land, a David Ben-Gurion, a Berl Katznelson, a Yitzhak Tabenkin. I knew and loved the man and his works for more than forty years and admired, indeed revered, his artist's personality until his death in 1973.

Hazaz's distinction as a novelist is in the extraordinary range and variety of his subject matter and in his rich and varied linguistic resources. His novels and stories embrace all the most decisive, far-reaching experiences of the Jewish people in his lifetime: the Russian Revolution; the fall of German Jewry; the messianic yearning of Yemenite Jewry to be restored to their historic homeland, and its fulfillment by the famous Magic Carpet operation that finally brought them to Eretz Yisrael; the coming of the survivors of the Holocaust; and the rise of the Jewish State. It is all there — intensely dramatized, known and felt with a passion that springs from total imaginative identification with the world and people he has created.

He worked hard to gain his insight. For example, to write his tetralogy, *Ya'ish,* about Yemenite Jewry, he lived among the Yemenites for seven years, studying and absorbing at close range what he needed to know for his saga. He did the same when he wanted to write about the Kurds, the Moroccans, and other Oriental communities. He lived among them, learning their language, immersing himself in their customs, practices, ideas, attitudes, embodying it all in his fiction with such stunning veracity that it was hard to believe the author was a Russian Ashkenazic Jew and not a born-and-bred Yemenite, Kurd, or Moroccan.

The magical authenticity was the effect, as much as anything, of his marvelous skill in creating a distinctive Hebrew language for each of the ethnic groups he wrote about. Most of them didn't speak Hebrew at all: the Yemenite Jews spoke Yemenite Arabic; the Kurdish Jews, Aramaic; the Russian Jews, Yiddish and Russian; the German Jews, German; and so on. Hazaz succeeded in finding for each of them a living mode of speech that was deeply rooted in traditional Hebrew sources, yet an invention of his own. In his creative exploration and utilization of the resources of the language, he seems to me to have no equal among modern Hebrew writers.

Hazaz started to publish in the early 1920s, when he was living in Paris. I was fourteen, and immediately ravished, when I first read his stories of the Russian Revolution. They addressed me with a peculiar directness and force, announcing that I had found "my" author. After that, I read everything of his I could lay my hands on, so by the time he settled in Eretz Yisrael in 1931, I knew his works well. Soon after Hazaz arrived, Berl Katznelson brought him to Ein-Harod for a visit and introduced us.

His first visit to Ein-Harod was an event in itself. The whole kibbutz gathered in the dining hall to hear Hazaz read the manuscript of a new play — which turned out to be the only play he ever published. Set in the seventeenth century — a period marked by the appearance of a series of false messiahs in the Jewish-populated towns of Turkey, Italy, and elsewhere — *The End of Days* dramatizes the spiritual tumult produced in a German town by the rumor that the Messiah is about to appear, heralding "the end of days." The theme is the archetypal one of the clash of the generations: between the young Jews of the town, who ardently want to carry out the revolutionary change of the promised redemption by a mass aliyah to Eretz Yisrael that will end the exile forever, and the Orthodox establishment, which, in spite of the suffering of the Jews crying out for redemption, wants to go on as it has always done, refusing to respond to the call of a messiah they deem to be false, arguing that "the time for redemption has not yet come," and that to pursue it would bring catastrophe on them all.

Hazaz's reading made an overwhelming impression. I remember his look, his voice, his message. He appeared to be thin and frail and a little shrunken when he rose to his feet, and his voice at the start was scarcely audible. But as he read, his voice grew stronger and stronger, his body seemed to become erect and taller; his eyes behind his glasses sparkled with the sheen of steel. His fine, grizzling beard moved violently as if blown by a wind, but it was his fervor that was moving it. His passion reached a peak as he read the fiery words of his young hero: "We will make the whole world boil in a midday sun." And when the hero cries out in fury, "The Jews don't *want* redemption!" the impact was electrifying. No one then could fail to recognize how tragically true this was of contemporary European Jewry: harassed and hunted by vicious anti-Semitism in every European country, yet failing to rise up and go to their redemption in Eretz Yisrael. When Hazaz finished reading, the audience sat in frozen silence for what seemed long minutes, then burst into wild applause, continuing as though they would never stop.

When Hazaz included the play in his collected works more than thirty-five years later, he dedicated it to the memory of his only son, called Zuzik, whose death in the War of Independence, Hazaz used to say, left him without a single blood relation in the world. He believed all his family had perished in the pogroms of the Ukraine after the First World War.

I met Hazaz often over the years, each time discovering a new facet of his complex nature, finding his passions and idiosyncrasies inexhaustibly interesting, moving, and delightful. Although his manner was austere and somewhat withdrawn, he could be a gracious and courtly host, and he was by nature a sociable person. But he was often oppressed by a deep sadness, and he was sometimes bitter about the world's injustices. Specific and general outrages affected him with equal intensity, and when he brooded over the condition of the Jews, both in Eretz Yisrael and elsewhere, hope and faith in the redemption he believed in tended to alternate with anger and despair at the lack of vision in his fellow Jews.

But he could also be full of humorous, light-hearted fancies. While I was on my mission to the Working Youth, we spent many a Sabbath afternoon walking along the Tel Aviv seashore, often accompanied by five-year-old Zuzik, who was beguiled by his father's imagination. "Look at those skimmers running around on the sand!" Hazaz would say. "This one is like a bride who has just come out from under the wedding canopy. That one is an impudent creature who sounds like a fishwife. And this one is a witch: see how viciously she's pulling that fish from the beak of her sister!" And so he went on until the child, tired of the talk, rushed at the birds and shooed them into flight.

One spring day, as we were passing a small sand dune, Hazaz

called my attention to the curious behavior of two crabs. The male crab had been scuttling in one direction, the female in the other, when suddenly they both stopped, turned back, and met, their claws tangling as they became, as the Bible says, "one flesh." "That's what you call love at first sight!" Hazaz said with a laugh. "That's the power of naked passion!" And, still laughing, he recalled a parallel example of fine naked passion between two young human beings. "It happened in the Metro in Paris as I was going up an escalator. On the step above me stood a young man with curly hair whom I had scarcely noticed. Suddenly we passed a young woman with gleaming blond braids on the down escalator. The young man turned his head toward her, and she gazed back at him. Instantly, without a moment's pause, he leaped across the handrail to the other escalator, landed a few steps above the young woman, rushed down and clasped her in his arms, and she happily surrendered herself to his embrace. Who knows the way of a man with a maid?" Hazaz concluded.

Intensely interested in the carnal side of human life, Hazaz used erotic scenes in many of his stories to explore sexual impulses and their connection with the highest spiritual aspirations. A memorable example is *Chatan Damim,* another of his key works, translated into English as *Bridegroom of Blood.* Written in Paris in 1928, it is a strange, powerful story in poetic prose, set in the desert and centering on Zipporah, Moses' wife, and her dramatic act of circumcising her small son, described in Exodus 4:24–25. Zipporah is sick with desire for Moses, but he keeps away from her, presumably because he is totally absorbed in his communications with God. In a frenzy of jealousy, thinking he is going back to Egypt to find "another Zipporah," she cries to the Almighty to "make her find favor in the eyes of her husband." Instead she has a waking dream of God Himself answering her sexual need: "Like a winged creature, or leaping like a lion from its cage, He conquered her. She still feels His enormous weight on her bones, the wild passion of His right hand. She still feels the searing fire on her lips, fire kissing her inner soul." Then she explicitly calls on God to be her lover: "Gradually she worked herself up, and became more and more excited. She stroked her breasts and undulated her belly, swaying her body with outstretched hands. Her ornaments shook, ringing loud. 'Oh God! Listen to my heart!

Awesome lover, glorious and brave! Run your hands over me!' "

Hazaz's bold originality is in intimating that Zipporah's motive for quickly, frantically, circumcising her son is not only the pious spiritual one attributed to her in the Bible — to save Moses from God's vengeance for having broken the covenant "between Him and his seed." Her motive is also to establish her own sexual covenant of blood with the Lord, which she proclaims by triumphantly crying out the words of the biblical text:

> Awful as a nightmare, her face blazing and her knees smeared with blood, like a woman on her first night, she opened her mouth and howled: *Bridegroom of blood! You are truly a bridegroom of blood to me!**

Hazaz's story in its first English translation caught the attention of T. S. Eliot, then editor of the *Criterion*. He wanted to publish it in his quarterly but didn't in the end because it was too long.

The interest in the erotic was typical of his novelist's curiosity about every facet of human behavior and motivation. But Hazaz was also passionately interested in the art of writing itself: in the problems of the art of fiction, in the conditions of the creative life, and in the special demands it made on the Hebrew writer. These were the topics he returned to again and again in our talks, illuminating them for me like no one else I have ever known. He had always lived in Jerusalem, and we usually met in one of his favorite cafés or for long walks in the quieter streets of the city or in the Valley of the Cross, which he particularly loved. In the last ten years or so of his life, I often visited him in his quiet, spacious apartment in Rehov Hovevei-Zion, a secluded road in Talbieh lined with low-walled old gardens from which tall trees spread their branches and dense green shrubs spill over the walls.

"There is no such thing as a final draft. Every draft is a first draft," Hazaz once said to me, adding that when a new book of his was published he was afraid to open it, knowing he would want to rewrite it from the first page. It confirmed what I had long suspected: that he was more of a perfectionist than any writer I had ever known, and he would never be fully at peace

---

*The quotations are taken from Haim Hazaz, *Bridegroom of Blood*, translated from the Hebrew by Shirley Kaufman with Aviva Hazaz and Shlomit Rimmon, published by Haim Hazaz Memorial Foundation, Jerusalem (1983).

with anything he wrote. Another time he spoke of the novelist's main problem in creating his fictive personalities. A character in a story, he said, has to stand solidly on his two feet. His development must have an inner logic, springing from his individual character and the conditions within which he operates. If he does not satisfy these requirements, he is nothing but a marionette controlled from behind the scenes. And the Hebrew story writer has a further problem, from which writers of other nations are happily exempt. He has to create a hero produced by a particular historical reality and, at the same time, he has to pour into this particularized mold the image of the Jew of the future that we dream of. In other words, the actual has somehow to be fused with the ideal. This, said Hazaz, is by no means a simple matter.

In my judgment, he often succeeded brilliantly: in his Jews of the Russian Revolution in *Gates of Bronze;* in the hero of his Yemenite tetralogy, *Ya'ish;* and in the young protagonist of his play *The End of Days.* This fusion of the actual and the ideal appears to have been intimately connected with his preoccupation with the theme of redemption. The Hazaz hero whose life centers on waiting for the Messiah and the redemption of the Jews and the whole world is always a creature of concrete historical time and place; at the same time, he embodies an exalted ideal: the spiritual quest for messianic redemption. This, for Hazaz, is the highest aspiration of which man is capable. It is this haunting leitmotif of his vision of the human condition that leads people to speak of his total body of work as a "messianic comedy," as Dante's is a "divine comedy" and Balzac's a "human comedy."

Still another theme he returned to again and again was that of the writer's life as an all-demanding vocation. You have to commit your whole life to writing, he used to say. If you don't or can't, or if you do it in a halfhearted, part-time way, you ought not to be doing it at all; you ought to be doing something practical instead — growing potatoes, breeding cows, baking bread, or building houses. There is no justification for writing, he seemed to be saying, unless you give to it all you have. But if you do, you are performing one of the greatest creative acts of man; yours is a priceless service to humanity. Then, remembering his own people (he never forgot them for long), he would say that literature has been our life's blood. Without it there would have been no Zion-

ism, no Jewish State, nothing — nothing of what is most precious
for our future, our survival. The fervor, the almost violent passion
with which he said it still rings in my ears. It impressed on me, not
for the first or last time, what a model he was of the dedicated artist and the visionary Jew, united.

I have written more poems about Haim Hazaz than about any
other human being except Susi. During his lifetime I wrote "ha-
Zayit" ("The Olive"), and dedicated it to him. After his death, I
wrote a long poem, *Yerushalai'im shel Hazaz* ("Jerusalem of
Hazaz"), on the analogy of the famous song "Yerushalai'im shel
Zahav," ("Jerusalem of Gold"), in which I imagine the heroes
and heroines of his stories marching in procession to his fresh
grave on the Mount of Olives and encircling it, with the name of
their creator on their lips.

It is a long procession, and they are all there: the Russian pioneers, the Yemenites, the Kurds, the Moroccans, the survivors of
the Holocaust — among them the Good Samaritan, who made it
her life's task to tend the sick and needy, and the former freedom
fighter, who marries a rich American man and goes to live in the
United States. Each representative figure in the poem is named
and briefly characterized. People who know Hazaz's works liked
the fancy and thought it a fair tribute to the immense variety of
the world he created in his fiction.

For my most recent book of poems, *The Well,* I wrote a cycle of
sixteen poems called "In the Steps of Hazaz." The epigraph of
each poem is a quotation from one of his stories, and the poem
reflects the theme expressed or hinted at in the epigraph. People
have teased me a little about my attachment to Hazaz. "Aren't
there other great Hebrew authors to write poems about?" they
ask. "What about Agnon? What about Alterman, Shlonsky, Lea
Goldberg, and so on?" I always agree that the others are great,
too, and ought to have sheaves of poems written about them. I
keep writing these poems because I think I shall never again have
a creative spirit enter and lodge itself in my deepest being as did
that of Haim Hazaz.

19

The Kibbutz: Changes and Continuities

WHAT HAS HAPPENED to Ein-Harod and the other kibbutzim since the establishment of the State of Israel? The answer is, There have been radical changes, and there have been continuities within the changes, and I think the two together are encouraging proof of the combined stability and flexibility of the kibbutz form of society.

The changes and continuities are often so intertwined that it is barely possible to consider them separately. But at least some continuities are almost undiluted by change. One is the role of the kibbutzim in the defense of the country. In proportion to their numbers (3 to 3½ percent of the Jewish population), they have continued to take a leading part in the Israel Defense Forces (IDF), the kingpin of the survival of the Jewish State. A significantly high percentage of the senior officers and field officers of the IDF have been members of kibbutzim, and each year a disproportionately high number of young men from the kibbutzim join the elite volunteer units: pilots, paratroopers, frogmen, and special commandos, under the direct command of the chief of staff, reserved for particularly dangerous (and usually top secret) missions. In addition, every young member of a kibbutz, men and women alike, give one year of extra national service. This is a universal practice of the kibbutzim, although the loss of manpower for another year is a serious economic hardship. The additional year may be spent in a combat unit, in an auxiliary army service, in a new settlement, usually in a dangerous border area, or in social or educational work in the youth movements or development towns.

The kibbutzim continued to lead the pioneer settlement movement immediately after the establishment of the State, founding many new kibbutzim, especially in border areas. They were very active again in the period following the Six Day War, when new kibbutzim were founded in rapid succession on the Golan Heights, in the Jordan Valley, and in the Gaza Strip across the Green Line (pre-1967 borders), and in the Arava south of the Negev inside the Green Line. Older kibbutzim like Ein-Harod have regularly sent veteran members to live in one of the new kibbutzim, for a year or longer, to act as advisers and guides in the initial, most difficult period. In spite of the hardships of building a new kibbutz from scratch, most of our young people seem to enjoy it; they presumably wouldn't go, and certainly wouldn't stay, if they didn't. It is pleasantly ironical to hear them, on their visits home, talk about the joys of living a simple life without the decadent luxuries of the parental kibbutz; they rejoice in the small size and the youth of their new society compared with the sprawling establishment of the old. They seem particulary happy about having responsible key work in their new settlements from the start, for in the older kibbutzim they have to wait, sometimes for years, for such jobs. I have often thought how lucky the kibbutzim are in being able to provide their young with this blameless way of cutting umbilical cords and getting away from their parents and parents' generation to make an independent life for themselves — all with the admiring approval of their elders, who cannot but rejoice and take great pride in the pioneering spirit of their sons and daughters, though they may secretly grieve not having them around in the home kibbutz.

The most radical changes, with the most far-reaching consequences, have been in the economic structure of the kibbutzim. Agriculture has become ever more completely mechanized and, most recently, computerized, keeping pace with the best scientific farming in the world, particularly in dairy farming, irrigation, and cotton growing. Sometimes we surpass world records in agricultural production. For example, our neighbor kibbutz, Merhavia, broke a world record with a cow that yielded 2600 gallons of milk per year; and in cotton growing, another world record was established with cotton fiber plants that produced more than 440 pounds of cotton per dunam. The best record, however, is that the kibbutzim produce 40 to 45 percent of the country's agricultural products though they represent only 3 to 3.5 percent of the total Jewish population.*

But the mechanization of agriculture has brought its own problems. The more mechanized a branch becomes, the fewer workers are required to run it, and the kibbutzim have faced the worldwide problem that results from mechanization — what to do with the redundant workers. The answer has been industrialization, and rapid industrialization of the kibbutzim in the last twenty-five years or so has been the biggest change in their economic organization. Finding work for displaced agricultural workers has not been the only reason, although it has been one of its good effects. The primary motive has been to create fresh sources of income for the community in line with the modern industrial development of the world as a whole.

Many kibbutzim have at least one factory or plant, and some of these enterprises have proved to be spectacularly successful. Kibbutz Na'an, one of the first kibbutzim to set up a factory, in the early 1950s, chose to manufacture sprinklers for farm and garden irrigation. Because the big industrial enterprises of the world find it uneconomical to produce small objects of this kind, Na'an managed to corner a world market for its sprinklers, quickly becoming an affluent society by kibbutz standards. Other kibbutzim have been similarly successful. Ma'agan Michael, on the coast between Tel Aviv and Haifa, has a world market for its plastic shopping baskets, supermarket carts, and other plastic products; one of its regular customers is Marks and Spencer. Kibbutz Ein-Dor (the traditional site of the Witch of Endor's activities) produces telephone coils almost exclusively for export; Kibbutz Gvat in the Emek sells plastic pipes for irrigation to South American and other countries, sending instructors to teach the buyers how to use them; Kibbutz Afikim near the Sea of Galilee has become wealthy from its big factory for wood products,

---

*The kibbutzim work 35 percent of the total farming land of the country: 1,500,000 dunams out of a total of 4,200,000 dunams.

made from timber imported from abroad. The kibbutzim have sensibly concentrated on light, consumer-oriented industries like plastic and rubber products, electrical and electronic equipment, canned fruits and vegetables, clothing and leather goods, toys, and pharmaceutical and chemical products. Several also have printing plants; the one at Kibbutz Be'eri in the western Negev prints the checks for most of the banks in the country. Science-based industries have become great favorites, producing medical instruments, electronically controlled irrigation equipment, and plastics of various kinds. They are popular because they give the kibbutzim an opportunity to use to capacity the brain power, education, and technological skills of their members and the kibbutz's special ability to adapt rapidly to the newest technological advances.

The success of the industrialization of the kibbutzim seems to me decisive proof of the purely economic benefits to be derived from the cooperative element of the kibbutz setup: what can be achieved by planned cooperative effort and communal ownership in contrast to cutthroat competition and private ownership. The profit motive is vigorously alive, but it is exercised for the benefit of the whole community instead of private individuals. The success of kibbutz industry, and the reasons for it, have been widely recognized by economic experts, including free-enterprise economists who are generally least sympathetic to the ideology of the kibbutz.

However, our very success in industry has produced problems that touch on some of the most fundamental principles of the kibbutz, including its traditional agricultural basis. In many kibbutzim, factories and plants have become the main source of income, leading to a significant reduction in the agricultural branches that are either unprofitable or demand an excessive amount of manual labor. Even though everyone has always recognized that the kibbutz has to get rid of economic enterprises that don't pay off, there is a good deal of ideological distress about what people regard as the erosion of the working-of-the-land and manual-labor ideals of the pioneer Zionist settlement movements. The process had been going on for a long time, even before the industrialization of the kibbutz. For example, Ein-Harod, for purely economic reasons, successively closed down its vegetable garden, its vineyard, and its fruit orchard, retaining its profitable grapefruit orchards and olive groves, and planting pecan trees and, most recently, avocados and mangoes because they promise to be profitable. But industrialization accelerated the process, and some people find it difficult to reconcile themselves to the shrinking of the agricultural element, no matter how economically justified.

The problem of hired labor has been a still more serious problem engendered by the industrialization of the kibbutzim. Again, industrialization only aggravated an existing problem, which came into being with the mass immigration of Jews coming from Arab lands in the early 1950s. The kibbutzim would have been ready to take in the new "Oriental" immigrants as members, but the vast majority of them had no desire whatever to join a kibbutz. They knew nothing about socialism, they didn't understand the cooperative-egalitarian principles of the kibbutz, and what they came to understand they didn't like. But they were poor, unskilled, often illiterate, and desperately in need of employment. David Ben-Gurion appealed to the kibbutzim to take in the new immigrants as hired laborers, even though to do so would oblige them to set aside their cherished egalitarian principle, which tolerated no employer-employee relationship in a kibbutz. Ben-Gurion's appeal created a severe dilemma for the kibbutzim. Most of them resisted; some capitulated, willing to try it out on an experimental basis; and the hired-labor question became a hotly disputed ideological issue throughout the 1950s.

The accelerating industrialization of the 1960s and 1970s sharpened and intensified the dilemma. In order to be profitable, the new kibbutz factories had to expand, and in order to expand, they needed more labor than the kibbutz could supply from its membership. Thus there was a strong temptation to hire unskilled workers from the neighboring development towns, whose people were constantly seeking employment. Many kibbutzim did, and some became rich as a consequence; but they lost a good part of their kibbutz character in the process, and members of these affluent kibbutzim often felt considerable moral discomfort at the knowledge that they owed their ever rising standard of life, partly at least, to the labor of hired hands.

A related problem that arises from the industrialization of the kibbutz is the danger of creating in the kibbutz factory a management-versus-workers dichotomy, leading to the growth of a managerial class that performs the highly skilled planning, executive, and administrative jobs and lords it over the hired semiskilled and unskilled workers. This aggravated form of employer-versus-employee flies in the face of the kibbutz principle of work equality, which insists that every form of productive work is equally important and honorable. It also introduces a creeping inequality between rank-and-file members of the kibbutz and the privileged factory managers, who constantly dash abroad on marketing business, to attend trade fairs, or to instruct their customers in the use of their products, while the ordinary kibbutz member gets one, or at most two, trips abroad in a lifetime.

These distortions and malfunctions are the result of objective circumstances and have generally occurred without ill will on anybody's part. The kibbutz factory managers don't deliberately set out to acquire privileges denied to their fellow members; it just happens that their jobs give them these privileges, and they are for the most part as anxious as their underprivileged brethren to find solutions consistent with kibbutz principles to the problems created by the phenomenon of industrialization. Seeking solutions to these and other problems has become one of the chief functions of the elected bodies of the kibbutz federation — ours, formerly the Kibbutz ha-Meuchad, is now the United Kibbutz Movement (UKM), Takam in Hebrew. Individual kibbutzim periodically turn to Takam for guidance and help in solving problems and, after long and intensive discussion with the individual kibbutz or group of kibbutzim plagued with the problem, and only with the approval of the majority of their membership, solutions are reached and put into effect.

Thus, on the management-versus-workers problem, the solution proposed is to rotate managerial staff every few years. This is being tried and seems to be working out well on the whole, even though it involves a certain amount of waste in the duplication of expensive skills and experience in the top managerial staff. But this is the price we have to pay for maintaining the principle of social equality in the kibbutz, and we think it worth paying.

Several solutions to the hired-labor problem have been proposed and implemented. The least radical is to keep to a minimum the percentage of hired people in the whole labor force, a solution intended for those small kibbutzim that would have to close down their factories if they were deprived of all hired workers. The most radical and best solution is, by common consent, automation. A fully automated factory does away with the need for any hired labor at all, because it requires the minimum of hands, and because the hands don't have to be particularly skilled. The factory can thus be worked entirely by members of the kibbutz, including older members who are no longer physically capable of working in the fields, the orchards, the cowshed, and so on. All new kibbutz plants aspire to total automation from the start, and older ones plan to introduce automation where possible or to close down their existing plants and replace them with new, totally automated ones.

An intermediate solution to the hired-labor problem takes the form of requiring kibbutzim that hire labor for their factories to pay a "fine," really a kind of tax, into a central fund, to be used for the purpose of helping kibbutzim that want to eliminate their hired force to meet the costs — primarily the severance pay due the workers, which can be very high. Ein-Harod was one of the beneficiaries of this fund when, in 1981, we decided to dismiss all the hired help in our stainless-steel factory. We had tried other solutions first, offering the workers a share in the ownership of the factory. But they had refused, preferring to be employees without the responsibilities and worries of ownership. So in the end they were paid off, receiving full compensation, along with a good deal of know-how, which enabled some of them to set up their own small workshops. Thanks to the help we received from the central fund, the workers had no cause for complaint about their severance pay and parted on excellent terms with Ein-Harod.

The hired labor problem extends beyond the factories of the individual kibbutzim to the regional plants usually owned by all or most of the kibbutzim of the area, often jointly with the moshavim. They are generally processing plants — for cotton, poultry, cattle fodder, and for sorting and packing citrus and other fruit — and are worked almost entirely by hired labor; the kibbutzim could by no means find the manpower for these regional plants as well as for their own factories. Although everyone knows the kibbutzim could not maintain their productive industries without these plants, the ideological objections to hired labor have nevertheless been discussed over and over again with great fervor. One solution, already implemented in some plants, is to share the profits with the hired laborers in the form of premiums or bonuses. Another is to invite the hired workers to participate actively in the plant's management. A third is to turn over ownership to or share it with the Histradrut, thus making the labor federation the sole or part employer. Those kibbutzim that have adopted the last plan have suffered financial losses but find the loss preferable to the hired labor problem.

The "materialization" or "bourgeoisization" of the kibbutzim has been another consequence of industrialization. The steep rise in the income of the kibbutzim with the most successful industries has led to a parallel rise in their standard of living. They can afford to give their members bigger houses, better furniture, air conditioners, TV sets, increased personal allowances, and private telephones (considered a great amenity), as well as higher education for those who want it, leave of absence for travel abroad, and other "treats" that were inconceivable in the 1950s. This has resulted in a greater preoccupation with the material things of life, at the expense, inevitably, of the spiritual, cultural, and ideological.

A further social problem, bearing on the materialism though not arising from the industrialization of the kibbutzim, has been created by "outside" sources of income or amenities that have become available to some members of the kibbutzim and not to others. German reparations payments to survivors of the Holocaust and their descendants have been one source since the early 1950s; bequests have become another, as has the property (houses, cars, money, and so on) of new members joining the kibbutz at a relatively mature age. Since these bequests and properties are often quite substantial, they have become particularly problematic. In earlier years such windfalls were turned over to the kibbutz for the use of the community, and in some kibbutzim that practice continues. In recent years, however, there has been a growing tendency to retain these funds or properties for private use, sometimes with the consent of the kibbutz, often without. With or without the community's consent, it obviously introduces a serious inequality between members in the matter of material possessions.

Less serious, but scarcely less embittering to the have-nots, are the relatively affluent grandparents, aunts, and uncles in Tel Aviv, or for that matter New York or Toronto, who love to send lavish gifts of money or clothes or round-trip air fares to their kibbutz grandchildren, nephews, and nieces. The kibbutz usually does not make a fuss about such gifts, but though the amenities they provide are trivial by the standards of the outside world, they are important for the traditional kibbutz ideal of absolute equality in the distribution of material goods and have become a source of resentment to members who see themselves as the victims — those who don't have rich relatives.

Takam again comes to the rescue, endeavoring to check the growth of inequalities. Its main concern is to equalize as far as possible the standard of living of the "poor" and "rich" kibbutzim. According to a recent rough calculation, 25 percent of the total of 262 kibbutzim are very badly off, 25 percent are very well off, and the remaining 50 percent fall somewhere between. Two hundred thirty kibbutzim have a total of more than 300 industrial plants. The remaining 32, generally young kibbutzim, have no industries.

At the urgent request of the kibbutzim, rich and poor alike, Takam issued standard-of-living guidelines for housing, living expenses per head, the use of cars, the proportion of the kibbutz's income to be spent on services as opposed to productive work, and so on. They are rigid about some things, flexible about others. The most rigid rulings are about dwellings, which are all required to be exactly the same size, though the permissible area tends to increase every few years; hours of work, which must be the same for each age group; number of days of annual holiday; average monthly living expenses per person, which includes the allowance per member for food, services, education, health, taxes, and so forth; and the use of cars, about which the rules are particularly strict, because this is one of the most sought after amenities. Private ownership of cars is not allowed; in addition, private use of cars supplied to people working outside the kibbutz is prohibited, no matter whether the car belongs to the kibbutz itself or to the outside employer. Cars are allowed to be used only for transportation to and from work; after working hours, they have to be turned in to the kibbutz pool to be available, at a fixed rate paid out of their personal allowances, to all kibbutz members for evening or Sabbath outings. The kibbutz goes so far as to pay outside employers a fee for the use of their cars in the common pool, just to make sure that no member has a car available for private use. To the outsider it may all sound very pedantic and complicated, but in practice it seems to work out well enough, and the list of applicants for evening or Sabbath or holiday use of the cars is always full.

The guidelines are more flexible about such amenities as television sets, air conditioners, and telephones, leaving it to each individual kibbutz to make its decision about them. They also propose optimal personal allowances, which are not always observed by the more affluent kibbutzim; optimal financial help to members' needy parents or relatives outside the kibbutz; and — a recent innovation — suitable severance pay to members, or the sons and daughters of members, who wish to leave the kibbutz to restart their lives outside.

What penalties or "sanctions" are available to Takam to enforce its rulings on any member kibbutz that persistently flouts or transgresses them? The most serious penalty is expulsion from the kibbutz federation, but to my knowledge it has never been used. The intermediate penalty is called severing relations with the transgressing kibbutz, which means that Takam withholds financial assistance for the kibbutz's investment and development projects, its cooperative purchasing, educational needs, cultural activities, teachers' and instructors' seminars, and other things. The threat of severing relations is evidently enough to persuade the violating kibbutz to mend its ways, for I can remember no case in which these economic sanctions have actually been applied. This generally healthy situation is doubtless a function of the totally democratic relationship between the kibbutzim and their federation. Takam is no autocratic body laying down the law to its member kibbutzim; it is in effect the member kibbutzim themselves actively coordinating and enforcing their own democratic decisions about the matters affecting their common welfare.

In addition to the effects of materialism on the rising standards of living of the kibbutzim, other more subtle, and in some ways more damaging, influences have been at work. These emanate from what one may call the worldwide skepticism of the younger generation about the validity of traditional idealistic values, and the worldwide permissiveness that springs from the skepticism. Although the kibbutzim, and indeed the country as a whole, have generally been free of the conflicts between the generations that have afflicted most of the world since the 1960s and beyond, the spirit of rebellion against accepted values has expressed itself among our young in a new tendency to insist on what they call self-realization — meaning the realization of what they deem to be good for them individually, without much reference to what may be good for the community as a whole. On the subject of study leave, for example: "I want to study now, this year. Not next year, or the following year, when it best suits the kibbutz's work schedules. And I want to study what interests me, not what the kibbutz needs." The kibbutz has gone a long way toward meeting the desire of the young to travel abroad, allowing them to go off for a year after their period of national service, on condition that they first spend one year working in the kibbutz and that they pay their own way. But if a young man wants to take his travel leave immediately after his service, and the kibbutz refuses to release him from the required year's work before he goes, he may find this sufficient cause to pack up and leave for good. The young have become much more choosy about their work in the kibbutz and are much more inclined to insist on working at what they personally find most interesting, refusing to reconcile themselves to do what is most urgent for the kibbutz. Thus, the kibbutz may be in great need of an extra kindergarten teacher, but the young woman who could fill the post wants to teach junior school, or physiotherapy, or gymnastics and dance, and won't hear of anything else. So she is sent to learn what she wants to teach, while the kibbutz has to hire the kindergarten teacher from outside its membership. If the kibbutz refuses to be accommodating, saying it doesn't need another junior school teacher or physiotherapist or gymnastics and dance teacher, the young woman is likely to leave the kibbutz and seek what she wants in the world outside, often successfully.

This drive toward self-realization, among other factors, has led to a significant increase in the number of *azivot* (departures). Since 1970, an average of 50 percent of the young members born and brought up in kibbutzim have left. Some return after a time, but many do not. This has been disturbing, of course, even though it is offset by the new kibbutzim being formed all the time by pioneering youth movements from Israel and from abroad. And it is further offset, but only potentially, by the hundreds of families who want to join a kibbutz and are prevented from doing so by the perpetual lack of suitable housing. It has been reckoned that the kibbutzim could take four to five thousand newcomers a year if the housing existed. Meanwhile, in 1983 our Takam group of kibbutzim alone absorbed twenty-five hundred adults and children, from Israel and abroad. So the situation is dynamic, as it has always been. People leave and people come; the newcomers are usually as good as those who left; the kibbutz population, totaling 120,000 adults and children, grows at the rate of about 2 percent per annum, and remains 3 to 3.5 percent of the total Jewish population of the country.

I have sometimes been asked whether the kibbutz has produced a New Man, a new human type, as its founders firmly believed it would. My answer is both no and yes. I say no when I consider how many kibbutz people seem to have retained unmodified some of the least noble traits of humanity as a whole. They can be as egoistical or insensitive or malicious or vengeful, and as crude and uncouth in their social behavior as the worst anywhere. Besides, the kibbutz setup may actually induce weaknesses of its own, especially in its more commonplace members. It may discourage individual initiative, just because the community as a whole has so much of it. And the absence of the competitive spirit may weaken those who need competition as a spur to achievement. Because kibbutz life is generally more leisurely, less pressured, than life outside, it may also produce a lack of stamina for standing up to the pace and pressure of modern life that might make adaptation to the big world difficult for anyone brought up in a kibbutz. Kibbutz life, in short, may in some ways be too protective, too easy, too undemanding, though, paradoxically, it is so exacting and challenging in other ways.

Yet, having given due consideration to the shortcomings, I feel that on balance they are outweighed by the merits and gains. An interesting circumstantial proof of this is the common reaction of the outside world to a kibbutz member who leaves his kibbutz and wants to start a new life outside. If the kibbutz member is thirty or older, he is likely to go straight into a managerial job in a Histadrut or independent enterprise and will probably quickly rise in the managerial hierarchy. This is because his exceptional expertise is immediately recognized and sought after, assuring him a secure place in the professional middle class of his new society. But what happens if the kibbutz leaver is a young person, say just out of the army and without any specialized qualifications? Such a young man or woman tends to find employment very quickly — more quickly than other job seekers. And why? Because the prospective employer, whether he is generally sympathetic or unsympathetic to the kibbutzim, is likely to think he will do well to have a former kibbutznik in his work force. He will think of him as dependable, responsible, capable of doing different kinds of work, capable of working with others, and probably also good at organizing his fellow workers, having learned this skill during his stint as work organizer in his kibbutz. The boss is likely to think of him as honest, more loyal, and more serious than others, and in general as somehow morally superior, in ways he may not always be able to define. What these attitudes suggest is that the outside world has come to recognize and value the educative effect of kibbutz life, what Aharon Zisling referred to when he spoke of *yishuvim mechanchim*, "settlements educate," meaning that the kibbutzim provide an education in values not easily found elsewhere.

I still believe this to be true, by and large because the kibbutzim have retained a great deal of their original character and vocation, especially in comparison with Israeli society as a whole. The comparison is relevant, because the kibbutzim have never been, and are less than ever, isolated rural communities out of touch with the outside world. Partly because of the small size of the country, mainly because of their active participation in the life of the nation, the kibbutzim are in close touch with what happens in the country and tend to be quickly and powerfully influenced by the prevailing currents of thought, opinion, attitude, and fashion in the country as a whole.

Nevertheless, the kibbutz has successfully retained some of its earlier principles and practices. It still fulfills its original Zionist-socialist ideal of a life based on work; and still, if possible, a combination of physical and intellectual work. Every member is a worker; there is no leisure class, and never will be. The principle of self-service also remains unchanged; all the work of the community is done by the members themselves, with a minimum of hired help. At Ein-Harod, for example, we have no hired labor except for the jobs that have always, from the start, required it: mainly builders — because the kibbutz has never been able to train enough from its membership to meet all its needs — and specialized professionals like doctors, dentists, and sometimes teachers. We also occasionally hire a nurse to take care of one of our aged.

What remains, too, is the ideal of productive work, that is, agriculture and industry, in contradistinction to work in services. More man-hours than formerly are given to nonproductive services of the kibbutz, but the emphasis is still overwhelmingly on productive work, whereas in the country as a whole there has been a growing trend toward a service mentality. People tend to disdain blue collar work, regard all white collar work as more prestigious, and prefer any boring office job or "business" to work in a factory, in building, farming, and so on.

The social structure of the kibbutz supports the absence of class distinctions that have tended to develop in the country as a whole. Men and women are still valued basically as human beings, not according to their possessions or the status of their work or their academic degrees. And most of the essential equalities that have made the kibbutz a uniquely egalitarian society remain unchanged. One kibbutz family may have a color TV set or a stereo or a closet full of American dresses while another doesn't, but everyone, without exception, lives in a house of exactly the same size; works the same number of hours according to his age group; receives the same education for the same number of years; and gets the same health care, with the same old-age care for elderly parents and grandparents. The totally democratic decision-making process also remains exactly the same as it was from the beginning. And there are still no criminals and no prisons in the kibbutzim.

Also, in spite of the perceptible drop in our young people's interest in ideological issues, I see no significant change in the kibbutz's habit of self-scrutiny and self-criticism, or in its passion for changing and improving whatever needs to be changed or improved — endlessly, it seems. And, most of all perhaps, the sense of community and the love of planning and participating in great communal events remains as intense as ever, and as exhilarating and moving to behold as it was when I arrived. The most regular communal events are the festivals, and though these have been greatly developed and elaborated upon since their beginnings in the 1920s, the original idea and pattern of the important festivals have been retained almost without change. Our celebration of Pesach is a good example.

Although Ein-Harod's Passover celebration remains the traditional festival of freedom commemorating the exodus from Pharaoh's Egypt, it has also acquired the character of a spring festival. This new element is expressed both in the original additions to the traditional Seder, the Passover Eve service, and in a beautiful new ceremony in the fields, Katzir ha-Omer, "First Harvest," which is held in the late afternoon before the Seder. The kibbutz members, with their families and guests — often more than four hundred (about as many as the number of members) — assemble in front of the dining hall and walk in procession to the field, music from loudspeakers accompanying us all the way.

Sitting on bundles of straw arranged in irregular rows facing the area set aside for the performers, we watch the ceremony against a backdrop of the glinting waters of the kibbutz fish ponds and the towering Gilboa. The ceremony begins by reading passages from the Bible that exalt and bless the harvesting of the first crops, imitating what our biblical forefathers did at this season. The words are then matched by the deed, depicted in a scene that might be titled "The Reapers." A group of kibbutz men carrying scythes appear and proceed in rhythmic order to cut down a long patch of the first ripened wheat while singing lines from a poem by Bialik inspired by Genesis 3:17–19: "Not dry bread /Not quail, not heavenly corn / But the bread of sorrow you will eat / The fruit of the labor of your hands." The reapers include a small number of veterans who actually scythed the crops in their youth and a much larger contingent of young men who have learned the

The Spring of Harod, 1984

art of scything for this ceremony. Meanwhile, the kibbutz combine harvester stands nearby, as if watching with interest the performance of a primitive ancestor.

As the reapers withdraw to loud applause, they are replaced by
young mothers and their children who gather the swathes into
heaps to the accompaniment of fresh music and song. Then follow
"The Dancers," young girls of the kibbutz dressed in long, flowing robes of biblical-oriental style in vivid colors, who dance in
from opposite sides of the stage area, gracefully miming the traditional prayers of thanksgiving for the first crops. A visitor once remarked that they looked like biblical figures out of a Poussin
painting, and I think the comparison does justice to the harmony
of color and movement the girls compose. The kibbutz choir, accompanied by the kibbutz orchestra and joined by the audience,

Girls' dance in the Katzir ha-Omer

sings songs of rejoicing; there are more readings from the Bible; then hordes of children run onto the stage from all directions and break into circle dances in groups, according to age, from kindergarten up. Although their miming of the symbolic acts of the first harvest is a trifle confused, they make up for it with their energy and enthusiasm and are applauded as the stars of the show. Then, as the light fades over the ponds and the valley and mountain beyond, the smallest children run in among the heaped-up swathes, tie them into sheaves, and carry them off for the opening ceremony of the Seder, which is held in the kibbutz dining hall about three hours later.

By half past eight in the evening, the great hall is packed to capacity. The members sit with their guests in family groups at long trestle tables loaded with the traditional fare of the Seder meal. Tradition has had to be simplified a little here and there because of the huge numbers; when did the Children of Israel have to feed over a thousand people at a single Seder? An army of kibbutz members have worked from five o'clock in the morning to set the tables, put out the cold fish, meat, and chicken, bowls of salads, platters of fresh fruit, bottles of festive wine, and the traditional matzo, bitter herbs, and so forth.

The hall is richly decorated with beautiful arrangements of fresh flowers and leaves hanging in baskets from the ceiling or standing in urns in every corner or in boxes on every free ledge. The walls above the long, wide windows are covered with large, posterlike horizontal panels of paintings and inscriptions in black and white on a golden green background. On one wall are quotations from the Song of Songs, illustrated by paintings full of traditional motifs: doves, gazelles, little foxes, bunches of grapes, King Solomon playing the harp, the Shulamit sleeping. On the opposite wall the theme is famous Jewish rebellions against foreign oppressors: the hasmonean revolt, Bar-Kochba's revolt, Jerusalem rising against Titus, the Palmach in the War of Independence. In the windows are smaller vertical panels, their lettering and illustrations in traditional colors of red, green, blue, and gold; by day the light shines through them, giving the effect of stained glass. And on the big square arch surmounting the west window is a single crowning panel in brilliant colors. All these paintings are the work of Chaim Atar, the Ein-Harod artist who was one of the founders of its art museum and is suitably commemorated each year by this living exhibition of his decorative work for Passover.

The kibbutz choir and its conductor file in and sit in rows at the back of the wide stage set up for the festival at the east end of the hall. The members of the kibbutz orchestra are in their places, and the pianist strikes the first resonant chords of the slow-movement melody that opens the Seder service. As she plays the last chords, more than a hundred kibbutz children, dressed in white, file into the hall from its northern entrance. They proceed along the narrow aisles between the tables, holding aloft the sheaves of wheat gathered in the field of the Omer a few hours before and joyously singing a traditional song of blessing of the first crops. The procession comes to an end on the stage, where they sing a last rousing refrain of the Omer song, joined by the choir and the whole audience.

Then come readings from the Book of Exodus that commemorate our suffering at the hands of the Pharaoh, celebrating our liberation from slavery in Egypt. The relevance of the biblical passages is too striking to be missed; they fit our relations with modern Egypt all too closely, especially in the time of Nasser. So we feel it as *our* suffering and *our* liberation; indeed, small children often become confused about what is past and what present and are likely to tell their parents, quite seriously, how fortunate it is that they, the parents, managed to get away from Pharaoh to Ein-Harod before they, the children, were born.

The readings from the Bible and other sources continue throughout the service, alternating with the singing of Passover songs, which, it is generally agreed, are the most beautiful in our repertoire of festival songs. Then, at a prescribed moment, a troupe of girl dancers, dressed this time in long white robes offset by broad sashes in brilliant jewel colors falling from their waists, glides onto the stage. They perform a slow oriental-style dance, all graceful fluid movements and stylized gestures of arms and hands. More reading and choral singing follow; and then comes the ritual question, "Why is this night different from all other nights?" The four questions and responses are chanted by six-year-old children, with the whole assembly joining in to repeat the responses. What is different, of course, is that the children pipe out the well-known words before a vast audience in a vast hall. Until a few years ago, the spectacle of these mites standing up on their chairs to chant the questions or responses, and the sound of their often surprisingly strong little voices carrying to the four corners of the hall, was a touching and hilarious experience that people did not soon forget. In the last few years, the children have been brought on stage to speak their questions and responses in front of the microphone, which has made their performance more businesslike but scarcely less moving and funny.

Among the additions to the traditional service in the Ein-Harod Haggadah are the passages of what might be called contemporary parallels and applications. The six million Jewish victims of the Holocaust are recalled in one passage. The sad, brave anthem of the heroes and martyrs of the Warsaw Ghetto and other ghettos destroyed by the Nazis, "Ani Ma'amin" ("I Have Faith"), is sung with the usual Passover songs. Each year a senior member of the kibbutz gives a short address on the Passover

theme of the passage from slavery to freedom as it applies to recent national events: for example, the mass immigration of Jews
arriving from Soviet Russia in the 1970s, the 1973 Yom Kippur
War, and the Lebanon War.

In the last section of the Haggadah, called Ge'ula (Redemption), we again follow traditional practice in striving to mitigate
the tragic elements of the Passover story. The whole assembly
with choir and orchestra sings the beautiful, haunting songs of redemption sung by Jews through the ages, "Karev Yom" ("Let a
Day Draw Near") and "Eliyahu ha-Navi" ("Elijah the Prophet").
"Karev Yom" speaks of the yearning for the day of redemption in
words that are mysterious and obscure, yet penetrate to the core
of the soul:

> Let a Day draw near which is neither day nor night;
> Tell us, Lord, for yours is both the day and the night;
> Raise up guards for your City all the day and all the night;
> Turn into the light of day the darkness of night.

In ringing cadences "Eliyahu ha-Navi" welcomes, with a symbolic flinging open of a door, the coming of the Messiah: "Elijah
the prophet / Elijah from Tishbe / Elijah from Gilead / Will
come to us quickly / with Messiah, David's son."

Then comes the finale, designed to dissipate every last shred of
sadness and melancholy. The children's choir walks onto the
stage, carrying a wonderful medley of musical instruments, to
perform the traditional "Chad-Gadya" — a merry round on the
pattern of "This is the house that Jack built" — composed in the
fifteenth century and still sung in Aramaic: "My father bought a
kid for a farthing / Came a cat and ate the kid / Came a dog and
bit the cat / Came a stick and beat the dog," and so on. They sing
with tremendous zest, with a clashing of cymbals, beating of
drums, tinkling of bells, clicking of castanets, and blowing of
horns that lifts the spirits of the whole audience to a peak of delight. The children troop off, beaming with pleasure at the thun-
derous applause, and the audience settles down at last to the
festive supper that has lain before them untouched for more than
an hour.

What happens behind the scenes of the great show we have just
witnessed is a separate story, one which isn't all beauty and grace.

The rehearsals for the performances — the dancers', the choir's, the children's — went on for weeks before Pesach, mostly in the evenings. Children staggered home after midnight, bleary-eyed with fatigue, and fretful parents were heard to say *"Is* it worth ruining a child's health just for the sake of Pesach?" But on the day itself, when cooking went on through the night, and the setting of the tables, arranging of the flowers, and so on started at five in the morning, tension is at its height. Nerves tend to become frayed, and you see the fur flying among the army of helpers. *"Don't* do it that way. *This* is the way to do it!" one woman says sharply to another about laying out the knives or forks or paper napkins, followed by a heated argument about the best way to set the table. Or there is a crisis about the compote, the traditional Seder dessert of stewed dried fruit. The compote team in the kitchen has poured the fruit from the huge vats into twelve hundred small bowls, one per person, instead of two hundred big ones, each for six people. The mistake is discovered only after several hundred small bowls have been placed precariously on the overladen tables; they have to be removed, and the operation has to be started all over again. The "commander in chief" (the woman member in charge of the whole Seder) shouts at the compote workers, "What's the matter with you all? Can't you *see* there isn't room for another teaspoon on those tables? How do you think we can push in another *twelve hundred* bowls?" The workers mutter resentfully that it always *used* to be one bowl per person, and no one told them about the change to the big bowls, so how could they know?

Even the flower arrangements are not exempt from the clash of human passions. At lunch I overheard one young woman saying furiously to another, "She's *impossible,* that So-and-so!" naming a middle-aged woman member we all know. "She's been doing the flowers in the baskets for the last twenty years, and she won't let anyone else *touch* them! Every flower has to be in exactly the same place every year, exactly the place *she* decided it has to be twenty years ago. And they have to be exactly the same flowers. If she can't find *her* flowers, it's a disaster — she won't do the baskets without them, and she won't let anyone else do anything else. I tell you, this kibbutz can drive you *mad.* I'm *fed up* with it; it makes me sick!" The last outburst is a common one; I've heard it for more than sixty years. If anything goes wrong, if someone annoys you — never mind about what — the kibbutz is going to the dogs, and it's impossible to go on living there. I remember how agitated I used to get about just this kind of thing when I was younger. But now I reflect that Ein-Harod has survived bigger crises, and it will probably survive the one about the flower baskets; I'm just selfishly glad that I'm not the one who has to settle the dispute, if it can ever *be* settled.

Our guests, however, know nothing about these backstage crises and conflicts. As we walk back to my house after the Seder, they can't stop talking about the wonder of it all. It's been an overwhelming experience, they say, and try to explain why. Its sheer beauty is one element: the singing, the dancing, the music, the flowers are a pleasure feast for the senses. The participation of the children is another. There is something uniquely moving and enchanting in the spectacle of a whole community of children singing, dancing, and playing musical instruments in celebration of the festival of spring, for are they not the symbol of the freshness and tender new growth associated with the season of renewal? Then there is the effect of the huge number of participants. A big family Seder may consist of thirty or forty people; a communal Seder, say in a Jewish hotel in a foreign land, may run to a few hundred guests; but who has ever attended a Seder with twelve hundred participants? The sheer numbers seem to make a qualitative difference, and to hear the familiar Passover songs rising in unison from so many throats is an experience in itself. Jews at Seders everywhere may well reflect that on this same evening in every corner of the world fellow Jews are conducting the same Passover service, commemorating the same ancient event in Jewish history, reading the same passages from the Haggadah, singing the same songs of sadness and joy; and the excitement and inspiration of this thought are somehow doubly and trebly intensified by participation in a Seder on Ein-Harod's magnificent scale.

As I sat at my fifty-seventh Seder at Ein-Harod, I felt the beauty and inspiration just as our guests did, and a certainty that they would never pall for me. But I also felt something else: pride in the knowledge that it was all the original creation of this one community. The dances had almost all been invented by Rivka

Sturman, our own choreographer, now over eighty and still teaching dance to the elderly. The choir, the soloists, the orchestra, the
conductors, were all members of Ein-Harod. The pianist was
Dalia Carmi, daughter of Moshe Carmi. The children's singing
and playing were the work of Rafi Lavie, younger brother of Gil
Lavie: Rafi's quiet, loving tutelage seemed to have the power to
draw a response from every child, the shy and timid and the
gifted and confident alike. One of the new songs was my composition, another Moshe Tabenkin's. The melodies were Shalom Pos-
tolski's, one-time member of Ein-Harod; the decorations were
Atar's; the simple, moving address on the Lebanon War was
Neria Zisling's. All, all the work of this community, grown now to
some eight hundred people, which started in 1921 in the encampment by Gideon's spring and has continued to develop — like our
fields, orchards, and woods, a creation of nature and human art
inseparably joined.

20

Ein-Harod, 1984

ON ITS FIFTIETH ANNIVERSARY in 1971 Ein-Harod produced a great musical comedy, a variant of the Rip van Winkle story, about Khonni ha-Me'agel (Khonni the circlemaker) who falls asleep for seventy years and wakes up to find a changed world around him.* I won't enumerate what Khonni saw when he surveyed Ein-Harod in 1971, but when I look around it today, I remember what it was like in 1931 when we completed our move to Kumi from the old site at Ma'ayan Harod.

The newest houses are a beautiful sight, glistening white in our eternal sunshine, their rising and dipping peaked roofs standing out against the skyline like a manmade chain of hills. The irregular rows of houses are separated by wide lawns broken at intervals by great spreading trees, and the brilliant colors of the gardens in front of the houses appear as frescoes against the white walls and green grass. Fortunately, the gardens can be somewhat untidy as well as beautiful, with children's bicycles, shabby bits of garden furniture, bathing suits hung on a line, and other household paraphernalia sticking out among the flowers and greenery, so that they are never *too* picturesque. The Gilboa, most of it now thickly forested, rises across the valley from the south, more than

*Khonni is called the circlemaker because he is said to have drawn a circle around himself and announced to the Lord that he would remain standing in it until He brought rain to the drought-stricken land. He is thus a kind of rain-maker or sorcerer.

ever exposed to view from the new open lawns and from every new road and path of the kibbutz. It seems to watch over us like a guardian spirit, our fixed, changeless symbol of continuity.

The new houses are about 555 to 740 square feet in size, the newest being the largest, in accordance with established practice. Each house contains a small bedroom for the parents, a more spacious one for the children, a well-designed and fully equipped modern kitchenette, in addition to the living room, which is almost big enough to be called a salon. The children sleep at home from birth to the age of fifteen, and families with three or four children who live in the older, smaller houses are already complaining of overcrowding. "How can you sleep four children aged three to fifteen in one room? Are we slum dwellers, or what?" they protest indignantly. So I expect a second children's room will be added before long, and everybody will be happy, for a while, anyway.

The communal amenities, to which the kibbutz still gives priority over the private or domestic, have also grown and improved, some slowly, others in big leaps at approximately ten-year intervals. For our sixtieth anniversary we gave ourselves two handsome gifts. One was a system, at last, of properly paved roads and paths to replace the mixture of dust tracks and dirt roads that we had lived with for fifty years. The main pedestrian walk that runs from the dining hall to the last rows of new houses on the edge of the fields is covered with elegant red, light gray, and dark gray flagstones flanked by a row of stately electric lamps that cast a milk-white light. It is so grand that we call it our Champs-Elysée, and feel very townish and sophisticated as we stroll along it. The other gift was the Founders' Wood (*Churshat ha-Rishonim*), a beautiful woodlands, all avenues of eucalyptus trees and green lawns, with our wheat fields — green in the winter, golden in the early summer — on its perimeter. A manmade stream, broken by small waterfalls, runs the length of it. Artful piles of rocks on one side look as natural as if they had been there from the beginning of the world, and rough wooden tables and barbecue pits have been placed on the other side. This wood has become a favorite spot for family suppers in the cool evening hours of a hot summer's day; for strolls in the shady avenues in the heat of the day; for paddling of little children's feet in the stream; and, of course, for communal picnics, wedding parties, summer camping, and so forth.

Most recently, the kibbutz has built a Founders', Heroes', and Martyrs' Memorial by the cemetery. It is dedicated jointly to the memory of the founding fathers and mothers of Ein-Harod, to its sons who fell in battle, and to the families of present members of the kibbutz who perished in the Holocaust. Separate memorial services are held for each: for the founders on Ein-Harod's birthday, Yud Chet Elul; for the heroes on our national Memorial Day; for the martyrs on national Holocaust Day. A row of irregularly shaped boulders at the entrance of the memorial commemorates the founders. Inscribed on one of them is an adaptation of a line from Leviticus 26:45: "I will remember for your sakes my covenant with your ancestors." Inside the entrance, a low curved wall, half enclosing a simple unpaved plaza, is paneled at irregular intervals with memorial tablets inscribed with the names of the fathers, mothers, brothers, and sisters killed by the Nazis, along with the names of the destroyed Jewish communities from which they came. Beyond the wall and plaza, a massive rectangular block of white chalkstone, resembling an ancient sacrificial altar, stands alone on a floor of large leaf-shaped slivers of basalt in the middle of a bare, open space that will eventually become green lawn and flowers. The beauty of this memorial to the fallen of Ein-Harod is in its plain, undecorated simplicity. A memorial flame will be lit in a shallow bowl scooped out of the altar-like chalkstone block each time we gather to commemorate the heroes.

At Ein-Harod the new has never succeeded in ousting the old, and so it is today. Alongside the dazzling new houses and other recent structures stand many shabby old buildings, still being used for one purpose or another. Some are badly in need of a fresh coat of paint, others require more radical renovation. But there is never enough money at one time to rebuild or refurbish all we want, and we console ourselves with the thought that if and when our factories become as successful as other people's, we will be able to make all sorts of improvements we can't undertake now. Our two older factories — one produces stainless-steel equipment, the other furniture, mostly for children — have not been failures;

New houses at Ein-Harod, with the Gilboa in the background

but neither have they been spectacular successes. Consequently, we remain less affluent than other kibbutzim, especially relative to our age and eminence. Our forthright young people sometimes make invidious comparisons between their personal allowances and those of their rich pals at Ma'agan Michael or Ein-Dor or Na'an and wonder pointedly whether we shall *always* be paupers. We hope that our newest plant, which produces special graph paper for medical machines, will be more successful.

There is another, historical reason for our nonaffluence. Thirty years ago, Ein-Harod, with almost all the other kibbutzim of the Kibbutz ha-Meuchad Federation, for complicated ideological reasons that I cannot attempt to explain here, split into two bitterly opposed camps. This tragic division ultimately led to our separation into the present Ein-Harod Meuchad and Ein-Harod Ichud, which built its new kibbutz farther up Kumi Hill. During the three to four years in which the communal property was being divided and other conditions of the painful divorce negotiated, practically all development came to a standstill. We of Ein-Harod Meuchad emerged deeply in debt; the process of economic recovery was a slow one, as was the recovery from the spiritual and emotional trauma of the breakup of the original community. The ideological wounds have since healed, and the United Kibbutz Movement, Takam, signifying the union of the two formerly distinct kibbutz federations, is proof of it. But the two Ein-Harods have remained separate. On economic and administrative grounds alone, there could be no question of remerging two kibbutzim that have since developed on independent lines, each into a distinct, complete social unit.

Relations between the two Ein-Harods are as friendly and natural now as they were not for many years after the split. But they remain separate, and whenever I walk up the hill to visit old friends at the Ichud, I feel great sadness about what happened long ago. But for the split, Ein-Harod would have had a population of some 1800, making it one of the two biggest kibbutzim in the country, second only to Givat Brenner, with its more than 2000. As I still believe firmly in the big kibbutz and its rich possibilities, I find it hard to reconcile myself to our reduced size.

However, I think of ourselves as diminished only when I remember the split, but certainly not when I think of the extended families of Ein-Harod, who are so typical of all older kibbutzim. I suppose nobody can beat the record set by the late Shmuel Stoler of Kibbutz Kinneret by the Sea of Galilee. A famous agronomist, with a fine Tolstoyan head and beard, Stoler begat seven children and derived from them a clan of some seventy souls. When we visited him a few years before his death, for a memorial service for his deceased wife, it was wonderful to see his living room fill up with his descendants, who arrived from kibbutzim in all parts of the country: sons, daughters, sons-in-law, daughters-in-law, grandsons and granddaughters with their spouses and offspring, pouring in seemingly endlessly. Stoler was horrified when someone asked if he could really remember all their names. He said he always knew exactly who was who, from which generation, and the finest points of the character and personality of each, down to the youngest great-grandchild.

Though no family at Ein-Harod is as vast as Stoler's, the Zislings don't do too badly with a total of fifty-seven — and still growing. To the time of her death at eighty-one, Sara Zisling made a daily round of visits to all twenty-four of her grandchildren, and we all wondered how she did it. At Passover, one long trestle table is scarcely enough to seat them all. The Tabenkins are next in order of descending magnitude. Yitzhak and Eva Tabenkin, if they were alive today, would certainly fill a Passover table with their three remaining children and spouses, thirteen grandchildren and spouses, and nineteen great-grandchildren. Behind the Tabenkins come the Gileads, my family, numbering thirty; after us are the Luzes, with thirteen grandchildren and a total of twenty-one. Sara Neumann is a case all by herself. All but one of her children have left Ein-Harod to live in other kibbutzim, but she has twenty-one great-grandchildren — the highest Ein-Harod record so far — who regularly come to visit her, making her the envy of all her contemporaries.

These figures are provided by my wife, Doris (Dorothea), who knows them better than I do. She pretends to be intensely competitive about their numbers and ours, keeps tracks of all new additions to the big families, and is constantly counting and recounting grandchildren and great-grandchildren to see who is overtaking whom, who is drawing level, who is lagging behind.

Though I can't compete with the Zislings and the Tabenkins in numbers, I am fortunate that my three daughters, sons-in-law, and eleven grandchildren live at Ein-Harod; as do my brother Yuval's widow, Eyra, with her four children, two sons-in-law, and three grandchildren. Counting Manya, my son-in-law Abbi's mother, who recently came to live at Ein-Harod, we do indeed, as Doris says, add up to thirty. I fear I am not capable of an objective assessment of the members of my family. To me, Tirza, Hanni, and Eyla are simply the prettiest, most gifted, most charming young women I know; and their husbands, Abbi, Ilan, and Mordi, are the finest, most upstanding young men a father could wish to have as his sons-in-law. The eleven grandchildren, to my fond eye, are all remarkably good-looking, intelligent, and spirited young creatures, each with his or her distinct character and personality, whose development I watch with keen interest. Some of them, I can't help noticing, look vaguely like me at their age; and at least two of the granddaughters strikingly like Susi. When I look at Tamar, aged three, I seem to be confronting a diminutive Susi, with her golden hair, her large, gray-green, slightly slanted eyes, her ravishing smile, and a laugh that has the very timbre of her grandmother's.

Eyra, my sister-in-law, a gifted graphic artist, is one of the

pretty, youthful grandmothers in which Ein-Harod seems to spe-
cialize. She lost Yuval when her youngest boy, Danny, was six
and Lipaz, her younger daughter, eleven. Yuval's death at the age
of forty-four was terrible for us. His talents and force of character
were known to his wide circle of friends at Ein-Harod and outside,
and they mourned the tragic waste of such a human being cut off
in his prime.

In the War of Independence Yuval had been mobilized into a
regional defense unit, fighting in some of its hard battles. He was
later a marine in the fledgling Israel navy, and finally a frogman
in a special naval commando unit. When the war was over, he returned to Ein-Harod to work in the fields, in the citrus groves,
and ultimately in the fish ponds, which became his permanent
job. When a woman guest remarked how handsome and romantic
he looked in his high boots and fisherman's outfit as he approached us in the evening light on his return from the ponds, I
agreed, glad to have my eyes opened to the appeal of Yuval's
manliness, which, in the usual way of families, I took for granted.
But I didn't take for granted, then or afterward, his sense of social
responsibility. A dedicated instructor to the Working Youth and
Youth Aliyah groups at Ein-Harod, he won the lifelong affection
and respect of his charges.

I expect the woman friend would have found Yuval even more
romantic as a sea captain. He had been attracted to the sea from
childhood, and by the early 1950s its call had become irresistible.
He received Ein-Harod's permission to take up seamanship as a
profession and became one of the leading spirits in the formation
of Kibbutz ha-Meuchad's small fleet of four merchant ships, rising to the rank of captain in a relatively short time. He never saw
any contradiction or conflict between his seaman's profession and
his passionate attachment to Ein-Harod. On the contrary, he
thought of himself as, specifically, a *kibbutz* seaman, and of his life
at sea as a natural extension of life in a kibbutz: the distinctive
milieu and values of the kibbutz transposed, as it were, to the
ocean. He succeeded in realizing the ideal of the kibbutz seaman
in his own life, according to John Auerbach of Kibbutz Sdot-
Yam, an author and fellow kibbutz seaman who was one of
Yuval's closest friends. "As we followed his coffin," Auerbach
wrote after his death, "an official of the Naval Officers' Union, an
old friend of Yuval and mine, turned to me and said, 'Do you

know what was special about him? That he was a *kibbutz* captain. I mean, of an honesty and integrity not to be found in any other kind. At most, in a few isolated cases you can count on the fingers of one hand — that's how special he was.' "

I think Yuval's integrity and honesty were the special marks of his character. His honesty was a severe, almost ruthless, sometimes brutal "straightness"; and it was somehow connected with a passion for justice and hatred of injustice that made itself felt very quickly in any encounter with him. He could be curt and brusque in talk, especially with strangers and people he didn't take to, in a way that was disconcerting and occasionally wounding. But with friends and people he liked, he was all affectionate warmth and talked copiously, with an animation, humor, and expressiveness that made him one of the most popular figures of his generation at Ein-Harod — even though everyone admitted he was "not an easy person," meaning, I suppose, stubborn, unconciliatory, and not inclined to suffer fools gladly.

But when he let himself go with his friends, what a range of interests he had, and what subjects for conversation. Seamanship and the life of the sea, for a start, of course; and the foreign places he had seen on his voyages — their people, their customs, their natural beauties, their art museums, their theaters. He seemed to have observed everything, and to remember everything he observed. He was just as interested in politics and the state of the nation, in agriculture and industry, in the newest technologies, in marketing problems and solutions, in education, literature, and art. He was remarkably well informed on all the subjects he discussed, had independent opinions about everything, and made no bones about expressing them firmly and sometimes dogmatically. But he cared most of all about justice and humanity, which he would talk about only to his closest friends. John Auerbach recalls one occasion when he did. "He was dedicated, with an almost tragic intensity, to personal honesty and justice. Not as philosophical concepts or 'principles' but as rules of day-to-day conduct. He said to me once, standing on the captain's bridge, 'Do you know what for me, in one word, is the whole doctrine of socialism — the whole doctrine of the kibbutz? It is: *be a human being!*' This naive doctrine," John concludes, "was the basis of our friendship in all the years I knew him."

Yuval was even more articulate, more completely himself, in

writing than in conversation. Because his seaman's life separated him from his family and friends for long periods, he wrote a good many letters and postcards. His gift for vivid, pictorial description of places, scenes, people, and episodes is conspicuous in the letters; they have a delicacy of fancy and humor he did not often display in his talk. The postcards to his children are intimate and affectionate, often illustrated with comic drawings, accompanied by rhymed verses, and overflowing with tender fancies. When at Eyra's request I read her collection of Yuval's letters after his death, I felt I knew him a great deal better than I did while he was alive.

When he was barely forty, he was struck down by the rare kidney disease from which we believe my father had died. He suffered for more than four years, terribly in the last two, before death delivered him from a life no longer worth protracting. He spent almost all of his last year in Tel Hashomer Hospital, getting whatever relief was possible from his devouring pain. He was visited by a constant stream of family and friends, eagerly using every respite from his pain to talk and joke, to bombard his visitors with questions about everything — Ein-Harod, the country, the world, old friends, new problems — and to offer his opinions about everything with his accustomed firmness. I remember thinking that it was as if he were trying by this talk to draw the torrent of life outside into his sick room and, by so doing, hold back the advance of death. But he hated the pain that racked his body, and he cursed and rejected it with his typical angry impatience. This is what I imagined him doing on his last voyage, standing alone on the captain's bridge.

> Incessant, without respite — this pain in the chest
> like waves on the hull of the ship. But the waves have a sweet smell
> and a strong taste of salt and the pain has no end and no cure.
> I'd rather have ten storms at sea than this bloody torture . . .
> If only I can keep my mind. If only I can stay lucid to the end.

He recalls the beautiful sight of "a greenback duck which appears in the rainy season," its "glistening head / reddish green and the violet eye in the white circle on its wing"; and grieves at the thought that he won't be able to show it to his small son. Then he relives in imagination "the nightmare of sailors" — the delusion he once experienced in a "far-off gulf" that the ship was foundering on a hidden reef. But these old terrors seem like children's games compared with this "darkness of pain":

> Here it comes again, boring away. Vicious, malignant.
> Give me a moment's rest. Let me breathe . . .

But it doesn't; and he gives up the struggle, surrendering himself to the last embrace of the sea he has loved all his life.

> Come, come — enclose me in your waves full of soft light
> and the restless foam will cover me, salt on my lips.

When Yuval died in 1973, I had been married to Dorothea, familiarly called Doris, for some five years, and she had been living at Ein-Harod since January 1969. Susi and I had first met her in Jerusalem about six months after she arrived from Cambridge in 1960 to take a senior lectureship in the English Department at the Hebrew University. Her fame as a brilliant lecturer and author of academic books had preceded her, and we were quite excited at the prospect of meeting this new superstar immigrant. Her best friends in Jerusalem were our friends Ruth and Natan Nevo, who took us to visit Doris in her first makeshift apartment in Beit-Hakerem. She had invited my old friend Lea Goldberg to dinner that evening, and when we came in to join them for coffee we were somehow reassured to see the superstar from Cambridge surrounded by dirty dishes and overflowing ashtrays, in a small salon full of shabby furniture, rocking with laughter over something Lea had said. As my English was practically nonexistent, I talked to Lea most of the evening, while Susi, whose English was much better, talked to Doris. By the end of the evening, they were friends, while I thought I had never heard anyone speak English so *fast*.

About a year after this meeting, Doris came with the Nevos to visit Susi in Tel Hashomer Hospital, where she had just had her second operation. Susi told me afterward that when Doris, with tears in her eyes, kissed her good-bye, she felt she was being kissed by an old, intimate friend. Remembering the happy, excited light in Susi's eyes as she told me this, I can scarcely think of it without emotion.

We met Doris again at the Nevos' in Jerusalem about a year before Susi's death. This time I listened in to her talk with Susi. Doris had become the assistant head of the English Department, and was describing a wonderful plan she had devised for student self-registration — a great streamlining operation, she explained to Susi, that would save scores of the valuable man-hours staff members wasted on the silly business of registering students individually. I didn't quite understand either the principles or the method, but Susi apparently did, and I can still hear her repeated peals of laughter at Doris's blow-by-blow exposition of her great plan, with all the amusing or absurd details suitably accentuated. It was my first experience of her talent for drawing out the comic ironies of situations, great or small, which, as my English (and her Hebrew) improved, I have enjoyed more and more.

When Susi died, Doris wrote us a beautiful letter, which I have kept to this day. My daughters were as moved by it as I was, and I know now, though I didn't at the time, that this letter was the beginning of my deeper feeling for her, which grew over the years that followed. Shortly before Susi's death, Doris had met Moshe Tabenkin in Jerusalem, where he was on a year's leave of absence. He was looking for someone to give him English lessons in exchange for Hebrew lessons, and an exchange was arranged by the Nevos. Although Moshe learned very little English and Doris very little Hebrew — because, Moshe told us, they spent most of their time arguing, in their own languages, about national politics — they became firm friends as a consequence. Soon after Susi's death, Doris began to pay regular visits to Ein-Harod as the guest of the Tabenkins. I saw her there each time, and occasionally in Jerusalem. Our friendship developed, and in due course we married. My daughters had come to know her well, had grown very fond of her, and were happy to have her as a stepmother, for their own and their children's sakes, and for mine most of all.

I have confined myself to the bare history of my second marriage because I find it difficult to talk freely about the co-author of this book — who is for once showing a reluctance to write down what I want to say. She also breathes down my neck all the time, saying "Keep it short, keep it short. There's no space for details. We've already overrun our word limit. We have to get this book *finished.*" This does not encourage tender reflections on my subject, so I shall stick to the external facts of our life together, keeping it short, leaving the tender reflections, as she suggests, for another time.

My marriage to Doris introduced all sorts of new elements into my life. The first was being assaulted on all sides in Jerusalem when she decided to resign from the Hebrew University and move to Tel Aviv University, to make my life easier. I couldn't be expected, she explained to her dean, to divide my life between *three* places — my home in Ein-Harod, my workplace in Tel Aviv, and Jerusalem as well; and though it was a wrench for her to be separated from Jerusalem, which she loved, she hadn't married me to make my life miserable. They feigned astonishment at this: what a strange woman — most women marry *just* to make their husbands' lives miserable. It was also suggested, at least half seriously, that the Kibbutz ha-Meuchad Publishing House simply move its offices to Jerusalem, and thus solve the whole problem. This was soon after the Six Day War, when Jerusalem had been reunited and declared the eternal capital of Israel, and as our kibbutz federation was known to be solidly behind this move, the proposal made good political sense — which was the point of the jest.

But Doris moved to Tel Aviv and was soon as much at home there as she had been in her twelve years at the Hebrew University. She divides her year between Tel Aviv and Ein-Harod, spending the academic year in Tel Aviv and the vacations in Ein-Harod, while I continue to divide my week spending more of it in Tel Aviv when she is there and less when she is at Ein-Harod. It is a somewhat complicated life, but an interesting one, and, she says, there's no place like Ein-Harod for carrying on with the study and writing she regards as the center of her life. The absence of distraction, the rural quiet, the bird song, the lawns and flowers, the Gilboa — she becomes quite lyrical about it all in talk with members of the kibbutz, who, of course, listen with great satisfaction.

It has been a great pleasure to me to see how quickly and easily she made a new life for herself at Ein-Harod. The only greater pleasure is what I have heard about her equally quick and easy adaptation to the country itself. She is one of those lucky Western immigrants, she tells people, who have never had any problems of absorption and integration. From the hour Doris set foot in Israel on her first visit in 1958, she loved it and identified with it completely, feeling immediately that she had "come home" out of exile, though she didn't know she was *in* exile, she says, until she had the experience. It's been the same at Ein-Harod. Within a very short time, she felt that it was her home in this country, made many good friends, and acquired a passionate interest in the kibbutz's history and growth.

She is on excellent terms with my daughters, who appreciate her affection and humor, her readiness to be helpful in any way she can, and her enthusiasm about their children — especially when she tells them, with the utmost objectivity, that they are the most beautiful, clever, adorable children in the world. Doris is not the ideal kibbutz grandmother who sees her grandchildren for at least three to four hours every day; she spends rather too much time in her study with her spiritual bridegrooms, as she calls them — Plato, Henry James, John Sergeant, and the rest — to meet this exacting standard. But she makes up in intensity for the lack of continuity of her grandmotherly activities, generally concentrating them into Sabbath morning entertainments. This is the morning the smaller grandchildren regularly come to have breakfast with me, starting to troop in at about seven o'clock, when Doris is still in bed having her four cups of early-morning tea. By the time they have finished their breakfast, she is ready to receive them, and then they are likely to spend up to an hour with her in our salon-bedroom, behind closed doors, getting up all sorts of fun and games, usually accompanied by a great deal of noise.

One of these mornings I was busy washing the breakfast dishes when I heard particularly loud, piercing yelps and squeals from behind the closed door. I opened it to see what they were up to, and found three of the children in the double bed with Doris, kicking and screaming ecstatically under the sheet. It was high summer, so there were no blankets; and though it was not yet eight o'clock it was unpleasantly hot. "What are you *doing?* Have you all gone mad?" I inquired. "Not at all," answered Doris, popping out her dark head above the sheet. "We're playing a new game called Bedouin Tents. We're pretending it's pouring rain and bitter cold outside, and a howling desert wind is trying to tear down our tent" — howling-wind noises from the children under the sheet — "but we're all warm and cozy inside; and we're cooking steaks and sausages over a Bedouin fire" — sounds of frying and sizzling from under the sheet. "Then we're going to eat them with chips and mustard" — loud chomping and smacking noises, with a crescendo of giggles — "and when we've finished eating we're going to tell Bedouin ghost stories. And then we're all flying to London to visit Anita!" The children knew all about Anita, Doris's youngest sister who lives in England, and constantly begged to be taken to visit her. "Yes, yes — to Lon-don, Lon-don, Anee-ta, Anee-ta!" chanted the children, finally showing their grinning faces above the sheet. I left them to it, thinking how lucky it was for their little game that none of them had ever seen the inside of a Bedouin tent.

The only thing Ein-Harod lacks, says Doris, are the research libraries she needs for her work. So about every two years I join her on her research trips abroad, usually to London or Cambridge, and once to the United States. Ein-Harod has been very good about allowing me to go, recognizing that she can't get on without the libraries, and that we can't easily get on without each other. Our journeys abroad have been an exciting extension of my experience. We usually manage to fit in a week or two in some European country en route to our destination — Italy, France, Switzerland, or Holland — then settle down for anywhere from six weeks to three months in our appointed place, where Doris spends her day in her library, and I wander about absorbing impressions or getting on with my own writing. At weekends, or any holiday time we feel we are entitled to, we make a round of visits to her numerous friends in London, Cambridge, and other parts of England. They put us up in grand guest rooms, give us sumptuous meals, and take us on wonderful drives and walks into the ever green English countryside. They love to hear about Israel and the kibbutz and don't seem to mind my poor English, so I tell them what I can and try to answer their dozens of questions.

My favorite house on our visiting list in England is a magnificent country estate in Norfolk owned by two of Doris's oldest and best friends. It is about twice the size of Ein-Harod, and while Doris has confidential talks with our hostess indoors, I enjoy wandering around the estate with our host, who is a distinguished scholar as well as estate owner. We compare farming notes, describe our latest machines and methods, and enjoy the bond that exists between serious farmers the world over. Another highlight of our visits to England is Doris's enchanting younger sister Anita. She now lives in a beautiful little cottage in the country, knows and loves all the trees, flowers, and birds of England, and takes me on the best country walks of all.

An old kibbutz like Ein-Harod is bound to have old people. This ought not surprise us, yet somehow it still does. Twenty years ago, when the kibbutz was just forty years old, there seemed to be very few; ten years ago there were more; and now the place seems to be full of them. I have a particularly warm feeling for them, and an advantage, I find, of having a good number of octogenarians and some nonagenarians about the place is that early septuagenarians like me are made to feel quite young — almost like striplings, in fact.

Care of the aged has thus become a problem for the kibbutz only in the last ten to fifteen years, and on the whole it has been successfully solved. In fact, gerontologists and social workers say the kibbutzim provide a model proof of their favorite doctrines about the care of the aged. To begin with, we have no official retirement age, so our oldest members can go on working as long as they like, for as many hours a day as they want to, and at any of a great variety of jobs suitable for them. The men work in automated jobs in the stainless-steel factory or perform administrative or clerical tasks in the kibbutz secretariat offices, in the factories, or in our two museums. The elderly women do light work in the kitchen and dining hall or set jobs of their own choice. For example, Rachel Tamarin, aged eighty-two, arrives in the kibbutz kitchen punctually at 5:00 A.M. to make all the omelets, fried eggs, and scrambled eggs for breakfast. She has been doing it for years and means to go on as long as she is physically capable. Many of the elderly women work in the big communal clothes store, mending, ironing, folding freshly laundered clothes and bed linens, and so on. They have plenty of congenial company there, and a limitless supply of work. The gerontologists say that to go on working is the basis of well-being for the aged or aging, and ours certainly seem to prove that to be kept busy, to feel you are continuing to contribute to your keep, and to know that what you are doing is appreciated by the community is the best protection against old-age melancholy, and the most effective way to maintain physical and mental health.

Our old people continue to live in their own houses as long as possible, surrounded by familiar possessions and spared the trauma of being removed to an institution before it is absolutely necessary. They are generally taken care of by their families: sons, daughters, and grandchildren clean for them, bring them food from the dining hall, make sure they have the medical care they need. Those who have no families at Ein-Harod, and even some who do, have these services performed for them by two women members of the kibbutz whose full-time job is to take care of the aged. So you see one of them, Sara Etz-Chaim, riding around on her motorized tricycle, equipped with spacious baskets for carrying food and other provisions to her old people and a special safety seat for ferrying them to and from the kibbutz clinic. She is devoted to her old folks, and they to her. The other member assigned to the aged, Lea Ben-Zvi, runs a recreational handicrafts center where her senior pupils gather to make soft toys, rugs, and other useful and ornamental objects that are proudly exhibited on festive occasions once or twice a year.

For collective transportation of the aged, the kibbutz has its own minibus, which picks up elderly members at appointed hours several times a day to take them to their workplace and back or to meals in the dining hall. It is also available for longer journeys to the cemetery for funerals and memorial services, to the art museum for exhibitions, or to the Founders' Wood or sports stadium, where most of the big communal celebrations are held. All lectures and performances given in the kibbutz are open to them, and the senior citizens also have special lectures and discussions once a fortnight at their Five O'clock Club in the kibbutz clubhouse.

When they contract the illnesses of old age and need round-the-clock care, our old people are transferred to a small home for the aged attached to the kibbutz hospital. So far the home consists of five one-room apartments; more will doubtless be added when they are needed. The hospital itself has five sick rooms, singles and doubles, so it can house fourteen aged, who are attended by a staff of four full-time women workers, with part-time help from

younger women and, occasionally, hired outside help. It is a pleasure to walk into the place: sparkling with new paint and cleanliness, furnishings in bright, cheerful colors, pictures on the walls,
fresh flowers everywhere. It also has the distinction of having almost the only bathrooms, rather than the usual shower rooms, in
the kibbutz. The apartments are, as much as they can be, replicas
of the occupants' original homes with their own furniture, pictures, ornaments, television sets, and so on brought to their new
quarters to make them feel the change as little as possible.

In spite of all these efforts to make them happy, our old people
often complain and grumble like old people everywhere. They
just don't like being old, and they can be querulous and cantan-
kerous, blaming everybody around them for the one misfortune
for which there is no remedy — being old and helpless. Those
who were always nice people tend to remain nice; those who were
never pleasant become worse — also an unalterable fact. But, ob-
jectively considered, their conditions and care are as good as the
best anywhere, and we are inclined to agree when people who
used to say "The kibbutz is a wonderful place for children" now
say "The kibbutz is a wonderful place for children and old people."

The doyen of the old-age corps is Slutzkin,* who at ninety-
eight is probably the oldest survivor of the pioneers of the Second
Aliyah. His mind is as lucid as a young man's, his memory unimpaired, his wit, humor, and compassion as fresh and delightful as
they have ever been in the long years I have known him. He has a
vast store of tales and anecdotes about the people he has known
and the events he has lived through, which he recounts with
lovely zest and good humor. Some of his best stories are about
Yitzhak Tabenkin and his family; he was a second father to the
Tabenkin children and knows every phase of their histories and
every quirk of their characters. He loved Berl Katznelson with
passion: he once told me he misses him to this day, and sometimes
feels he wants to cry from yearning for his companionship. I go to
see Slutzkin as often as possible, feeling each time the restorative
power of his ageless mind and personality.

*Slutzkin, Sorkin, Greenberg, and others have always been called by their surnames;
few people outside their families know their first names.

Then there is Sorkin, at ninety-two the oldest cowman of the kibbutzim and of the whole country, who has received more prizes and certificates of merit than he can count for his sixty years of continuous service as a cowman. He still works six hours a day in the cowshed, finding this the best cure for all the ills of old age. Until a short time ago, he walked with the straight firm gait of a healthy man of fifty; only in his ninety-third year did he begin to feel a certain stiffness of the limbs, and he now goes about in the motorized tricycle. But he still attends almost all the General Assembly meetings on Saturday nights and participates actively in the discussions and arguments, and he is always in the front row at lectures and festive performances. He reads enormously, more than he ever read in his younger years — because, he explains, he now does a mere half-day's work, from 4:00 A.M. to 10:00 A.M., and it's good to have a long day left for the reading and study he had always wanted to do.

Among the octogenarians, Greenberg, eighty-three, heads the list for energy and good spirits. He keeps physically fit by swimming every day of the year, and when our swimming pool is closed during the winter months, he trots briskly up the hill to Ein-Harod Ichud's pool, which is open all year. He learned to paint in his late seventies, pursued his new recreation with great industry, and has treated us to several exhibitions of his charming neoprimitive paintings. He takes a week's holiday in Jerusalem every summer and after his latest sojourn, he stopped me on a path and for some twenty minutes told me what a wonderful week he'd had. Something different every day, he said, glowing with remembered excitement as he spoke: excursions, archaeological digs, museums, theaters, the Old City, the new Hebrew University on Mount Scopus, and more. I felt quite ashamed to think that I had never contrived to see half as much in a week in Jerusalem.

Our women octogenarians outnumber the men, forming a little society of their own. They sit in twos or threes on the benches along the paths, resting on their way to or from work, the dining hall, their grandchildren, or wherever. I usually stop to ask how they are, and as often as not get a spate of reminiscences in return. Their memories are extraordinary. When I tell Miriam Givol, who is eighty-five, that we are writing this book, she tells me she hopes I won't forget to "put in" my grandmother. (Everybody, I may say, constantly urges us to "put in" somebody; if we put them all in, this book would be three times the length it is.) "What a Bolshevik she was!" says Miriam, chuckling over her young woman's recollections of my Russian grandmother and proceeding to recount episodes in which she figured — with many digressions and much historical and ideological commentary. Then there is Hadassah, aged eighty-seven, who walks with difficulty but remembers the minutest details of every Passover Seder meal she prepared in the long years she was Ein-Harod's chief cook. She also recalls with satisfaction the hot meals-on-wheels she cooked and personally delivered, often risking life or limb to do it, to the soldiers of Battalion 13 stationed in the Emek during the War of Independence. One of those soldiers, Ahuvia Tabenkin, still remembers how good it was to get those meals in their defense posts, and remains devoted to Hadassah.

Utiya, eighty-one, likes to retell the dramatic tale of her time as a Prisoner of Zion in Soviet Russia in the 1920s and how she made her escape to Eretz Yisrael. And Lillia, eighty-five, has one overriding passion — her writing. For some fifty years she was a member of the editorial board of the journal of the national working women's organization, formerly *Dvar ha-Po'elet*, now *Na'amat*, regularly contributing to it articles and sketches about the life of the kibbutz, the problems of women in the kibbutz, and of the working women of the country as a whole. A few years ago she published a selection of them in book form and, to everyone's surprise, the book has been a great success with the younger generation of women, who see Lillia as a pioneer of women's rights in the country and are fascinated by her record of the milieu and problems of the early pioneer women. Among her best-known sketches is that of a curious domestic practice of that early time, the *primus*. For lack of living space, a young married couple was obliged to share its one-room quarters with an unmarried young person who might be out all day but was certainly there at night, sleeping in the other bed. This person was the primus, and Lillia feelingly describes her suffering from the intrusive presence of this third person. Her record, which is as moving as it is funny, has been much appreciated by surviving fellow sufferers, who also cannot forget their ordeal of the primus.

The oldest cowman in the country, ninety-two-year-old Sorkin still finds six hours a day in the cowshed the best cure for the ills of old age.

Lillia, however, is no more than a representative case. There would have been no Bible, people have said, but for the recording passion of the Jews. This is generally true of our people, and Ein-Harod, from this point of view, is Jewish through and through. The passion burns steadily in a relatively high proportion of our members. The most devoted recorder in recent years has been Neria Zisling, who diligently and patiently extracted from members of all age groups their life histories, along with their impressions and recollections of Ein-Harod, for our massive fiftieth anniversary volume *Pirkei Yovel.* Neria continues her good work, collecting material for future anniversary volumes, making sure that no member's story remains unrecorded. Then there are the memorial booklets for all the Ein-Harod members who have passed away. It is our established practice to commemorate every member, distinguished and ordinary alike, in a small volume recording the stories of their lives, with photographs, other people's recollections of them, and letters or extracts from their writings. It means a great deal to the families to have this mark of the community's recognition of their dead, and the booklets are a valuable addition to the records of Ein-Harod, collectively giving a fair picture of its human composition in each period of its history.

Besides these communally sponsored records, there are those of individual members. Yitzhak Luz, aged eighty-five, recently completed a small book of personal memoirs written, he insists, only for his grandchildren; but I am sure that in time they will find an honorable place in the kibbutz archives. He is not the only grandfather, nor will he be the last, to record his personal history "for family circulation only." Then there is the relatively new phenomenon of the "research theses" of our eighteen-year-olds. For matriculation they are required to produce a fairly extensive piece of research on any approved subject of their choice, and several of our young people have chosen to research a particular period or event or personality in the history of Ein-Harod. The theses I have read have struck me as genuinely original and solid contributions to our records, with a freshness of approach and style that is especially engaging. One, for example, surveyed the published literary remains, chiefly letters, of the young men of Ein-Harod and other kibbutzim killed in our wars from the War of Independence to the Yom Kippur War, and attempted to

bring out the special characteristics of the young of each generation shown in this material. Another inquired into the lives and
personalities of the people buried in our old cemetery at the foot
of the Gilboa in the period 1922–1938, describing them with great
sensitivity. A third studied the group of Second Aliyah pioneers
from Kibbutz Kinneret who, with the pioneers of the Third
Aliyah, founded Ein-Harod. This one was beautifully written as
well as historically accurate, showing a great power of imaginative identification with its heroes and heroines.

Whether these young people's productions are one-time efforts
or the promise of more to come remains to be seen. Meanwhile,
the more formal publications of the members of Ein-Harod testify
to our recording passion: the books, articles, essays we somehow
keep producing, in all circumstances and conditions. I cannot resist quoting a review by Shlomo Shumani, a learned bibliogra-
pher of the National and University Library at the Hebrew
University, of the bibliography of publications by members of
Ein-Harod that we produced in 1973 as another gift to ourselves
on our fiftieth anniversary.

Israel is known to be a land of unique phenomena. This time I can
offer you an unparalleled tale about a village of 800 persons of
whom one-third are authors.

On the occasion of the fiftieth anniversary of Ein-Harod, the
kibbutz has published a most remarkable bibliographical booklet,
compiled by Yocheved Bat-Rachel. This bibliography lists about
3000 articles written by 240 members of the kibbutz. These articles
do not represent the total number of publications of the Ein-Harod
population. This bibliography lists only the articles which appeared in the kibbutz's own periodicals.

This fact, of course, makes one curious to know what these
wide-awake people have written outside of their kibbutz publications.

Browsing through the titles in this booklet reveals what an extremely rich diversity of interests the members of Ein-Harod pursue. To be sure, kibbutz and labor problems, as well as Israel and
world problems, occupy a prominent place. Economic and organizational problems of the kibbutz movement account for about a
quarter of the bibliography. However, there is almost no topic, including poetry and literature, which is not represented.

A large number of the entries are, of course, by the leaders and known authors of the kibbutz. The late Yitzhak Tabenkin is responsible for about 400 entries and the poet Zerubavel Gilead for more than 100.

Nothing demonstrates better than this bibliography does the overwhelming role which kibbutz people play in the cultural activity of our country. We are all aware of the disproportionate part which kibbutz youth plays in the armed forces, and now we have documentary evidence of the imposing role played by kibbutz people in our intellectual life.*

And the writing goes on. As we work on our book, Yosef Tabenkin is writing a book on the history of the Harel Brigade; Yisrael Odem has in press four books on the theory and practice of graphology and is preparing a fifth; and Ze'ev Ivyansky is awaiting the publication of his new book *Terrorist Warfare: The Story of Pilsudski and the Bojowka 1904–1909*. So it seems we are destined to remain, in the true Jewish spirit, a writing and recording community — if our third and fourth generations carry on the tradition. The third (my daughters') generation give little sign of this. They seem to be fighting shy of all writing, either imaginative or scholarly, a phenomenon the sociologists explain as a natural reaction against the overproductivity of their parents and grandparents. But the fourth generation, they promise us, may well pick up where we left off. So I watch my own and other people's grandchildren with interest for the first signs of incipient authorship; meanwhile remembering the wise words of Haim Hazaz, the dedicated writer who intimated that there are services to humanity other than writing.

*Shlomo Shunami, "Ein-Harod's Writers," *The Jerusalem Post,* December 1, 1973.

Epilogue:

Birthday

ON MY SEVENTIETH BIRTHDAY we made a great family excursion into the biblical Land of Ephraim, also called Samaria, which lies on the other side of the Gilboa, stretching on to the Judean hills. I had known it well in my boyhood from our excursions with Moshe Carmi into this neighboring area of the undivided Eretz Yisrael. Then, in 1948, we were cut off from it until the Six Day War of 1967; and though I had been back several times since then, it was a different experience to revisit it now in the company of my family.

We traveled in a kibbutz vehicle called a *masa'it,* a big truck that can be converted into a regular bus. Almost all the family were there: Doris; Tirza and Abbi, with three of their four children, Ayelet, Dror, and Moran; Hanni and Ilan, with three of theirs, Shoshanni, Sigal, and little Yuval (born soon after the death of my brother and named after him); Eyla and Mordi, with two of their three children, Yiftach and No'a. Ori, Tirza's eldest boy, was missing, because he was in the army and couldn't get leave for his grandfather's birthday; the two babies, Hanni's Tamar and Eyla's Gil, had been left behind in the children's house. Eyra was there, with two of her children; and Manya, Abbi's widowed mother, had come from Tel Aviv especially to join us. Our expert driver — one needs a special license to drive the truck — had brought his family, too, so we were a party of some forty people. Huge picnic hampers were piled in the back of the vehicle, with every other provision for a good day's outing: you can trust the experienced organizers of a kibbutz excursion to think of everything.

The brilliant sunshine of the winter's day was a stroke of luck, and there was pure physical pleasure in breathing the cold crisp air of the Samarian hills, and in the beauty of the long vistas of fields and valleys and tree-covered hills that hove into sight almost every time our bus turned a corner in the ascents and descents of its winding route. My daughters had planned it all: we were to return to the places I had seen in my boyhood, and when we reached each place, I would tell the grandchildren about my first visit there and any dramatic or humorous events associated with it. It was not a difficult prescription. I found the recollections coming in a flood as I stood again in the immemorial places, most of all when we stood facing the Valley of Sanur, where Moshe Carmi had taken us on an unforgettable expedition in 1927.

Moshe had first heard of this little known valley from an Arab peddler we met on one of our excursions. It lay somewhere to the east of the road from Jenin to Sebastia, and was called in Arabic *Marj-el-Rarak,* (Valley of the Swamps), or alternatively *Marj Sanur* (the Valley of Sanur), after the name of the village that stood at its entrance. It was very fertile, said the Arab peddler, so fertile that the crops there ripen twice a year, and the corn grows so high that a man on a horse is invisible as he rides through it. In his subsequent investigations, Moshe tracked down a fascinating story in the history of Sanur, recorded in *Field Crops of the Land,* a book by Rabbi Yehohasaph Schwartz, a Jewish traveler in the area in the early nineteenth century.

Rabbi Schwartz related that several times in the late eighteenth century the village of Sanur was a center of rebellion against the rule of the pashas, and in one of these rebellions Abdullah Pasha of Sanur turned for help to his friend and ally, Bashir Pasha of Damascus and Lebanon. Among the contingent of soldiers Bashir sent him was a group of Jewish fighters from the ancient Jewish villages of Hasbaya and Dir-el-Kamar. These Jews, writes Schwartz, were "strong men, fighters and farmers, like the peoples of the mountains." (Hasbaya, which figured prominently in the Lebanon War as a stronghold of the Lebanese Druse, is at the foot of the eastern slope of Mount Hermon, and the mountains Schwartz referred to are doubtless the surrounding mountains inhabited, then and now, by Lebanese Druse.) These farming and fighting Jews from the mountains subdued the rebels of Sanur; "and to this day," Schwartz concluded, "their fame lives on after them."

We had reason to surmise that perhaps their descendants, too, lived on after them in Sanur when we went there with Moshe. Passing through Jenin, south of Ein-Harod, we turned off east from the main road leading to Sebastia, Nablus, and Jerusalem, onto a dirt track and proceeded on foot for two to three hours. As we approached the valley, Moshe told us it was seven and a half kilometers long and more than three kilometers wide, and closed in on all sides. Consequently, the heavy winter rains, having no outlet into the Jordan, turned the middle of the valley into a huge swamp (hence, Valley of the Swamps), which never dried out completely. At its southwest entrance, we observed the fortified village of Sanur, standing on a high hill, dominating the valley.

On entering the valley, we saw the Arabs of the village plowing and sowing for the summer crops. The whole village seemed to be in the fields: men, women, and children, all doing their own jobs. Deep-green fields of corn stretched all around us. In the fields at the foot of the hills plowmen walked behind their plows, which were drawn by small black oxen with square heads. Women and children in ragged, colorful garments bent over beds of vegetables, chattering like running water. The tinkle of cow bells and braying of donkeys mingled with the cries of babies and the shouts of a plowman cursing an ox for refusing to move.

Then they saw us. Immediately, all activity stopped, and everyone surged forward in great excitement to surround us, waving a welcome as they approached and calling out long, elaborate blessings. The women caressed the dresses of our girls and gazed admiringly at their blond hair. The young men looked at us in wonder, smiling all the while. And the older men talked to us, singly and in groups, like old friends. Before we could answer the question one had asked, another leaped in with a fresh question. And all of them, each in his own style, kept returning to one question, asking eagerly, almost yearningly: "Have you come to buy land?" Or, more positively: "We knew you would come to us — you have come to buy land!"

This completely baffled us, until someone explained. "This valley has been waiting for you," said the spokesman, smiling happily. "There, at the edge of the mountain in the east, in a place hidden from us, is a hole your ancestors blocked many, many years ago, before they went into exile. From that time to this, there has been no outlet for the water that collects here in the rainy season: it is soaked up by the earth, ruining the whole of the middle part of the valley, making it impossible to work any part of it. But, our fathers and grandfathers told us, the day will come when the Jews will return to this place. Then they will open up the hidden hole, releasing the imprisoned water, and bring back blessings to the earth and purification of the air. This is why we ask, and ask again, 'Have you come to buy land?' "

As we talked further, it transpired that many of them had Old Testament names, which is uncommon among Arabs of the villages. Such names as Ibrahim (Abraham; in Hebrew, Avraham), Isshak (Isaac; in Hebrew, Yitzhak), Ya'akub (Jacob; in Hebrew, Ya'akov), Yussuf (Joseph; in Hebrew, Yosef), and Mussa (Moses; in Hebrew, Moshe). Said one man, "My name is Ya'akub, and my father's name Isshak. I am sure there is someone among you whose name is the same as mine — and whose father's name is the same as my father's. And why? Because the one father of our fathers was called Ibrahim!"

They went on to tell us other stories connected with the valley and the Jews. One, told by a very old Arab with bleary eyes, centered on the hill to the east of the valley called *Tel Khaibar el-Yahud*, the Hill of the Khaibar Jews, Khaibar being the name of a tribe of Jewish Bedouins who lived in the Arabian Desert and were never converted to Islam. As a boy, said the old man, he used to pasture his sheep near this hill; and one day, "Behold, there appeared a long line of horsemen — very grand, very important-looking people — all Jews, dressed like Frenchmen [meaning in European garb]. They dismounted and entered the ruins on the hill. Each drew out of his bosom a big map, spread it out in front of him, and found from this map the grave of his grandfather. Then each sat down on the ground in front of the grave of his father's father, and wept."

The old man did not have a chance to complete his story. Children came running up to us, crying "The sheik, the sheik is coming!" We gazed in the direction they were pointing and saw approaching on the path between the trees a magnificently attired old man riding on a horse, his sword on his thigh, his servant running behind him with the sheik's saddlebag slung over his shoulder. This was the Sheik of Sanur and the lord of its lands. Everyone bowed low before him, and Moshe Carmi bowed, too, touching his forehead and chest in deferential greeting.

The sheik dismounted, turned to Moshe, and asked, "From where, to where, with God's blessing?" Moshe told him. When he heard the name Ein-Harod, the sheik smiled, but said nothing. Continuing to bless us, he invited us to be his guests in his house. Moshe thanked him warmly but said we had decided to spend the night on the top of the hill and would have to start moving to avoid arriving there in the dark. He explained that he wanted to get us to the top of the hill for the night to avoid the malarial mosquitoes of the swamps. Then he thanked the sheik again for his kind offer of hospitality and invited him to come and visit us at Ein-Harod as our guest.

At this, the sheik could hold back no longer. "I have already been at Ein-Jalud!" he said, using the Arabic name for Ein-Harod and enjoying the surprised looks on our faces. Surprise, however, changed to shock and embarrassment when he added, "But they would have driven me out if it had not been for one man!" We could hear the dismay in Moshe's voice as he asked, "How *could* that have happened? Please tell us, what happened?" The sheik then told his story. "One day," he said, "I was riding in the Emek to Zari'in [biblical Yizre'el] to visit some of my relatives there, when I saw next to the Jalud [the spring of Harod] an encampment of tents and huts. I was curious to see what the *moskobim* [the Muscovites] had done there; so, having watered my horse in the stream, I started to walk up toward the encampment. Suddenly there leaped out at me some young men with wild hair, wearing short pants, who laughed among themselves as if they were mocking me in a language I did not understand, and shouted at me, 'Yalla! Yalla!' [Be off; get out quickly!]. I had not asked them for so much as a drop of water, or a handful of barley for my horse. I only wanted to look around. But they pointed toward the road to Zar'in and just shouted again, 'Yalla! Yalla!'

"I was about to turn away, feeling very hurt and insulted, when one of their men appeared: red-haired, tall, broad-shouldered, dressed in long trousers and a white shirt, and with good bright eyes. He scolded the young men and sent them away. Then he turned to me, spoke to me in the language of friendship and respect, and invited me to his home. He didn't know me — I was only a passer-by — I with my horse beside me. But he took the bridle out of my hand, led the horse to the stable, and there, in spite of my protests, gave it barley and oats — a good big helping. Then he took me to his room in one of the wooden huts, offered me coffee and talked to me as if we were brothers. This man's name was Chaim Sturman — I suppose you know him? He is surely a son of the sons of our father Ibrahim. For, like our ancient father, he saw in every guest first a human being. Our father Ibrahim saw even angels that appeared at the entrance to his tent as human beings."

The old sheik embraced Moshe, patted him on the shoulder, and said, "By your face I can tell you are among the friends of Chaim. If you are, these children are in good hands — you will make human beings of them!" We said good-bye to the sheik and the villagers, climbed up the hill, entered the *madaffi*, and settled down for the night. The sheik had told us we would be perfectly safe there, for it was a sacred place and any thief who came to rob there knew that his hand would wither in the act.

Nevertheless, when darkness fell and it began to be very cold, we were astonished to see an aged man appear at the door of the madaffi. Wrapped in a sheepskin, he sat down in front of the door and told us the sheik had sent him to act as our guard. He carried no weapons, only a heavy stick. Moshe could not persuade him to come inside. Nor was he moved by Moshe's reminding him that this was a holy place and therefore in no danger of robbery or attack. He just said the sheik had sent him to watch over us, and that is what he would do.

He did, right through the night, until we rose at dawn. Before we set out on our day's expedition, Moshe asked the aged guard to deliver a note to the sheik. He told us what he had written: "I invite you again to come to Ein-Harod to be our guests. And I promise you we shall be hosts like our father Abraham — and like you."

* * *

These were the tales of Sanur I recounted to the attentive grandchildren. The older children, who knew something about Moshe Carmi, Chaim Sturman, and Arab sheiks, seemed to understand everything; the smaller ones only half understood, but listened entranced all the same. And my devoted daughters listened, too, as they had listened to my stories ever since they were the ages of the grandchildren.

From Sanur we moved on through Nablus to the foot of Mount Eyval, where we had our picnic lunch. Eyval, "the mountain of curses," faces Mount Grizim, "the mountain of blessings," which is the traditional sacred place of the Samaritans. From Eyval we took the main road that leads through the Valley of Shilo to Jerusalem, turning west into the hills to make a brief tour of two new settlements, Elkana and Emmanuel; then we wound our way down to the coastal road for the journey back to Ein-Harod.

As I sat in the bus on the homeward journey, in the silence that falls on an excursion party at the end of a long day of sightseeing in the open air, I was conscious of a strange mixture of joys. Each was distinct, and all blended into one surpassing joy. There had been the joy of reliving my first boyhood experience of these places, breathing the fresh, carefree happiness of the springtime of life. Then there was the joy of having survived to revisit. No Jew in the Eretz Yisrael of the last sixty years takes survival for granted, and for a long moment my memory filled and brimmed over with the faces of the friends and comrades who had not survived to revisit. The beauty of the day and the magnificence of the Samarian hills had been another joy, intimately familiar to me, never palling by familiarity. But the surpassing joy was the simplest of all. It was the joy of my mother when, more than sixty years ago, she broke into her wild little dance on the bleak Tel Aviv sands, crying with tears in her eyes, "We're in Eretz Yisrael, Eretz Yisrael!" I didn't mind the tears in my own eyes, unobserved by the daughters and grandchildren, as I recognized once more that this is what counts most: being in Eretz Yisrael. No matter where — Ma'ayan Harod, Kumi, Tel Aviv, Jerusalem, Sanur, Shilo, Gilgal — all, one and indivisibly, Eretz Yisrael.

Yes, that is the great, positive, sustaining thing. I linger over it, gazing at it as if it were a living thing, wanting to enjoy its loveliness, wanting to find peace and rest in it. As I gaze, a shadow crosses it, an old familiar shadow. It is the fear that is always mixed with the joy. A vague but potent fear: that we may not survive after all; that the enemy without waits to destroy us, or worse, that the enemy within may accomplish what the enemy without can't. So I can't rest; I can't be complacent. I fear what others seemingly don't, and I call silently for the lost hero who might restore us to ourselves.

The thought of the lost hero mingles in my mind with a biblical figure who has long haunted me: Elika the Harodite, the man from Ein-Harod, the Spring of Harod, which is Gideon's spring. In 2 Samuel 23:25 he is named as one of David's thirty heroes who went out to battle with him in the Judean Desert. After David's victory, twenty-nine of the heroes are named again, along with the high office each received as a reward for his valor and loyalty. Only Elika's name is missing, and is never mentioned again, which leads me to wonder: What happened to Elika? Was he killed in the battle? Where is the lost hero?

Elika
Rain with the crash of thunder and earth
in full flood
and the darkness beats on a huge drum
crying,
"Elika, Elika, where are you?"

Like me he lived here on the banks of the stream,
and the Bible mentions his name just once:
Elika the Harodite, one of David's heroes,
the thirty heroes who stood with him in the desert
facing war.

There is no mercy in the roar of the heavens
and all the men are asleep:
none is anxious, none afraid,
only my eyelids are like birds
galloping swiftly on the day of doom
between lightning and the rage from the crests of the rocks:
"Elika, Elika, where are you?"

Chronology

Glossary

Historical Chronology of Key Events

1516–1917   Turkish (Ottoman) rule in Palestine
1882–1904   First Aliyah: arrival of 25,000 immigrants, marking begin-
            ning of modern Jewish resettlement of Eretz Yisrael
1904–1914   Second Aliyah: 40,000 immigrants
1909   Hashomer founded
1910   Kibbutz Degania, the first kibbutz, founded
1914–1918   First World War
1917   Balfour Declaration, promising support of British govern-
            ment for creation of national home for Jewish people in
            Palestine
1917   General Allenby conquers Palestine, marking end of Turk-
            ish rule
1919–1923   Third Aliyah: 35,000 immigrants
1920   British Mandate established in Palestine
1920   Histadrut (Labor Federation) founded
1920   Haganah founded
1920   G'dud ha-Avoda (Labor Legion) founded: first country-
            wide commune of Jewish workers in Eretz Yisrael, dedi-
            cated to working the land, forming pioneer settlements,
            advancing Jewish self-defense, and other pioneering tasks
1921   Kibbutz Ein-Harod founded by G'dud ha-Avoda; settle-
            ment of Emek begun
1920–1921   First Arab riots, mainly in Jerusalem and Jaffa areas
1921   British introduce quota on Jewish immigration to Eretz
            Yisrael

1924–1928	Fourth Aliyah: 90,000 immigrants
1927	Kibbutz ha-Meuchad Federation established
1929	Arab riots: massacre of Jewish communities in Hebron and Safad
1929–1939	Fifth Aliyah: 225,000 immigrants
1933	Hitler and Nazis assume power in Germany
1934	Aliyah Bet begun
1936–1939	Arab riots
1939	British White Paper, further restricting Jewish immigration to Eretz Yisrael
1939–1945	Second World War
1939	First Palestinian Jews join British army as volunteers
1941	Palmach established
1941–1942	First news of Holocaust reaches Eretz Yisrael
1943–1944	Rescue mission of Hanna Szenesh and comrades
1943	Revolt of Warsaw Ghetto
1945–1946	End of Second World War
1945–1947	Struggle of Jews of Eretz Yisrael against British rule and White Paper preventing rescue of survivors of Holocaust; Aliyah Bet intensified; tragic drama of S.S. *Patria, Struma,* and *Exodus.*
November 29, 1947	United Nations decision to establish Jewish State in Palestine
November 1947	Arab riots against U.N. decision, marking beginning of War of Independence
May 14, 1948	Declaration of Independence; State of Israel established
May 15, 1948	British Mandate in Palestine ends; State of Israel invaded by five Arab armies
1948–1949	War of Independence
1949	Armistice agreements with Egypt, Jordan, Lebanon, and Syria
1949–1950	New kibbutz settlements established on borders of State in Galilee, Jerusalem Corridor, and Negev
1949–1952	Mass immigration of Jews from Arab lands in Middle East and North Africa; increased immigration from eastern, central, and western Europe; new settlements (moshavim and development towns) established to absorb new immigrants; Jewish population of State of Israel more than doubled, from 650,000 in 1948 to 1.5 million by 1952; development of Negev begun; port of Eilat on Red Sea founded 1952

1952   Crisis in Kibbutz ha-Meuchad movement. Along with other kibbutzim, Ein-Harod splits, becoming Ein-Harod Meuchad and Ein-Harod Ichud.

1954–1956   Egypt and Jordan repeatedly violate armistice agreements by terrorist attacks across borders; Israel answers with reprisal raids; attacks and counterattacks lead to war with Egypt

October 1956   Sinai Campaign. IDF conquers Gaza Strip and entire Sinai Peninsula in 100 hours, stopping 16 kilometers from Suez Canal; under pressure from United States and Soviet Union, Israel evacuates Sinai and Gaza Strip; buffer United Nations Emergency Force (UNEF) posted to keep peace

1957–1967   Rapid development in all areas of national life; in the kibbutzim, accelerated mechanization of agriculture and growth of industry; frequent terrorist infiltrations from Egypt and Jordan, and Syrian attacks from Golan Heights on settlements in Hula Valley; Syrians attempt to close off water sources of Jordan River

1964   Palestine Liberation Organization (PLO) established: avowed aim to liberate all of Palestine as homeland exclusively for Palestinian Arabs by totally liquidating State of Israel; PLO declared sole legitimate representative of Palestinian Arabs, reconfirmed at Rabat Conference of Arab States in 1974; from 1964 PLO practices indiscriminate terror against Jews in Israel and abroad, and against Arabs prepared to make peace with Israel; in early 1970s establishes its power base in Lebanon

May 1967   Gamal Nasser, President of Egypt, blockades Tiran Straits; calls for a *jihad* (holy war) against Israel; orders withdrawal of United Nations buffer force from Sinai; marches 100,000 troops and 900 tanks across Sinai Desert to Israel's borders, ready for invasion

June 5–10, 1967   Six Day War. Israeli air force destroys Egyptian air force in a few hours on June 5; IDF conquers Gaza Strip and Sinai up to Suez Canal, driving Egyptian army back across canal; Jordan attacks Jerusalem in spite of messages from Israel urging it to stay out of war; IDF conquers East Jerusalem, including Old City and West Bank up to Jordan River; Syria intensifies attacks from Golan Heights; IDF conquers Golan Heights on June 10

June–
September 1967

Israel offers to restore some conquered territories in return for peace treaties on basis of Allon Peace Plan; Arabs refuse

September 1967

Khartoum Conference of Arab states; announces Three No's policy toward Israel: No recognition, no negotiations, no peace

1967–1973

Development of country continues; Labor governments establish new settlements, roughly according to Allon Plan, in Jerusalem area, Hebron area, Jordan Valley, and Golan Heights

1969–1971

War of Attrition. Egypt, supported by Soviet Union, resumes attacks across Suez Canal and Jordan across Jordan River; IDF suffers heavy casualties to stop attacks

1971–1973

Constant threats of war from Egypt and Syria, forcing repeated mobilization of IDF

October 1973

Yom Kippur War. Surprise attack by Egypt in south and Syria in north; fighting lasts nineteen days; IDF suffers heaviest casualties since War of Independence but succeeds in pushing Egyptian forces (except Third Army) back across Suez Canal and Syrians out of Golan Heights; military disengagement agreements with Egypt and Syria

May 1977

Likud coalition (roughly equivalent to Conservative party in Britain) defeats Labor alignment in general election; first Likud government formed after twenty-nine years of continuous Labor rule; holds doctrine of *Shlemut ha-Aretz* (Integrity of the Land), which rejects any peace plan that entails giving up territories taken in Six Day War; in particular, refuses to give up Judea and Samaria (West Bank) which, with East Jerusalem, are regarded as inseparable parts of historic Eretz Yisrael; Jewish settlement begun in Judea and Samaria, including settlement near or in Arab-populated centers

November 1977

Egyptian President Anwar Sadat makes historic visit to Jerusalem; declares readiness to make peace with Israel, on condition that Israel return whole of Sinai to Egypt and commit itself to negotiated settlement of political future of Judea, Samaria, and Gaza

1978

Camp David accords signed by Egypt, Israel, and United States

1979

Egypt-Israel Peace Treaty signed at White House; Israel undertakes to withdraw from Sinai in three stages spread over three years and to negotiate autonomy for Judea, Samaria, and Gaza

1978–1981	Israel completes first two steps of withdrawal from Sinai; Jewish settlement in Judea and Samaria intensified
November 1981	Second Likud government elected
April 1982	Last stage of withdrawal from Sinai completed, despite violent resistance from nationalist Stop the Withdrawal movement; town of Yamit in northern Sinai razed by Israeli bulldozers; traumatic experience for all Israelis
1981–1982	PLO attacks from Lebanon on northern Galilee intensified; massive buildup of PLO military forces in Lebanon, centered in Beirut; PLO terrorism abroad intensified; attempted assassination in London of Shlomo Argov, Israel ambassador to Britain
June 1982	Lebanon War (Operation Peace for Galilee) starts; IDF invades Lebanon, destroys PLO strongholds in South Lebanon and as far north as outskirts of Beirut; Israel air force bombs Beirut in effort to destroy PLO forces, including leadership, hiding in Palestinian refugee camps; PLO forces expelled from Beirut
September 1982	Pro-Israel President of Lebanon, Bashir Gemayel, killed by anti-Israel, Syrian-inspired forces; succeeded by brother, Amin Gemayel
1982–1983	Peace negotiations between Israel and Lebanon; accord signed but not ratified, owing to violent Syrian opposition; multinational peace-keeping force, including U.S. Marines, set up; IDF in Lebanon and multinational force under constant terrorist attack from anti-Israel and anti-American Lebanese factions
1983–1984	IDF withdraws southward to Awali River; Israel-Lebanon accord abrogated under Syrian pressure; multinational force withdrawn
July 1984	Israel general election results in virtual draw between Labor and Likud; National Unity government formed of Labor, Likud, and smaller parties
November 1984	Negotiations started between Israel and Lebanon for complete withdrawal of IDF from Lebanon, subject to adequate arrangements for security of Israel's northern border; one certain gain (so far) of Lebanon War destruction of PLO base in Lebanon

Glossary

Aliyah (literally, "ascent"). *Aliyah* refers to immigration to Eretz Yisrael exclusively. The usage originated in the period of Ezra and Nehemiah, when the Jews who returned from Babylonian exile to rebuild the Temple were said to "ascend" to Eretz Yisrael.

Aliyah (plural *aliyot*) is also used in a collective sense to mean an immigration movement or wave of immigration. There were five main waves of Jewish immigration or *aliyot* in the pre-State (before 1948) period of Zionist resettlement: the First Aliyah (c. 1882–1904), Second Aliyah (c. 1904–1914), Third Aliyah (c. 1919–1923), and Fourth Aliyah (c. 1924–1928), all mainly from Russia and Eastern Europe; and the Fifth Aliyah (c. 1929–1935 and 1936–1939) of Jews from Germany and central Europe fleeing the Nazi terror, along with illegal immigrants from these countries and Eastern Europe.

Ashkenazic and Sephardic pronunciations. In Ashkenazic pronunciation, called *milel* ("from above") and used primarily by European Jews, the first or second syllable in words of more than one syllable is stressed; the Sephardic pronunciation, called *milra* ("from below") and spoken mainly by Oriental Jews, puts the accent on the last syllable. Thus the name Zerubavel is pronounced Zrŭ-bă-vēl in Sephardic Hebrew and Zrŭ-bāh-vĕl in Ashkenazic. There is also a difference in the pronunciation of a few vowels and one consonant: the short *a* in Sephardic (Zrubavel) becomes a short *o* in Ashkenazic (Zrubovel); the short *o* in Sephardic (as in *cholem,* "he dreams") becomes *oi* in Ashkenazic (*choilem*); the soft *t* in Sephardic (as in *bayit,* "house") becomes *s* in Ashkenazic (*bayis*).

The Sephardic pronunciation was adopted from the start for mod-

ern spoken Hebrew in Eretz Yisrael and has remained the only "received" pronunciation. However, modern Hebrew poets who wrote or
began writing their poetry in Europe (Bialik and Tchernichovsky, for
example) accented it in the Ashkenazic way, making it sound very
odd to the ears of native Hebrew speakers in Eretz Yisrael and still
odder when their works were set to music and sung — as were many of
Bialik's poems. The Ashkenazic pronunciation tended to become an
object of mirth and even ridicule, and to this day in Israel it is a recognized form of popular humor to pronounce individual words or recite
a poem or deliver a mock speech in the Ashkenazic *milel.*

Chassidic. From *Chassidism,* the revivalist movement in Judaism founded
in the eighteenth century, which emphasized enthusiasm, joy, and ecstasy in religious worship. Chassidic Jews use dancing and singing to
express the fervor of their piety.

Eretz Yisrael ("Land of Israel"). Designates the biblical land of the Jewish people (People of Israel) in the area afterward known as Palestine.
The name came into common use at the end of the period of the Second Temple (c. 538 B.C.–A.D. 70) and was used by Jews throughout
the nearly two thousand years of dispersion. During the British Mandate in Palestine (1920–1948), the Hebrew letters *aleph yud,* the initial
letters of "Eretz Yisrael," were written after the name "Palestine" in
all Hebrew documents and communications.

Hashomer ("The Watchman"). The first Jewish self-defense organization
in Eretz Yisrael, active c. 1909–1920. It guarded and helped develop
Jewish settlements in new areas and was the forerunner of the Haganah, the underground Jewish defense force during the British Mandate. The *shomrim* often wore a mixture of Arab and Circassian dress,
carried modern weapons, and usually rode on horseback.

Moshav (plural, *moshavim*). Another form of pioneering cooperative settlement. Moshavim retain some private ownership but, like the kibbutzim, practice mutual aid on collective principles. Nahalal, founded in
1921, was the first moshav.

Moshava (plural *moshavot*). Noncommunal agricultural village.

Sephardic pronunciation. See *Ashkenazic and Sephardic pronunciations.*

Stockade and watchtower (*Homa u'Migdal*). Under an Ottoman law recognized by the British Mandatory government, any structure that had
been in existence for at least twenty-four hours could not legally be
pulled down. This gave Jewish pioneers the idea of stockade-and-
watchtower settlements, which could be set up in twenty-four hours,
usually between the evening of one day and the next. "Portable barri-
cades, huts, and a wooden watchtower would be transported through
the night to the point of settlement, accompanied by members of the

Haganah. On the following day, defended by the Haganah, the structures would be assembled. By sundown, a new village was born." (Moshe Pearlman, in *The Army of Israel*.) About 118 settlements of this type were set up between 1936 and 1938; the first was Nir-David in the Beit-She'an Valley.

Zionist Executive in Palestine. The body representing the World Zionist Organization in Eretz Yisrael (Palestine). Its task was to execute Zionist policy in Eretz Yisrael, especially in settlement, absorption of immigrants, economic development, and political relations with the British Mandate authorities.